AF713391

TRUMP 2.0

PRESIDENTIAL ACTIONS

RESTORING FREEDOM OF SPEECH AND ENDING FEDERAL CENSORSHIP

EXECUTIVE ORDER

January 20, 2025

By the authority vested in me as President by the Constitution and the laws of the United States of America, and section 301 of title 3, United States Code, it is hereby ordered as follows:

Section 1. Purpose. The First Amendment to the United States Constitution, an amendment essential to the success of our Republic, enshrines the right of the American people to speak freely in the public square without Government interference. Over the last 4 years, the previous administration trampled free speech rights by censoring Americans' speech on online platforms, often by exerting substantial coercive pressure on third parties, such as social media companies, to moderate, deplatform, or otherwise suppress speech that the Federal Government did not approve. Under the guise of combatting "misinformation," "disinformation," and "malinformation," the Federal Government infringed on the constitutionally protected speech rights of American citizens across the United States in a manner that advanced the Government's preferred narrative about significant matters of public debate. Government censorship of speech is intolerable in a free society.

Sec. 2. Policy. It is the policy of the United States to:

(a) secure the right of the American people to engage in constitutionally protected speech;

(b) ensure that no Federal Government officer, employee, or agent engages in or facilitates any conduct that would unconstitutionally abridge the free speech of any American citizen;

(c) ensure that no taxpayer resources are used to engage in or facilitate any conduct that would unconstitutionally abridge the free speech of any American citizen; and

(d) identify and take appropriate action to correct past misconduct by the Federal Government related to censorship of protected speech.

Sec. 3. Ending Censorship of Protected Speech.

(a) No Federal department, agency, entity, officer, employee, or agent may act or use any Federal resources in a manner contrary to section 2 of this order. . . .

THE WHITE HOUSE,

January 20, 2025.

TRUMP 2.0

Executive Power and the First Amendment

TIMOTHY ZICK

CAROLINA ACADEMIC PRESS
Durham, North Carolina

Copyright © 2026
Timothy Zick
All Rights Reserved

Library of Congress Cataloging-in-Publication Data
is available at loc.gov

ISBN: 978-1-5310-3493-1
eISBN: 978-1-5310-3494-8

The photograph on the the cover has been cropped to focus on the President. The original, uncropped version (P20250207DT-0103) can be found on whitehouse.gov at the following link:

https://www.whitehouse.gov/wp-content/uploads/2025/02
/p20250207dt-0103_54325856729_o_128d74.jpg

Carolina Academic Press
700 Kent Street
Durham, North Carolina 27701
(919) 489-7486
www.cap-press.com

Printed in the United States of America

CONTENTS

3 ▪ EXECUTIVE ORDERS AND OFFICIAL ORTHODOXIES 45

4 ▪ HIGHER EDUCATION 73

5 ▪ IMMIGRATION ENFORCEMENT 107

FOREWORD

By Ronald KL Collins

The book you are about to read is like none other. How so? Well, there are several reasons—let's start with the following six:

1. Professor Timothy Zick's book is the only one that offers, as much as possible up to this date, a near-comprehensive account of one of the most brazenly repressive and vindictive periods in First Amendment history.
2. This account reveals, in example after example, the often-unprecedented techniques employed by the second Trump Administration to suppress and chill free speech.
3. This work shows how, in many instances, traditional types of judicial review are ineffective in protecting a range of First Amendment rights.
4. Given the relative novelty of some of the actions taken by President Trump and his cabinet, the absence of "on-point" judicial precedents has required informed and resourceful lawyering to contest various abridgments. This point, ably made by Professor Zick, reminds us that the First Amendment is as much about what practicing lawyers do as what judges say.
5. All of the above occurs against an orchestrated plan by the Trump Administration to "*flood the zone*" with abundant violations of free speech. In the dizzying swirl of things, it is easy to lose track of what occurred last week, let alone last month. For that reason alone, this superbly timed book provides a major contribution to the literature about the Madisonian amendment.
6. Given the "flood the zone" problem, this book offers both detailed and documented examples of abridgments along with useful topical categories by which to best grasp the nature of various free speech violations.

A UNIQUE DANGER

I cannot recall anything like this. I've been defending First Amendment rights since 2006, and this is the most serious of threats I can recall.

—**WILL CREELEY** (First Amendment lawyer)

As superbly documented in this book, under President Trump, the rule of law, including free speech law, has been corrupted such that agency officials (especially the Attorney General and the Director of the FBI) must pledge allegiance to the President over and above the Constitution and the laws of the nation. There has been a relentless effort to erase ideas and history deemed incompatible with the President's own personal and ideological predilections. There have been similar attempts to control, directly or indirectly, the operations of law firms, universities, and libraries. Open attacks have been leveled by the President and those serving under him against judges whenever they dare to rule against the Administration.

In case after case, the Trump Administration has used patently unlawful methods (violative of basic due process norms) to chill the speech of those persecuted as well as those countless other bystanders who could face a similar fate. And time and again, President Trump has exceeded his constitutional authority in violation of powers entrusted to Congress—also in violation of the First Amendment. And yet a subservient and timid majority of the House and Senate has succumbed to his imperious will.

Finally, mountains of government information have either been destroyed or removed from public access. Though not a technical First Amendment violation, such destruction and suppression of information runs contrary to the spirit of the First Amendment.

THE PRACTICE OF PRETENSE

There is also the hypocrisy so much at play here. Consider, for example, what Donald Trump promised on the occasion of his inaugural address: "After years and years of illegal and unconstitutional federal efforts to restrict free expression, I will also sign an executive order to immediately stop all government censorship and bring back free speech to America." Then, in his Executive Order of January 20, 2025, the new

President issued an order titled "Restoring Freedom of Speech and Ending Federal Censorship." In it, he declared: "Government censorship of speech is intolerable in a free society." Let none forget what then-designate Attorney General *Pamela Bondi* pledged during her confirmation hearing: *"Under my watch, the partisan weaponization of the Department of Justice will end. America must have one tier of justice for all."*

Know this: It is not partisan to first expose and then denounce the actions of a President and his Administration whenever they abridge our free expression rights. In that respect, Donald Trump is no more or less beyond condemnation than John Adams (the Alien and Sedition Acts) and Woodrow Wilson (the Espionage Act of 1917 and the Sedition Act of 1918), among others.

THE NEED FOR CREATIVE LAWYERING

Professor Zick's book sheds needed light on the breadth and depth of actions taken by the 47th President in breach of his constitutional oath of office when it comes to the First Amendment. While these are real breaches occurring in real time, their number alone places them beyond the content of traditional First Amendment casebooks. Moreover, since so much of legal education is premised on notions of Supreme Court review (federal and state), the absence of such review typically means the absence of any meaningful examination of the kind of major issues facing Americans today—the kind documented and discussed in this book.

If this book is like none other, it is because in so many ways we live in times like none other. And that raises at least one major question, one addressed by Professor Zick: *How do we respond to such abridgments of our free speech freedoms?* For example:

- How should lawyers counsel clients even before the wolf has come to their door? (This is important for First Amendment agents—e.g., librarians and university presidents—who elect to stand on their rights.)
- How should lawyers litigate such novel cases?
- How should they strategize relief for their clients when judicial relief alone would not make them whole?
- And then this: How should law professors teach such matters?

Having said all of that, you now should have some idea why Professor Zick's book is unique, timely, and indispensable to any meaningful account of the state of First Amendment freedom in these perilous times. Real defenders of the First Amendment owe him a great debt, whatever ideological flag they may fly.

Inform yourself. Think critically. Stand up. Speak out. And finally this: Heed what Justice Hugo Black exhorted in his dissent in *In re Anastaplo*, 366 U.S. 82, 116 (1961): "We must not be afraid to be free."

Ronald KL Collins is a retired law professor and editor of First Amendment News (hosted by FIRE, the Foundation for Individual Rights and Expression).

TRUMP 2.0

INTRODUCTION

During his first term, as the Nation's forty-fifth president, Donald J. Trump's words and deeds raised many red flags when it came to freedoms of speech and press. President Trump railed against the "enemy" press, threatened and in some case attempted to use the powers of his office against political rivals, and frequently expressed disdain for public protest and other forms of dissent.[1] Before it had reached its one hundredth day, it was clear that President Trump's second term, as the forty-seventh president, would be far more consequential for freedom of expression. What had been mostly idle threats or bluster morphed into a flurry of Executive Orders and agency actions affecting First Amendment rights and principles across society.

At his second inaugural address, President Trump promised: "After years and years of illegal and unconstitutional federal efforts to restrict free expression, I will also sign an executive order to immediately stop all government censorship and bring back free speech to America." As promised, in an Executive Order issued on January 20, 2025 (reproduced as the book's frontispiece), the President declared: "*Government censorship of speech is intolerable in a free society*."[2] What has happened since suggests the President and his Administration are not committed to this principle. In fact, while boasting about an executive order that criminalizes flag burning, President Trump declared, "We took the freedom of speech away because that's been through the courts and the courts said, you have freedom of speech."[3]

Trump 2.0 policies and actions have had broad censorious and chilling effects. Indeed, the use of executive power during Trump 2.0 represents the greatest governmental threat to the First Amendment since the McCarthy Era of the 1950s. As of publication, more than *forty* Executive Orders, "Fact Sheets," and Presidential Memoranda issued by President Trump, along with a bevy of enforcement actions by federal agencies and officials, have affected the First Amendment rights of millions of Americans and foreign visitors. Among other actions, President Trump and officials serving in his Administration have:

- Retaliated against law firms for their advocacy and representation of specific clients.
- Investigated and indicted current and former government officials based on their criticism of the President or expression of disfavored ideas.
- Fired federal prosecutors and Federal Bureau of Investigation employees for working on cases relating to President Trump and the January 6, 2021, Capitol riot.
- Terminated billions of dollars in federal funding to universities in an effort to alter their ideological cultures and control their core academic operations.
- Conditioned federal research and other funding on the agreement not to practice or promote "Diversity, Equity, and Inclusion" or "gender ideology" and to teach only "patriotic" curricula in K-12 schools.
- Arrested, detained, and subjected to deportation international students and foreign scholars based on their viewpoints and political activism, and revoked the visas of foreign nationals based on political expression.
- Retaliated against the press by excluding specific media outlets from White House events based on their viewpoints and reporting.
- Threatened to revoke broadcast licenses based on networks' editorial decisions.
- Restricted reporters' access to unclassified defense-related information held by the Pentagon.
- Sued newspapers and publishers for defamation, consumer fraud, and "election interference."
- Defunded libraries and public broadcasters.
- Scrubbed historical, scientific, and other data from federal agency websites.

- Ordered the removal of "anti-American" displays in national museums.
- Terminated grants for scientific research and removed scientific papers from government databases because the research referred to forbidden terms relating to race, gender, or environmental justice.
- Threatened to sanction advocates who assist officials with prosecutions in the International Criminal Court.
- Directed the Attorney General to prosecute individuals who burn the U.S. flag because the expressive act is "uniquely offensive and provocative" and communicates "contempt, hostility, and violence against our Nation."
- Declared "Antifa" a "domestic terrorist organization" and directed federal agencies to investigate and prosecute political violence linked to the expression of "anti-Americanism," "anti-capitalism," "anti-Christianity," "extremism on migration, race, and gender," and "hostility towards those who hold traditional American views on family, religion, and morality."
- Suggested that individuals protesting immigration raids are members of "organized crime" syndicates.
- Federalized and deployed the National Guard and active duty United States Marines to several American cities in response to public protests.

Most challenges to free expression emanate from Congress or, more commonly, state legislatures or state and local officials. In First Amendment casebooks and scholarship, it is customary to focus on these sources of law—and, of course, the Supreme Court decisions that address their constitutionality. However, as Trump 2.0 has shown, it is equally imperative that we reckon with *executive* threats to freedom of expression. The text of the First Amendment states, "Congress" shall make no law abridging expressive freedoms. A literal reading of that text might suggest the only federal institution or actor bound by the First Amendment is Congress. However, the weight of authority concludes that the President and agencies he directs are also bound by the First Amendment.[4]

Presidents are unique government officials, in part because they possess all the executive power the Constitution confers. The President's primary function is to *execute* the laws Congress enacts. But as Trump

2.0 has demonstrated, with the stroke of a pen the President can issue new interpretations of federal laws and institute policies that affect not just government institutions but vast swaths of the private sector as well. As President Trump has demonstrated, an aggressive executive can bypass Congress or usurp its powers, including the power to spend federal funds. A federal bureaucracy can implement policies in ways that implicate or violate the First Amendment rights of regulated parties including broadcasters, universities, and non-profit organizations.

The Trump Administration's second act is a stark reminder that executive power can significantly threaten or violate First Amendment rights—indeed, for reasons examined in this book, it may pose even greater threats to free expression than ordinary legislative acts. President Trump has shown the Nation's Chief Executive can use his powers to direct, influence, suppress, and coerce private expression. Executive Orders cannot override federal statutes or the Constitution. However, as Trump has demonstrated, the laws of Congress may be of little consequence if a President chooses to ignore them and Congress does not respond. Although courts can invalidate Executive Orders and agency actions, that check may not be sufficient to remedy the First Amendment harm they produce.

The President's uses—and potential abuses—of executive power suggest we are experiencing a change in basic assumptions concerning how to understand and address "abridgments" of expression. These changes, in turn, have raised important questions about how we ought to teach and study the First Amendment during and beyond the Trump Era.

- What is the relationship between executive power and free expression?
- Are Executive Orders a form of government speech or a means of suppressing private expression?
- What kinds of governmental actions constitute governmental suppression or censorship of speech forbidden by the First Amendment?
- To what extent can the President use threats to terminate federal funding or other actions to influence or coerce expression?
- How well-equipped are First Amendment doctrines and principles to respond to new threats by presidents and executive agencies under their direction?

By focusing on the actions of the President and the agencies he directs, this book fills an important gap in the study of the First Amendment. It documents the variety of ways in which executive power can independently threaten freedom of expression, and the ways in which executive actions differ from legislation in that respect. It also addresses how instructors, scholars, and students can use Trump 2.0 events to deepen their understanding of freedom of expression and perhaps suggests revisions to First Amendment doctrines.

Although especially relevant in the academic setting, the subject matter of the book is important to *anyone* who supports, defends, relies upon, or indeed exercises First Amendment rights. We ought all to be aware of current executive challenges to free expression and how various actors—including courts, the press, lawyers, universities, and other regulated parties—have responded to them.

RECORDING EXECUTIVE THREATS TO FREE EXPRESSION

Trump 2.0 has been a chaotic period characterized by intense executive activity implicating free expression. One of the goals of the book is to organize potential threats to the First Amendment so they can be more systematically studied. Creating a record of Trump 2.0 threats to free expression is independently important. Imagine, for example, having access to a contemporaneous record of McCarthy Era violations of First Amendment rights. A repository of the various executive actions affecting Americans' First Amendment rights during the Trump Era is an invaluable resource for current—and future—students of this period.

This is not simply a matter of recording events for posterity. Although this is a book about Trump 2.0, we ought to put what has happened so far into historical perspective. Some might suggest the events of Trump 2.0 represent "business as usual" or are simply "more of the same" when it comes to executive actions implicating or violating First Amendment rights. As historians and scholars have observed, presidents have threatened or violated First Amendment rights throughout American history. John Adams had wartime political opponents, including members of the press, prosecuted and jailed under federal "sedition" laws.[5] Pursuant to the Sedition Act and Espionage Act, Woodrow Wilson's administration convicted and imprisoned a thousand wartime activists and prosecuted twice that many.[6] Richard Nixon threatened to subject individuals on his "enemies list" to Internal Revenue Service investigations and other sanctions.[7] First Amendment conflicts have also arisen during more recent presidencies. For example, President Obama initiated prosecutions of reporters in connection with national security investigations. And President Biden's Administration pressured social media platforms to remove falsehoods about the 2020 presidential election, Covid-19 misinformation, and other content.[8]

However, in terms of threats to free expression, Trump 2.0 has been historically exceptional. No past president's actions affecting expression likely would have merited a chapter, much less an entire book, after only the *first 100 days* of a term. This book (and a companion online resource*) chronicles the breadth and depth of Trump 2.0 actions affecting free speech and press.

One could argue that since the Trump Administration has not generally imprisoned speakers (other than several international student activists), threats to free expression are not as acute as they were during previous eras. However, we should not use the excesses of wartime suppression, or periods in which the Supreme Court showed little regard for First Amendment rights, as benchmarks for contemporary First Amendment freedoms. In any event, as far as both past and more recent presidencies are concerned, the materials in the book show that the Trump Administration's actions represent an unprecedented executive threat to free expression.

One driver of this threat has been President Trump's historically unmatched reliance on Executive Orders as a means of top-down governing.[9] President Trump has demonstrated the Nation's Chief Executive needs only a pen and paper to issue both narrowly speech-retaliatory Orders and sweeping directives affecting expression within and far beyond government. As noted, of the more than two hundred Executive Orders and Memoranda Trump has issued thus far, a significant number target or affect freedom of expression. Even those that do not directly or explicitly target speakers or speech may threaten First Amendment

---

* I have compiled a comprehensive online repository of First Amendment-related Trump 2.0 Executive Orders, litigation challenging executive actions, and commentary, which is available at *Trump 2.0: Executive Power and the First Amendment*, First Amendment Watch, https://firstamendmentwatch.org/deep-dive/trump-2-0-executive-power-and-the-first-amendment/. The resource, which is updated weekly, can be used to further explore First Amendment issues raised by Trump 2.0 executive actions.

rights, depending on how agencies execute or administer them. For example, President Trump's directives relating to the increased use of federalized National Guard and other military personnel to respond to civil unrest may significantly affect the right to protest in public.[10]

President Trump has wielded the Executive Order as a retributory weapon. When he ran for president in 2024, Trump told his supporters, "I am your retribution."[11] He vowed to use the powers of his office to retaliate against individuals and institutions he and his supporters perceived as political and cultural foes. Trump was borrowing from President Richard Nixon's playbook. Nixon's White House Counsel, John Dean, described the Nixon Administration's "enemies list" project as aspiring to "*use the available federal machinery to screw our political enemies.*"[12] The Nixon Administration could not convince the IRS to participate, and the project was never fully implemented. Indeed, Nixon's retribution campaign would later become a political liability during Watergate.

By contrast, President Trump has been far more successful at instituting and leveraging executive power to seek retribution against political and ideological enemies. Several of President Trump's Executive Orders target and retaliate against individual institutions or speakers based on their disfavored expression. For example, *six* of the President's directives target law firms based on their representation of clients and advocacy for causes the President disfavors.[13] Two Presidential Memoranda target former Trump Administration officials who engaged in disfavored expression, including declaring the 2020 presidential election was free and fair.[14] Through Executive Orders and agency enforcement actions, the Trump Administration has also retaliated against the American Bar Association, media outlets, universities, and international student activists. President Trump and officials in his administration have also vowed to investigate and sanction others, including former public officials and celebrities who have criticized Trump or his policies.

Executive Orders are only the tip of the regulatory iceberg. As President Nixon recognized, it helps to have a federal bureaucracy fully committed to carrying out the President's directives and agenda. Agency actions implementing President Trump's Executive Orders have dramatically expanded threats to First Amendment rights. The Executive Orders are a general blueprint for a campaign aimed at punishing enemies for speech, controlling civic institutions, insisting on governmental truths or orthodoxies, deporting lawful resident aliens, and suppressing the distribution of information and scientific and other research. All federal agencies under President Trump's command are now loyally enforcing this blueprint, in what amounts to a whole-of-government campaign.

So far, that campaign has included more than *twenty* separate agencies including the Federal Bureau of Investigation, the Department of Justice, the Department of Homeland Security, the Department of Education, and the Agency for Healthcare Research and Quality. The President has also relied on Department of Justice prosecutors, who have threatened to investigate universities, scientific journals, and others for allegedly teaching, researching, or writing about disfavored concepts or ideas singled out in Executive Orders.[15]

Agencies across regulatory areas are enforcing presidential edicts that direct them to scrub data and information from public websites and agency materials, and to sanction individuals or institutions that do not accept official "truths." Pursuant to Executive Orders, federal agencies have investigated private employers, broadcasters, and universities based on their alleged support for Diversity Equity and Inclusion ("DEI") or "radical gender ideology"; targeted law firms based on their clients and causes; arrested, detained, and subjected to deportation international students based on their political advocacy; initiated proceedings against broadcast stations based on their editorial decisions; subpoenaed media records based on alleged participation in advertiser boycotts; removed scientific papers from public databases; and removed books from Department of Defense school libraries.[16]

President Trump and officials in his administration have made no secret of the fact that they want to control public narratives, punish and suppress disfavored speech, bring the media to heel, alter the ideological culture on university campuses, and influence scientific inquiry. Toward those ends, President Trump and executive officials have used various tactics to expand the reach of Executive Orders. These strategies have produced whole-of-society effects on freedom of expression and the free flow of information. They have affected expression across the Nation and beyond including in boardrooms, classrooms, laboratories, libraries, scientific journals, museums, and international courts. It is vitally important to understand *how* the Executive Branch has had such a broad impact on First Amendment freedoms in such a short period of time.

First, many Executive Orders rely on the threatened or actual termination of federal funding as an enforcement mechanism. Federal funding affects nearly every aspect of American life, including education (at all levels), commerce, agriculture, health care, immigration, the practice of law, broadcasting, and scientific research.[17] The Trump Administration has used a chainsaw rather than a scalpel when terminating funds for alleged violations of federal law. In contrast to prior administrations and in many cases contrary to federal law, agencies have terminated *all* funding rather than just those portions relating to alleged violations.

Second, in many instances, the Trump Administration has failed to provide the process required under federal law to deny or terminate federal funding.[18] This has enhanced the coercive and chilling effects of agency enforcement actions. By accelerating the denial of millions of dollars in federal funding, grantees have little time or recourse to contest often vague allegations or charges of wrongdoing prior to the denial or termination.

Third, because some of the Executive Orders lack meaningful specificity about concepts and terms, including "DEI," "radical gender ideology," "patriotic" curricula, and "divisive ideology," federal grantees cannot be certain which words, phrases, or ideas will result in a denial of often-critical funding. The vagueness of the standards in Executive Orders has produced significant uncertainty for universities, hospitals, businesses, and other funding recipients.[19] That uncertainty, in turn, has led to significant instances of *anticipatory compliance*—including changes in expression on a scale far beyond what federal anti-discrimination or other laws require.[20]

Fourth, for many of the above reasons, the Orders have engendered a repressive fear in federal fund recipients and those who have been or might be targeted—a fear "born of direct or veiled demands for loyalty" and the specter of punishment for dissent.[21] Thus, words and phrases must be removed, lectures canceled, and "deals" inked that trade away First Amendment rights and academic freedom for relief from facially retributive, disproportionate, and likely unconstitutional Executive Orders.[22]

The administration's reliance on anticipatory compliance and fear underscore just how widespread the effects of its actions on First Amendment rights and principles can be. By virtue of their breadth, procedural violations, vagueness, and coercion, President Trump's Executive Orders and agency enforcement actions have produced far more regulation and suppression of speech than ordinary executive action —which is constrained by (among other things) resource considerations and the obligation to comply with federal laws. Corporations have responded to Executive Orders by terminating activities and programs recognizing the value of a diverse workforce. Universities have scrubbed websites and other materials of references to the values of diversity in education or canceled lectures based on concerns that the "anti-government" tone of presentations might offend the Trump Administration.[23] Legal counsel at hospitals have even warned staff not to use "triggering" words like "vulnerable" or "diverse" to describe patients in presentations and other work.[24]

In short, as the book will show, President Trump has used executive power in unique ways to control what many millions of Americans can say and the information they can receive. In a remarkably brief period of time, President Trump and his administration have significantly impacted individual First Amendment rights and the broader American speech culture.

THE FIRST AMENDMENT LESSONS OF TRUMP 2.0

The goal of the book is not simply to record what has happened during Trump 2.0 regarding threats to First Amendment freedoms. Once we appreciate the breadth and depth of potential First Amendment harms from the Trump Administration's actions, questions arise concerning *whether* and, if so, *how* to address them in the classroom and more generally in discussions relating to the First Amendment.

The "whether" question is straightforward. Whatever else it will produce, Trump 2.0 and, for that matter, the entire Trump Era will be one of the nation's most significant historical periods when it comes to freedom of expression. To ignore or minimize this period would deprive students, scholars, and others interested in the First Amendment of essential information concerning the nature and scope of First Amendment freedoms. One cannot fully understand the current state of the First Amendment without examining how it has been affected, and as importantly how its doctrines and principles have performed, during this critical era.

How, though, does one teach and study one of the most impactful and fraught periods for free expression since the 1950s? And what lessons can we learn by studying the free expression controversies of Trump 2.0?

The book uses events of the current era to deepen our understanding of the First Amendment. As noted, we must first highlight and examine *executive* challenges to freedom of expression—something most First Amendment courses spend little time examining in any detail. We must better understand how the Executive Branch can use its powers to control, coerce, and suppress expression. President Trump and agency officials have revealed some of the mechanisms of this vast regulatory power, including Executive Orders, threats to federal funding, reliance on vague directives and guidance, anti-discrimination investigations, and prosecutorial "inquiries" to universities and scientific journals.

The book examines how these uses of executive power implicate First Amendment doctrines and principles. Each chapter contains a synopsis of the principal doctrine(s) under consideration. Trump 2.0 actions have intersected with a variety of traditional First Amendment doctrines and principles—for example: content neutrality, government speech, vagueness, unconstitutional conditions, newsgathering, and access to the public forum. Exercises of executive power have placed unique stress on these longstanding doctrines. The Trump Administration's actions have also affected doctrines and principles typically receiving little, if any, attention in First Amendment courses or discussions. For example, Trump 2.0 actions and policies have implicated doctrines prohibiting government from retaliating against speakers based on expression and forbidding "jawboning" and other informal means of coercing or suppressing speech. Executive actions have also raised questions about the First Amendment rights of noncitizens and the free flow of information.

The materials in the book support a standalone seminar on executive power and free expression. They could also be used to supplement traditional First Amendment casebooks, which will likely contain little, if any, discussion of Trump 2.0's unique free speech and press challenges. The book could also be used as a supplement in a course on executive power. Finally, the materials would provide students in First Amendment clinics with real-world references to the most critical issues of our time and, perhaps more importantly, how lawyers have sought to address them. In all these contexts, the book can be used both to reinforce the study of traditional doctrines and expand coverage to include doctrines and principles invoked to challenge recent exercises of executive power.

Most First Amendment courses focus on the decisions of the Supreme Court. This book is unique. To the extent it relies on judicial decisions, they are from lower courts—primarily district courts. Some of these decisions relate to pre-enforcement actions and preliminary relief. Supreme Court decisions are, of course, mentioned in discussions, briefs, and other materials. However, none of the issues examined in the book have yet been presented to the Supreme Court. Indeed, it is not clear how many (if any) Supreme Court decisions will result from Trump 2.0 First Amendment litigation. In contrast to other significant First Amendment eras, it is possible this period may not produce even one blockbuster Supreme Court precedent.

The absence of Supreme Court and, in general, other appellate decisions may be a virtue. Teaching law through the vehicle of appellate court decisions minimizes what occurs before appellate courts, including the Supreme Court, decide First Amendment claims.[25] Long before this happens, governments announce policies and take steps to implement them, and regulated and other affected parties decide whether and how to respond. Courts must then decide whether to grant injunctive or other relief, often based on pleadings or thin records.

Lawsuits are, of course, critical to understanding Trump 2.0 First Amendment controversies. As of this publication, more than *fifty* lawsuits raising First Amendment claims have been filed by law firms, universities, media, scientists, international students, professional associations, and others affected by executive actions. As noted, the book presents excerpts from decisions in some cases. However, in terms of materials, it differs from a conventional casebook. In addition to judicial decisions, the book contains texts of Executive Orders, pleadings, agency compliance letters and responses, public comments in agency proceedings, and other materials to examine First Amendment controversies. This mix of resources highlights both the variety of First Amendment issues raised by executive actions and the challenges of responding to them—often in a compressed time frame.

In this and other ways, the book focuses on the *practical realities* facing lawyers and their clients as they consider how to respond to executive actions. Although First Amendment precedents, doctrines, or standards may not directly address an issue, lawyers must still:

- Determine how to respond to Executive Orders that threaten to terminate billions of dollars in university research and other funding, unless the client accepts conditions that may undermine campus speech, academic freedom, and institutional independence.
- Counsel law firms targeted by Executive Orders concerning whether to file a lawsuit or make a deal with the White House.

- Counsel private companies concerned about federal anti-discrimination investigations.
- Represent legal resident and other aliens arrested, detained, and subjected to deportation proceedings based on their expressive activities.
- Counsel scientific journals that have received inquiries about their editorial processes from federal prosecutors.
- Defend a newspaper or broadcast station in a civil suit filed by the President of the United States.

To highlight the complexities of these and other situations, each chapter in the book contains a *Problem Exercise* that encourages discussion of relevant First Amendment doctrines and practical considerations affecting how to respond to executive action. For example, students will be asked to counsel celebrities targeted by Executive Orders, universities considering how to comply with unclear agency directives, newspapers excluded from official events, corporate executives wanting to support a diverse workforce, and scientists whose research projects have been canceled. These lessons will facilitate learning relevant First Amendment doctrines and standards but also encourage discussion of the on-the-ground realities of representing clients targeted by the President of the United States or affected by executive policies.

The book also invites consideration of broader concerns. For instance, Trump 2.0 has raised important questions about the extent to which courts can be relied upon to preserve First Amendment rights and civic institutions when they are under attack. Although lawsuits are an important check on executive power, one lesson of Trump 2.0 is that courts alone cannot address the full extent of threats to expressive freedom. For one thing, as we have seen, not all targeted or affected parties will challenge executive actions in litigation. Indeed, many will decide, as have prominent law firms, universities, and broadcasters, that the best course of action is to negotiate a "deal" or simply comply with Orders in advance of their enforcement—even when they strongly believe the executive's actions are unlawful.[26] Another consideration is that the Supreme Court has made it more difficult for courts to enter *nationwide* remedies, which may mean challengers will need to file in many jurisdictions to obtain relief or obtain judicial certification for class actions.[27]

The book also raises important questions about the efficacy and strength of First Amendment rights. To what extent did First Amendment doctrines prevent President Trump or his administration from inflicting harm on political enemies, starving universities of federal funding, or deporting legal resident aliens and temporary visa holders who engaged in political expression? How well did First Amendment doctrines, including the bar on retaliation for expression, vagueness, unconstitutional conditions, and viewpoint neutrality, fare when subjected to the stress test of Trump 2.0? To the extent these doctrines are deemed insufficient, what revisions might be made to strengthen or improve them?

In sum, we should endeavor not just to record events in this critical era but to make sense of how new threats to the First Amendment arose and, more importantly, how to effectively respond to them. This book is an early—and, given its timing, necessarily *preliminary*—effort to facilitate these goals.

1

A DOCTRINAL OVERVIEW

The Trump Administration has flooded the zone with Executive Orders, agency actions, and other measures that implicate the First Amendment. This makes it challenging to organize and understand the implications of its actions for First Amendment rights. However, in terms of First Amendment doctrines, a select few have played a prominent role in Trump 2.0 First Amendment controversies. This chapter provides a general overview of the primary First Amendment doctrines implicated in legal challenges to Trump 2.0 actions and policies. Subsequent chapters will remind readers, through *doctrinal synopses*, of the First Amendment standards that apply to covered topics. The chapters will then discuss application of specific doctrines in both actual and hypothetical situations.

A. EXECUTIVE ORDERS: GOVERNMENT SPEECH OR SPEECH REGULATION?

Federal statutes and regulations are familiar sources of law. By contrast, the legal and constitutional status of Executive Orders, and their relationship to the First Amendment, are less well understood. President Trump's Executive Orders are at the center of most of the conflicts discussed in the book. Unlike federal statutes, these Orders are not laws. Typically, they communicate the Executive's enforcement priorities and policies. But Executive Orders can also have significant regulatory effects.[1] As we will see, they often direct federal agencies and officials to take certain actions that affect First Amendment rights. In that respect, Executive Orders resemble other governmental actions having the force of law.

The First Amendment imposes restrictions on governments when they *regulate* private expression. Several of these limits are discussed below. For example, First Amendment doctrine establishes that speech regulations that target the idea or viewpoint of a speaker are presumptively invalid.[2] However, First Amendment doctrine also recognizes that when government is *speaking*, it may say what it wishes and can refuse to include or publish contrary views.[3] Among other things, this means that when the government communicates it need not comply with content neutrality standards. To take a very simple example, the Executive Branch can communicate its support for Israel without also being obligated to communicate speech supporting Palestine.

Are Executive Orders a form of government speech or a means of regulating private speech? As Genevieve Lakier has observed, Executive Orders "often merely declare administration policy, at a high level of generality. In this sense, they are akin to a political speech."[4] However, as noted, these presidential directives can have significant legal consequences. Consider an Executive Order directing agencies to terminate federal funding grants if grantees engage in "Diversity, Equity, and Inclusion" or "gender ideology" activities. Professor Lakier asks, "Does the statement of policy articulated in orders of this kind unconstitutionally coerce private silence, in violation of the First Amendment, or is it merely the kind of political rhetoric that is protected by the freedom of government speech?"[5]

Thus, one recurring question raised by the book's materials is how to characterize Executive Orders. Lawyers defending the Trump Administration have argued that President Trump's Executive Orders communicate the government's views and policies or merely articulate a policy to investigate or sanction unlawful discrimination or other conduct. By contrast, challengers have argued the Orders carry significant legal consequences, including the potential termination of federal funding and the initiation of investigations, which may deter or chill speech, and therefore are subject to First Amendment standards and limitations.

Whatever their legal status, parties targeted or covered by Executive Orders must decide how to respond to them, if only to avoid running afoul of any policies they articulate. Courts must decide, without much guidance from Supreme Court decisions, how to characterize and review these presidential directives.

B. VIEWPOINT DISCRIMINATION

As noted, although the government can communicate its own views, it is generally prohibited from suppressing the viewpoints of private speakers. First Amendment doctrine treats both laws that single out specific *subjects* and those that target *viewpoints* or *ideas* as presumptively unconstitutional.[6] These content-based speech regulations must meet a "strict scrutiny" standard requiring they further a compelling governmental interest and be the least speech-restrictive means of doing so.[7]

While all content-based regulations are suspect, the Supreme Court has described viewpoint discrimination as "an egregious form of content discrimination."[8] Thus, it has directed: "government must abstain from regulating speech when the specific motivating ideology or the opinion or perspective of the speaker is the rationale for the restriction."[9] Targeting speech based on its disfavored content or viewpoint is a quintessential First Amendment violation. As the Court has observed, "[i]f there is any fixed star in our constitutional constellation, it is that no official, high or petty, can prescribe what shall be orthodox in politics, nationalism, religion, or other matters of opinion or force citizens to confess by word or act their faith therein."[10]

A recurring issue in Trump 2.0 free expression controversies is whether presidential directives, agency actions, and other Executive Branch initiatives single out ideas, ideologies, or beliefs the administration disfavors. As we will see, the Trump Administration has offered two general defenses to such claims. The government has argued its actions constitute government speech and thus that it may choose among competing viewpoints. The Trump Administration has also defended against viewpoint discrimination claims by asserting that its actions target unlawful *conduct*, for example unlawful discrimination, rather than viewpoints regarding race, gender, or other matters.

C. RETALIATION BASED ON PROTECTED EXPRESSION

During the 2024 presidential election, Donald Trump told his supporters, "I am your retribution."[11] The President has delivered on that promise, in part by attacking political opponents and others whose expression he dislikes. As a result, a common challenge to Trump 2.0 executive actions is that they constitute official retaliation against speakers for speaking out. In civil actions, law firms, universities, private associations, broadcasters, international students, and others have alleged the administration has retaliated against them based on protected expression.

The First Amendment prohibits government officials from subjecting individuals to retaliatory actions for engaging in protected speech.[12] To succeed on a First Amendment retaliation claim, a plaintiff must typically prove: (1) they engaged in a constitutionally protected activity; (2) the government's actions would "chill a person of ordinary firmness" from continuing to engage in the protected activity; and (3) the protected activity was a substantial motivating factor in the defendant's conduct—*i.e.*, that there was a causal nexus between the defendant's actions and the intent to chill speech.[13] Proving retaliatory motive is not sufficient. The speaker must demonstrate the government would not have taken the adverse action absent a retaliatory motive.[14]

In most of the retaliation actions discussed in subsequent chapters, there is no dispute plaintiffs were engaged in protected expression. However, as noted, they must also demonstrate a causal link between the expression and the government's action. That may prove difficult, especially during early stages of litigation. Even if retaliation claims survive a motion to dismiss, government defendants prevail if they have a valid non-speech basis for their actions. As we will see, in many cases the Trump Administration has argued it acted not to retaliate against a speaker but to investigate and sanction unlawful conduct.

D. VAGUENESS

The Supreme Court has held that, like other laws, those regulating expression must be drafted with sufficient clarity that a person of "common intelligence" can understand how to comply.[15] As the Court has observed, "It is a basic principle of due process that an enactment is void for vagueness if its prohibitions are not clearly defined."[16]

This requirement is rooted not in the First Amendment but in the Due Process Clause. However, vague governmental directives are especially dangerous when enforced against speakers. Because they provide no meaningful warning as to what expression the law prohibits, vague laws and regulations offend basic principles of fairness. As the Supreme Court has observed, "[v]ague laws may trap the innocent by not providing fair warning."[17] Further, the failure to provide clear standards raises the specter of arbitrary and discriminatory enforcement.[18] Vague speech regulations may also "chill" expression by causing speakers to "steer far wider of the unlawful zone ... than if the boundaries of the forbidden area were clearly marked."[19] In particular, the Court has emphasized the chilling effects of broad governmental directives and investigations aimed at suppressing disfavored viewpoints or ideas.[20] For all these reasons, "[s]tandards of permissible . . . vagueness are strict in the area of free expression."[21]

Like First Amendment retaliation claims, vagueness arguments have played a prominent role in early challenges to Trump 2.0 directives and actions. Challengers have argued that Executive Orders lack the requisite clarity. For example, President Trump's Orders prohibit funding recipients from engaging in "Diversity, Equity, and Inclusion" (DEI) but do not define "DEI." Grantees and others have argued this fails to provide clear standards regarding what they must do to comply, which has led to self-censorship and anticipatory compliance.

E. "JAWBONING" AND INFORMAL SPEECH SUPPRESSION

Suppression and censorship of expression can take many forms. Regulations sometimes directly prohibit or restrict expression. However, governments sometimes rely on more *indirect* forms of speech suppression. For example, as the vagueness doctrine recognizes, governments could use unclear laws strategically to cause or encourage speaker self-censorship.

The problem of "jawboning," or the use of *informal* means of coercion and pressure to suppress expression, has begun to receive greater attention from courts and scholars.[22] Although governmental reliance on informal means of censorship is not a new problem, courts have had difficulty applying a consistent principle to this practice.[23] In a recent decision, *National Rifle Ass'n v. Vullo*, the Supreme Court announced a categorical rule against government using informal means to accomplish unconstitutional ends.[24] The Court unanimously held New York officials violated the First Amendment when they used informal communications and other forms of indirect pressure against regulated businesses, in an effort to prevent them from working or associating with the

National Rifle Association. It concluded the officials' communications "can be reasonably understood as a threat or as an inducement."[25]

In *Vullo*, the Court held that "[a] government official cannot coerce a private party to punish or suppress disfavored speech on her behalf."[26] The Court also established a broader principle. It held government officials cannot "rely[] on the 'threat of invoking legal sanctions and other means of coercion . . . to achieve the suppression' of disfavored speech."[27] Shortly after *Vullo* was decided, the Court heard a case in which plaintiffs alleged Biden Administration officials had pressured and coerced social media platforms to remove information about Covid-19 and other topics.[28] In that case, the Court did not reach plaintiffs' claims that the federal government had indirectly suppressed expression because it determined they lacked legal standing to sue.

Vullo is a significant precedent. Indeed, owing to how the Trump Administration has used executive power, it could turn out to be the *most* important First Amendment precedent of the Trump era. The administration has frequently relied on threats to terminate federal funding and investigations based on "DEI" and other practices. The Court's rule against "jawboning" speakers is rooted in a basic understanding that the government's use of threats, intimidation, and leverage can be just as dangerous to speakers' rights as laws or regulations directly regulating expression.

To be sure, as we will see, the line between lawful government persuasion and coercion that violates the First Amendment can be difficult to identify. As some of the Trump 2.0 policies and actions show, that uncertainty may provide space for government officials to use the threat of sanctions and other leverage that can be as—or even more—effective than direct regulation of expression. Left unchecked, "jawboning" and other coercive measures can produce broad-scale anticipatory compliance and chill protected speech.

F. UNCONSTITUTIONAL CONDITIONS

One way the government can apply pressure to control expression is to condition the receipt of federal funding on the grantee's agreement not to engage in certain speech or associational activities. Congress has the power to appropriate and spend monies. However, many Trump 2.0 initiatives rely on the *executive's* purported authority to terminate federal education, scientific, and other funding. For this reason, the doctrine of "unconstitutional conditions" has played an important role in early Trump 2.0 legal challenges. According to the doctrine's central principle, the government is not required to fund any activity but if it does so it cannot deny funding on a basis that infringes an applicant's First Amendment or other constitutional rights.[29]

Unconstitutional conditions doctrine consists of a complex and confusing set of standards. However, as they relate to Trump 2.0 controversies, the basic contours of the doctrine can be readily identified. Start with the principle that the federal government is not legally or constitutionally obligated to distribute funding for educational, scientific, or any other activities. In cases challenging the termination or threatened withholding of federal funding, the Trump Administration has frequently invoked the government's broad funding discretion. (Many plaintiffs have challenged the exercise of this discretion on separation of powers grounds, arguing that Congress's funding directives control.)

Challengers have pointed to two First Amendment limitations on executive discretion. One limit is if government chooses to fund private expression, it cannot deny funding to speakers or associations in order to suppress ideas or viewpoints.[30] A second limit is that although government can restrict the use of federal funds to activities it chooses to support, including its own expression, the Supreme Court has held it cannot "leverage funding to regulate speech outside the contours of the funding program itself."[31] In other words, the government cannot use the spending power as an indirect means of suppressing private speech. For example, it cannot condition university funding for *scientific* research on the medical faculty speaking out publicly against "gender ideology."[32]

Under the unconstitutional conditions doctrine, defining the *scope* of the government's funding program is often a key consideration. The critical question, in many cases, is when does the government's attempt to control funding cross the line into a form of unlawful leveraging? As Michael Dorf has put it, "At some point, the relation between the projects being funded and the objectionable speech (or conduct) is so attenuated that the government should be understood to be impermissibly leveraging the funding power."[33] For example, regarding the Trump Administration's termination of university funding, one question is whether withholding billions of dollars in scientific, educational, and other funding is sufficiently related to its concerns regarding campus anti-Semitism and alleged "DEI" practices.[34]

G. THE FIRST AMENDMENT RIGHTS OF NONCITIZENS

As discussed in Chapter 5, the Trump Administration has arrested, detained, and initiated deportation proceedings against several international students and foreign scholars who engaged in pro-Palestine political advocacy.[35] The administration's actions against these foreign nationals, who were present in the U.S. pursuant to temporary student visas or Green Cards, have raised questions about the First Amendment rights of noncitizens and the intersection between federal immigration law and freedom of expression.

Most First Amendment courses and casebooks devote little, if any, space to considerations of the rights of noncitizens. The Trump Administration's immigration enforcement policies highlight the need for greater attention to this area. Unfortunately, case law is somewhat sparse and binding precedent hard to come by. The Supreme Court has indicated that "[f]reedom of speech and of press is accorded aliens residing in this country."[36] However, it has not clarified the precise relationship between enforcement of the nation's immigration laws and the First Amendment. In particular, the Court has not decided whether noncitizens in the U.S. enjoy the *same* First Amendment rights as citizens.

The leading precedent from 1952, *Harisiades v. Shaughnessy*, suggested Congress has broad powers over deportation. However, *Harisiades* was decided during the Red Scare, when First Amendment protections were far less robust—even for citizens—than they are today.[37] Further, the Court's discussion of congressional power over deportation occurred in a section of the opinion addressing the Due Process Clause. The relatively brief First Amendment discussion rested on the Court's determination that active membership in the Communist Party was not protected, for citizens or noncitizens, by the First Amendment. This ruling has been significantly undermined by subsequent precedents.[38] However, lower courts have issued conflicting decisions regarding the application of the First Amendment in the deportation setting. Some courts have concluded resident aliens enjoy the same protections as citizens,[39] while others have ruled that the federal government has nearly unlimited or "plenary" power to exclude or deport aliens—including based on their political expression.[40]

The lack of clarity is somewhat understandable. Since the mid-twentieth century, presidential administrations have not asserted a *general* power to detain and deport lawfully resident aliens based solely on their political expression. The First Amendment question has not been squarely presented to the Supreme Court. Meanwhile, the Court has not formally overruled its decisions from the 1950s, and subsequent decisions continue to recognize the executive's broad power to revoke visas.[41] In recent legal challenges, the Trump Administration has either avoided answering the First Amendment question (relying instead on other grounds for detaining and deporting noncitizens) or asserted that lawful resident aliens do not have the same First Amendment rights as citizens based on Red Scare era and other precedents.

H. THE FREE FLOW OF INFORMATION

As discussed in Chapter 7, the First Amendment protects the right to gather, distribute, and receive information. The Supreme Court has sometimes collectively referred to these activities as encompassing the "free flow of information."[42] Trump 2.0 activities and policies have affected the free flow of information in several ways. The administration has removed scientific and other data from government websites, restricted scientific research, defunded public broadcasters and libraries, and removed books from school libraries.

The free flow of information is not a discrete, substantive First Amendment doctrine. Rather, it is a general principle that recognizes the importance of free and unfettered discourse, with a special emphasis on the right to receive information. That right furthers First Amendment values including self-government, the search for truth in marketplaces of ideas, and individual self-fulfillment.[43]

Protecting the free flow of information is a longstanding First Amendment concern. Early commentators emphasized its importance. Alexander Meiklejohn, whose work focused on the importance of free expression to self-government, wrote that "the point of ultimate interest is not the words of the speakers, but the minds of the hearers . . . [w]hat is essential is not that everyone shall speak, but that everything worth saying shall be said."[44] Thomas Emerson, another prominent early commentator, emphasized that government must "undertake positively to promote and encourage freedom of expression, as by furnishing facilities, eliminating distortions in the media of communication, or making information available."[45]

Modern First Amendment precedents and doctrines have incorporated this wisdom. Thus, the Supreme Court has emphasized that discourse on matters of public concern must be "uninhibited, robust, and wide-open."[46] Toward that end, it has recognized the rights of reporters to gather information and of listeners and viewers to receive commercial, scientific, political, and other kinds of information.[47] The Court's decisions have also established or supported safeguards, including the requirement of content neutrality, limits on the government's authority to remove books from libraries, and principles of academic freedom, which protect the production and distribution of information from governmental censorship and interference.[48]

Supreme Court precedents have specifically recognized a concern with the right of audiences to *receive* information.[49] When invalidating a state law that prohibited corporations from making expenditures in referendum campaigns, the Court wrote, "the First Amendment goes beyond protection of the press and the self-expression of individuals to prohibit government from limiting the stock of information from which members of the public may draw."[50] The Court has invalidated laws prohibiting adults from possessing obscene matter in the privacy of their homes because the "right to receive information and ideas, regardless of their social worth . . . is fundamental to our free society."[51] It has warned against governmental efforts "to control the flow of ideas to the public" and observed that "the State may not, consistently with the spirit of the First Amendment, contract the spectrum of available knowledge."[52] In its decisions, the Court has also urged government to *promote*, through its laws and regulations, "the paramount interest in a free flow of information to the people."[53] Finally, the Court has recognized that when it communicates with the public, the government contributes to the free flow of information.[54] In sum, as the Court observed in *Citizens United v. Federal Election Comm'n*: "The right of citizens to inquire, to hear, to speak, and to use information to reach consensus is a precondition to enlightened self-government and a necessary means to protect it."[55]

As is true of all constitutional rights, the right to receive information is not absolute. Thus, the Court has not interpreted the First Amendment as if it is a freedom of information act. For example, it has rejected claims that the public enjoys a First Amendment right to access *all* information in the possession of government.[56] And the Court has recognized significant limitations on the right to publish or receive information in the context of federal funding, where government has wide latitude to determine what messages to convey and what activities to support.[57]

2

RETRIBUTION AND RETALIATION

Plaintiffs in a variety of contexts have challenged Trump 2.0 actions on the ground that they constitute retaliation against speakers or associations based on protected First Amendment activities. This Chapter introduces the First Amendment anti-retaliation doctrine. It focuses on executive actions targeting law firms and the Bar. The President has issued *six* Executive Orders directing executive agencies to take various regulatory actions against specific law firms. It has also threatened to withhold federal funds for projects supported by the American Ban Association. The *Problem Exercise* asks how you would advise a different kind of presidential target—the rock star Bruce Springsteen.

A. LAW FIRMS

Executive Order 14230: Addressing Risks from Perkins Coie LLP

90 Fed. Reg. 11781 (March 6, 2025)

By the authority vested in me as President by the Constitution and the laws of the United States of America, it is hereby ordered:

Section 1. Purpose. The dishonest and dangerous activity of the law firm Perkins Coie LLP ("Perkins Coie") has affected this country for decades. Notably, in 2016 while representing failed Presidential candidate Hillary Clinton, Perkins Coie hired Fusion GPS, which then manufactured a false "dossier" designed to steal an election. This egregious activity is part of a pattern. Perkins Coie has worked with activist donors including George Soros to judicially overturn popular, necessary, and democratically enacted election laws, including those requiring voter identification. In one such case, a court was forced to sanction Perkins Coie attorneys for an unethical lack of candor before the court.

In addition to undermining democratic elections, the integrity of our courts, and honest law enforcement, Perkins Coie racially discriminates against its own attorneys and staff, and against applicants. Perkins Coie publicly announced percentage quotas in 2019 for hiring and promotion on the basis of race and other categories prohibited by civil rights laws. It proudly excluded applicants on the basis of race for its fellowships, and it maintained these discriminatory practices until applicants harmed by them finally sued to enforce change.

My Administration is committed to ending discrimination under "diversity, equity, and inclusion" policies and ensuring that Federal benefits support the laws and policies of the United States, including those laws and policies promoting our national security and respecting the democratic process. Those who engage in blatant race-based and sex-based discrimination, including quotas, but purposefully hide the nature of such discrimination through deceiving language, have engaged in a serious violation of the public trust. Their disrespect for the bedrock principle of equality represents good cause to conclude that they neither have access to our Nation's secrets nor be deemed responsible stewards of any Federal funds.

Sec. 2. Security Clearance Review. (a) The Attorney General, the Director of National Intelligence, and all other relevant heads of executive departments and agencies (agencies) shall immediately take steps consistent with applicable law to suspend any active security clearances held by individuals at Perkins Coie, pending a review of whether such clearances are consistent with the national interest.

(b) The Office of Management and Budget shall identify all Government goods, property, material, and services, including Sensitive Compartmented Information Facilities, provided for the benefit of Perkins Coie. The heads of all agencies providing such material or services shall, to the extent permitted by law, expeditiously cease such provision.

Sec. 3. Contracting. (a) To prevent the transfer of taxpayer dollars to Federal contractors whose earnings subsidize, among other things, racial discrimination, falsified documents designed to weaponize the Government against candidates for office, and anti-democratic election changes that invite fraud and distrust, Government contracting agencies shall, to the extent permissible by law, require Government contractors to disclose any business they do with Perkins Coie and whether that business is related to the subject of the Government contract. . . .

(b) The heads of all agencies shall review all contracts with Perkins Coie or with entities that disclose doing business with Perkins Coie under subsection (a) of this section. . . .

Sec. 4. Racial Discrimination. (a) The Chair of the Equal Employment Opportunity Commission shall review the practices of representative large, influential, or industry leading law firms for consistency with Title VII of the Civil Rights Act of 1964, including whether large law firms: reserve certain positions, such as summer associate spots, for individuals of preferred races; promote individuals on a discriminatory basis; permit client access on a discriminatory basis; or provide access to events, trainings, or travel on a discriminatory basis. . . .

Sec. 5. Personnel. (a) The heads of all agencies shall, to the extent permitted by law, provide guidance limiting official access from Federal Government buildings to employees of Perkins Coie when such access would threaten the national security of or otherwise be inconsistent with the interests of the United States. In addition, the heads of all agencies shall provide guidance limiting Government employees acting in their official capacity from engaging with Perkins Coie employees to ensure consistency with the national security and other interests of the United States.

(b) Agency officials shall, to the extent permitted by law, refrain from hiring employees of Perkins Coie, absent a waiver from the head of the agency, made in consultation with the Director of the Office of Personnel Management, that such hire will not threaten the national security of the United States.

DOCTRINAL SYNOPSIS I: GOVERNMENT SPEECH

- The First Amendment limits governmental regulation of private speech but does not limit the government's own speech.
- When the government acts as a speaker, it is entitled to determine what it wishes to say.

DOCTRINAL SYNOPSIS II: FIRST AMENDMENT RETALIATION

- The First Amendment prohibits government officials from subjecting an individual to retaliatory actions for speaking out or engaging in protected expression.
- To prevail on a First Amendment retaliation claim, Plaintiff must show (1) they engaged in conduct protected under the First Amendment; (2) Defendants took some retaliatory action sufficient to deter a person of ordinary firmness in Plaintiff's position from speaking again; and (3) there is a causal link between the exercise of a constitutional right and the adverse action.

Perkins Coie LLP v. U.S. Dept. of Justice

783 F. Supp. 3d 105 (D.D.C. 2025)

HOWELL, D.J.

No American President has ever before issued executive orders like the one at issue in this lawsuit targeting a prominent law firm with adverse actions to be executed by all Executive branch agencies but, in purpose and effect, this action draws from a playbook as old as Shakespeare, who penned the phrase: "The first thing we do, let's kill all the lawyers." WILLIAM SHAKESPEARE, HENRY VI, PART 2, act 4, sc. 2, l. 75. When Shakespeare's character, a rebel leader intent on becoming king, hears this suggestion, he promptly incorporates this tactic as part of his plan to assume power, leading in the same scene to the rebel leader demanding "[a]way with him," referring to an educated clerk, who "can make obligations and write court hand," *id.* l. 90, 106. Eliminating lawyers as the guardians of the rule of law removes a major impediment to the path to more power. *See Walters v. Nat'l Ass'n of Radiation Survivors*, 473 U.S. 305, 371 n.24 (1985) (Stevens, J., dissenting) (explaining the import of the same Shakespearean statement to be "that disposing of lawyers is a step in the direction of a totalitarian form of government").

The importance of independent lawyers to ensuring the American judicial system's fair and impartial administration of justice has been recognized in this country since its founding era. In 1770, John Adams made the singularly unpopular decision to represent eight British soldiers charged with murder for their roles in the Boston Massacre and "claimed later to have suffered the loss of more than half his practice." DAVID MCCULLOUGH, JOHN ADAMS 68 (2001). "I had no hesitation," he explained, since "Council ought to be the very last thing that an accused Person should want in a free Country," and "the Bar ought . . . to be independent and impartial at all Times And in every Circumstance." 3 DIARY AND AUTOBIOGRAPHY OF JOHN ADAMS 293 (L.H. Butterfield et al. eds., 1961).

When the Bill of Rights was ratified, these principles were codified into the Constitution: The Sixth Amendment secured the right, in "all criminal prosecutions," to "have the Assistance of Counsel for . . . defence," U.S. CONST. amend. VI, and the Fifth Amendment protected "the right to the aid of counsel when desired and provided by the party asserting the right," *Powell v. Alabama*, 287 U.S. 45, 68 (1932). This value placed on the role of lawyers caught the attention of Alexis de Tocqueville, who in reflecting on his travels throughout the early United States in 1831 and 1832, insightfully remarked that "the authority . . . intrusted to members of the legal profession . . . is the most powerful existing security against the excesses of democracy." ALEXIS DE TOCQUEVILLE, DEMOCRACY IN AMERICA 301 (Henry Reeve trans., 2002) (1835).

The Supreme Court, too, has recognized the importance of lawyers to the functioning of the American judicial system, since "[a]n informed, independent judiciary presumes an informed, independent bar." *Legal Servs. Corp. v. Velazquez*, 531 U.S. 533, 545 (2001). This is so because Congress may legislate, the President may implement, and courts may adjudicate, "but only the lawyers can prepare and submit the great issues of human justice under law in such manner and form that courts, in the ultimate, may be effective." *Williams v. Beto*, 354 F.2d 698, 706 (5th Cir. 1965). Absent their crucial independence, lawyers would "become nothing more than parrots of the views of whatever group wields governmental power at the moment." *Cohen v. Hurley*, 366 U.S. 117, 138 (1961) (Black, J., dissenting).

The instant case presents an unprecedented attack on these foundational principles. On March 6, 2025, President Trump issued an Executive Order entitled "Addressing Risks from Perkins Coie LLP." By its terms, this Order stigmatizes and penalizes a particular law firm and its employees—from its partners to its associate attorneys, secretaries, and mailroom attendants—due to the Firm's representation, both in the past and currently, of clients pursuing claims and taking positions with which the current President disagrees, as well as the Firm's own speech. In a cringe-worthy twist on the theatrical phrase "Let's kill all the lawyers," [the Order] takes the approach of "Let's kill the lawyers I don't like," sending the clear message: lawyers must stick to the party line, or else.

Using the powers of the federal government to target lawyers for their representation of clients and avowed progressive employment policies in an overt attempt to suppress and punish certain viewpoints, however, is contrary to the Constitution, which requires that the government respond to dissenting or unpopular speech or ideas with "tolerance, not coercion." *303 Creative LLC v. Elenis*, 600 U.S. 570, 603 (2023). The Supreme Court has long made clear that "no official, high or petty, can prescribe what shall be orthodox in politics . . . or other matters of opinion." *W. Va. State Bd. of Educ. v. Barnette*, 319 U.S. 624, 642 (1943). Simply put, government officials "cannot . . . use the power of the State to punish or suppress disfavored expression." *NRA v. Vullo*, 602 U.S. 175, 188 (2024).

That, however, is exactly what is happening here. For this reason, and those explained more fully below, [the Order] is unconstitutional, and the findings and instructions to Executive Branch agencies issued in its Sections 1 through 5 cannot be allowed to stand.

[Government Speech]

The government's argument suggests that to the extent the Section 1 statements amount merely to President Trump's protected speech, at least that section (and potentially the full Order) may not be enjoined. Not so. While government officials may, under the First Amendment, "share [their] views freely and criticize particular beliefs," they may not "use the power of the State to punish or suppress disfavored expression." *Vullo*, 602 U.S. at 188. Courts may, therefore, properly "scrutinize" cases where "the application of state power" is called into question. *Id.* at 188.

The government's attempt to reframe this case as about governmental speech is subterfuge. Plaintiff has not sued at any point over the last almost decade when President Trump, either when serving in an official role as President or as a private citizen and political candidate, made derogatory statements about the Firm and its current or former employees. The claims that the government seeks to dismiss in this lawsuit challenge the use of governmental power, not governmental speech. More specifically, plaintiff seeks to enjoin the use of the Section 1 statements by executive branch actors to justify adverse actions toward plaintiff, on grounds that actions based on those statements would constitute unlawful retaliation and other violations of plaintiff's and its clients' constitutional rights.

. . . Plaintiff does not seek, nor would this Court grant, an injunction to prevent President Trump from sharing his views or criticizing particular beliefs. At the same time, however, plaintiff may challenge the application of state power against plaintiff based on statements qualifying as "findings" used to justify an order with which Executive branch agencies must comply.

[Retaliation]

As the Supreme Court has explained, the First Amendment protects the right of "all persons . . . to think and speak as they wish, not as the government demands." *303 Creative*, 600 U.S. at 603. One obvious implication of these First Amendment protections is that government officials may not subject individuals to "retaliatory actions" after the fact for having engaged in protected speech. Such official reprisal for protected speech threatens to inhibit exercise of the protected right.

This prohibition also extends to retaliation against individuals for the specific viewpoint expressed by their First Amendment protected activities, since the government may not "use the power of the State to punish or suppress disfavored expression," *Vullo*, 602 U.S. at 188, nor use threats of legal sanctions and other means of coercion to achieve the suppression of disfavored speech. Retaliation and threats of retaliation to effectuate viewpoint discrimination is uniquely harmful to a free and democratic society. Ultimately, punishing or denying a benefit to an individual on the basis of constitutionally protected speech or associations violates the Constitution.

In this case, plaintiff claims that [the Order] targets the Firm for unconstitutional retaliation based on two different types of viewpoints expressed by plaintiff in the exercise of First Amendment protected activities. First, plaintiff alleges that the Executive Order singles out and punishes Perkins Coie for its association with, and advocacy on behalf of, the President's political opponents in the 2016 and 2020 elections, attributing those viewpoints to plaintiff and retaliating against the firm on that basis. Second, plaintiff claims that [the Order] unconstitutionally retaliates against plaintiff for statements in favor of diversity and inclusion.

[The Order] openly acknowledges that plaintiff engaged in speech and other activities protected by the First Amendment. Section 1 of the

Order, which sets out its "Purpose," cites three reasons for the enumerated action items in Sections 2 through 5 that federal agencies are ordered to take against plaintiff: (1) the Firm's representation of "Hillary Clinton" during the 2016 presidential election; (2) the Firm's involvement in litigation against "election laws, including those requiring voter identification"; and (3) the Firm's alleged discrimination in "hiring and promotion" and efforts to "purposefully hide the nature of" this alleged discrimination "through deceiving language." The associated fact sheet adds a fourth: "Perkins Coie LLP has filed lawsuits against the Trump Administration," which are also described as "partisan lawsuits against the United States." These four reasons are the sole rationales provided for the issuance of [the Order] and each, on their face, implicate First Amendment protected activities.

Well-settled law establishes that advocacy by attorneys to the courts falls within the category of private speech protected by the First Amendment, *see NAACP v. Button*, 371 U.S. 415, 429 (1963) ("[T]he First Amendment . . . protects vigorous advocacy, certainly of lawful ends, against governmental intrusion," including litigation, which "is thus a form of political expression."), meaning that plaintiff's representation of a political opponent of the current President and involvement in election litigation and lawsuits against the Trump Administration explicitly qualifies as core First Amendment speech.

Moreover, as part of plaintiff's involvement in election litigation, [the Order] further states that plaintiff "worked with" what is described as "activist donors," specifically naming "George Soros," in bringing these cases. This relationship explicitly invokes core First Amendment associational rights. *See, e.g.*, *Button*, 371 U.S. at 430 (affirming "the right 'to engage in association for the advancement of beliefs and ideas'"). So, too, does plaintiff's representation of and association with President Trump's former presidential opponent.

Both [the Order] and the accompanying fact sheet additionally make clear that President Trump and his administration disfavor the specific messages conveyed by plaintiff through involvement in these activities. For instance, the Order expresses disapproval of the election-related lawsuits litigated by plaintiff challenging actions supported by President Trump or his campaign and with other lawsuits filed by plaintiff on behalf of its clients "against the Trump Administration" and "against the United States."

The Order also takes issue with plaintiff's representation in the 2016 presidential election of President Trump's political opponent and, as part of that representation, some of plaintiff's former employees associated with an opposition research firm, Fusion GPS. Finally, the fact sheet disparages plaintiff as "partisan" three separate times, making explicit that those in power disagree with the political and litigation positions taken by clients of plaintiff.

As to the third reason—that plaintiff supposedly engages in unlawful discrimination—the record also demonstrates that this claim refers to plaintiff's First Amendment protected speech in favor of diversity. . . . [The] government's briefing reveals the true motivation lurking behind the façade of discrimination allegations: the administration's disapproval of plaintiff's speech in favor of diversity.

The second requirement for a retaliation claim, that plaintiff show the actions taken against the Firm were sufficient to deter a person of ordinary firmness in plaintiff's position from speaking again, is satisfied by plaintiff's showing of irreparable harm, and further bolstered by the reactions of plaintiff's peer law firms. . . . The fact that Paul, Weiss quickly negotiated a deal, including an agreement to provide "the equivalent of $40 million" in free legal work, rather than face the potential injuries of the similar Executive Order targeting that firm, demonstrates the coercive power of such targeting by the Trump Administration. This conclusion is further confirmed by the reaction of additional peer law firms that chose to negotiate deals with the Trump White House to avoid being targeted by similar Executive Orders.

Each additional deal provides further evidence to satisfy the second element of plaintiff's retaliation claim, given that each of these firms, presumably possessing "ordinary firmness," sought successfully to avoid being targeted by similar Executive branch actions, with each law firm committing the equivalent of $100 million or more as part of the price to do so.

Finally, the record is clear that [the Order] is motivated by retaliation for plaintiff's First Amendment protected activity. Resisting this conclusion, the government protests that [the Order] does not retaliate against plaintiff for First Amendment activity but instead takes action "based on what it believes to be in the public interest." Here, however, these arguments are merely two sides of the same coin. The four reasons provided by the Order to justify targeting plaintiff all refer to President

Trump's objections to plaintiff's protected speech and associations. Neither the Order nor the accompanying fact sheet provide any basis to find that plaintiff threatens the public interest or national interest other than the stated disagreements with plaintiff's First Amendment protected activity. That plaintiff's protected activities are the only reasons provided by the Order itself to justify the actions directed is strong evidence that the Order retaliates against plaintiff for engaging in those protected activities.

In addition to the text of the Order, President Trump's repeated prior statements about plaintiff and lawyers formerly associated with the Firm provide probative context that informs assessment of the retaliatory purpose of the Order as a whole. Since 2017, President Trump has repeatedly attacked plaintiff and its former employees for representing clients involved in the 2016 and 2020 presidential elections, as well as the 2018 midterm election, accusing the Firm of involvement in "[c]ollusion" during the 2016 campaign; criticizing the Firm's "dishonesty"; accusing Marc Elias of "stealing" elections and engaging in election fraud; and sharing online articles claiming that plaintiff and Michael Sussmann tried to "[c]orrupt a Presidential Election." President Trump's nearly decade-long preoccupation with plaintiff's election litigation and representation of Democratic political candidates, as well as his grievances about the Firm's work in those client matters, are reflected in the purpose of the Order, which justifies the actions taken against plaintiff, in part, on the Firm's representation of his political opponent during the 2016 presidential election and election law litigation.

That the Order was issued as retribution for plaintiff's work and President Trump's grievances is further confirmed by President Trump's statements during the 2024 presidential campaign, when he continued to attack plaintiff and its former lawyers, Marc Elias and Michael Sussmann, and explicitly promised to take some form of action if he were elected. These retaliation threats have now come to fruition against plaintiff, through the issuance of the Order, which outlines in the "Purpose" section some of these same longstanding grievances.

President Trump's multi-year history of lodging public attacks critical of plaintiff, his promises during the 2024 campaign to act on his displeasure toward plaintiff if he won, and the subsequent issuance of the Order—which repeats many of the same attacks on plaintiff—further demonstrates that [the Order] was issued to seek retribution against plaintiff for the Firm's representation of clients in political campaigns or litigation, about which President Trump expressed disapproval, dating back to 2017. This purpose amounts to no more than unconstitutional retaliation for plaintiff's First Amendment protected activity.

* * *

[The Order] . . . and the context surrounding the Order's issuance each express President Trump's disapproval of plaintiff's First Amendment activity and demonstrate that it targeted plaintiff because the Firm expressed support for employment policies the President does not like, represented clients the President does not like, represented clients seeking litigation results the President does not like, and represented clients challenging some of the President's actions, which he also does not like. That is unconstitutional retaliation and viewpoint discrimination, plain and simple. Plaintiff, therefore, is entitled to summary judgment.

DISCUSSION

1. *Litigation and First Amendment Rights.* In addition to freedom of speech, Judge Howell observed that the Perkins Coie Executive Order affected the right to *associate* with clients and others for expressive purposes. *See, e.g., Roberts v. United States Jaycees*, 468 U.S. 609, 622 (1984). Filing and pursuing lawsuits also constitute forms of protected *petitioning* under the First Amendment. *See Borough of Duryea v. Guarnieri*, 564 U.S. 379, 387 (2011) ("This Court's precedents confirm that the Petition Clause protects the right of individuals to appeal to courts and other forums established by the government for resolution of legal disputes.").

2. *Deal or No Deal?* As of this writing, lower courts that have ruled on Executive Orders targeting law firms have all invalidated them. However, as Judge Howell observed, not all law firms targeted by the President challenged his actions in court. *Nine* firms decided to enter unwritten "deals" with the Trump Administration. As Judge Howell observed, they agreed to provide *pro bono* legal services totaling approximately $1 billion in cumulative value. Some law firms defended the deals by explaining to their employees and the public that the Orders threatened the very existence of the firms and, more-

over, the agreements to provide *pro bono* services were consistent with their missions.

- Imagine you are a *partner* with one of the targeted law firms. Would you want the firm to file a lawsuit or make a "deal" with the President? What factors would you consider when making this decision?
- Imagine you are an *associate* at one of the targeted law firms. How would you want the firm to proceed? What considerations would influence your thinking?
- Imagine you are a *lawyer representing the federal government.* Would you appeal the district court's decision? Are some provisions, such as the security clearance and employment discrimination directives, valid exercises of executive power? Would filing an appeal communicate to other firms that the President is committed to issuing similar Orders?

3. *The Right to Counsel.* The law firm Executive Orders and the "deals" made with President Trump may undermine the role of lawyers and the rule of law. In addition to violating the First Amendment, Judge Howell held that the Perkins Coie Order violated the Fifth Amendment and Sixth Amendment rights of plaintiff's clients—by interfering with Perkins Coie's ability to represent its clients and the clients' rights to choose their own lawyers. The court interpreted the Order to mean Perkins Coie lawyers could not enter federal buildings to meet with prosecutors for plea negotiations and clients would be forced to choose between retaining Perkins Coie lawyers and future federal contracts. Based in part on these concerns, the American Bar Association filed a lawsuit on behalf of itself and its members challenging what it referred to as the Trump Administration's "Law Firm Intimidation Policy." *See American Bar Association v. Executive Office of the President*, No. 1:25-cv-01888 (D.D.C.).

4. *Pro Bono Representation.* As noted, the "deals" some law firms have made with President Trump include requirements that they provide thousands of hours in *pro bono* work, for causes the President (and presumably the law firms) support. Although the law firms' leaders have said they will choose their own clients, President Trump indicated that targeted firms would help negotiate trade deals and support

other government functions. Two firms appear to have participated in such work, although it is not clear whether they were paid for their services. Targeting law firms may also affect certain kinds of *pro bono* representation. For example, law firms facing potential Executive Orders may decline to represent immigrants subject to deportation orders or other clients challenging Trump Administration policies. The President issued a Memorandum, *Preventing Abuses of the Legal System and the Federal Court*, which directed the Attorney General "to seek sanctions against attorneys and law firms who engage in frivolous, unreasonable, and vexatious litigation against the United States or in matters before executive departments and agencies of the United States." The Memorandum singles out immigration lawsuits. The Justice Department has moved to sanction at least one lawyer who represented an alien *pro bono* in a deportation case. Why did the President focus on *pro bono* work in his "deals" with law firms? *See* Scott Cummings, *There's a Darker Reason Trump Is Going After Those Law Firms*, N.Y. Times (May 15, 2025) (arguing President Trump is seeking to handicap left-leaning causes by controlling access to legal representation).

5. *Vagueness.* Judge Howell also held that the EO's provisions relating to "Diversity, Equity, and Inclusion" were unconstitutionally vague. As noted in Chapter 1, the Due Process Clause of the Fifth Amendment requires that the federal government provide adequate *notice* regarding which speech or other activities are prohibited by law. As we will see, vagueness has been a recurring theme in challenges to Trump 2.0 Executive Orders, especially those targeting "DEI." Judge Howell wrote:

   > The terms diversity, equity, and inclusion, taken collectively or individually, however, could refer to a wide range of actions and programs, formal or informal, as well as basic thoughts and beliefs. The Order provides no definition or guidance as to what form of program possibly described by these terms is considered unlawful discrimination by the Trump Administration, leaving plaintiff to guess at what is and is not permissible in the government's view, while already facing the threat of adverse actions during the guessing.

B. THE AMERICAN BAR ASSOCIATION

The Trump Administration's actions against the Bar have extended beyond elite law firms. Consider the following excerpts from a district court opinion addressing the Department of Justice's denial of federal funds to the American Bar Association.

American Bar Association v. Dep't of Justice

783 F. Supp. 3d 236 (D.D.C. 2025)

COOPER, D.J.

Deputy Attorney General Todd Blanche issued a memorandum prohibiting all Department of Justice ("DOJ") lawyers from participating in events sponsored by the American Bar Association ("ABA") on official time. The reason, Blanche candidly explained, was that the ABA had recently joined a lawsuit against the Trump Administration [challenging the Administration's freeze on international development grants to the U.S. Agency for International Development and the Department of State]. The next day, DOJ cancelled a series of grants with the ABA that funded services to victims of domestic and sexual violence. The only explanation offered for the cancellation was a terse statement indicating that the grants "no longer effectuate DOJ priorities."

... The First Amendment bars government retaliation for protected speech. The ABA has made a strong showing that Defendants terminated its grants to retaliate against it for engaging in protected speech.

First, the Blanche Memo openly acknowledges that plaintiff engaged in speech and other activities protected by the First Amendment. It identifies the catalyst for the memo and DOJ's change in policy as to the ABA: "[T]he ABA filed a lawsuit against the United States." And it describes the ABA's history of "tak[ing] positions on contentious legal, policy, and social issues" that "frequently have not aligned with the positions advanced by [DOJ]" and its "litigat[ion] in support of activist causes." This activity is protected under the First Amendment.

Second, DOJ's termination of the grant funding is an action sufficient to deter a person of ordinary firmness in plaintiff's position from speaking again.

Third, the ABA's allegations, accepted as true, plausibly plead that the government's proffered justification for terminating the grants is pretextual, and that the real reason was retaliation. The Blanche Memo explicitly spells out how DOJ will be changing its approach toward the ABA in light of the ABA's lawsuit against the United States. And the temporal proximity between the Blanche Memo and the termination of the ABA's grants is probative of Defendants' retaliatory motive. The Memo may not have mentioned the ABA's grants specifically, but it promised to stop funding ABA events because of the DOJ's duty to be a "careful steward of the public fisc."

The government claims that it had a nonretaliatory motive for terminating the grants: They no longer aligned with DOJ's priorities. But the government has not identified any nonretaliatory DOJ priorities, much less explained why they were suddenly deemed inconsistent with the goals of the affected grants.

And the government's different treatment of other grantees suggests this justification is pretextual. DOJ did not terminate any other OVW [Office on Violence Against Women] grants, and, at oral argument, the government conceded that other grant recipients continue to conduct similar training functions with OVW money. The government has offered no nonretaliatory explanation for why it continues to fund these other OVW grantees after terminating the ABA's grants, or why these other grantees' projects still effectuate DOJ's priorities while the ABA's do not.

Finally, DOJ also purported to terminate two grants that, by their terms, had already ended, making it even less plausible that DOJ conducted an individualized analysis of whether each grant aligned with DOJ policy. Based on all this, the Court cannot but conclude that the ABA is likely to succeed on its claim that Defendants terminated the agreements because of its protected activity in violation of the First Amendment.

DISCUSSION

1. *Government Contractors and Funding.* The ABA receives federal funds to provide a variety of programs and services. In general, the government may not cancel contracts with private organizations based on the organizations' First Amendment activities. *See, e.g., Bd. of Comm'rs v. Umbehr*, 518 U.S. 668 (1996). The same is true of termination or denial of grants. *See, e.g., Agency for Int'l Dev. v. Alliance for Open Soc'y Int'l*, 570 U.S. 205 (2013).

2. *DOJ's Position.* The Memorandum distributed by the Deputy Attorney General stated, in part:

> The ABA is free to litigate in support of activist causes, including by inserting itself into pending litigation as an *amicus curiae*. But '[p]ublic service is a public trust.' The Department of Justice must, consistent with the Constitution, be careful stewards of the public fisc, represent all Americans regardless of ideology or political preferences, and defend the policies chosen by America's democratically elected leadership-as reflected in Congressionally enacted statutes and Presidential policy choices. . . . Put simply, the Department's own speech—which includes employee speaking engagements and written publications that rely upon taxpayer-funded resources—must be focused on achieving the Department's core Constitutional mission and advancing the legitimate and lawful statutory and policy decisions made by the political branches of our government.

The Memorandum also proclaimed: "The Department of Justice will no longer use taxpayer funds to pay for any travel to or engagement with ABA events. Additionally, Department employees may not, when acting in their official capacities, speak at, attend, or otherwise participate in events hosted by the ABA." Should a government agency or department have the authority to restrict which organizations it will financially or otherwise support? Why is it obligated to finance the activities of organizations that oppose the administration in court?

3. *Retribution Targets.* President Trump has sought or suggested retribution against a wide variety of individuals and institutions based on their expression. The list includes officials that served in President Trump's first administration, Department of Justice lawyers and Federal Bureau of Investigation employees who worked on cases pertaining to the January 6 Capitol riot, universities, celebrities, and members of Congress. These actions are inconsistent with the President's vows to "de-weaponize" government and "end censorship" and raise substantial First Amendment issues.

C. PROBLEM EXERCISE: REPRESENTING "THE BOSS"

At concerts in the U.S. and abroad, legendary rock star Bruce Springsteen criticized Donald Trump and his administration as "corrupt, incompetent and treasonous." After Springsteen continued to speak out against Trump's actions and policies, the President posted to Truth Social: "This dried out 'prune' of a rocker (his skin is all atrophied!) ought to KEEP HIS MOUTH SHUT until he gets back into the Country, that's just 'standard fare.' Then we'll all see how it goes for him!" Trump also called Springsteen a "pushy, obnoxious JERK."

In a follow-up post, President Trump called for a "major investigation" into whether Springsteen's endorsement of Kamala Harris during the 2024 presidential election, which included a public concert, violated campaign finance laws. The President wrote: "HOW MUCH DID KAMALA HARRIS PAY BRUCE SPRINGSTEEN FOR HIS POOR PERFORMANCE DURING HER CAMPAIGN FOR PRESIDENT? WHY DID HE ACCEPT THAT MONEY IF HE IS SUCH A FAN OF HERS? ISN'T THAT A MAJOR AND ILLEGAL CAMPAIGN CONTRIBUTION?" Trump continued: "Candidates aren't allowed to pay for ENDORSEMENTS, which is what Kamala did, under the guise of paying for entertainment . . . IT'S NOT LEGAL! For these unpatriotic 'entertainers,' this was just a CORRUPT & UNLAWFUL way to capitalize on a broken system. Thank you for your attention to this matter!!!"

Assume President Trump has just signed an Executive Order, *Addressing Risks From Paid 'Celebrity' Endorsements*, in which he directs the Federal Election Commission to "investigate the phony and illegal paid endorsements by musicians and other entertainers and enforce campaign finance laws to their full extent." A partner at your law firm has connections to Mr. Springsteen, who has scheduled an appointment at the firm to discuss the Executive Order. The partner has asked you to join the meeting with "The Boss" and to be prepared to discuss his legal options. In preparation, the partner has asked you to draft a brief memo outlining steps the firm might take in its representation of Springsteen. What advice would you provide? [**Note**: You have learned that Springsteen's production company received $76,000 from the Harris campaign after he performed as a musical guest at a Harris campaign rally in Georgia. You have also investigated the campaign finance laws and discovered that they require candidates to pay fair market value to any vendors for their services. Thus, the *failure* to pay the production company would have been an unlawful in-kind contribution to the campaign.]

3

EXECUTIVE ORDERS AND OFFICIAL ORTHODOXIES

In a series of Executive Orders, President Trump addressed race, gender, American history, and patriotism. The President directed agencies to implement his administration's views concerning these topics. Some of these directives have been challenged by educators, diversity officers, and other regulated parties. Agencies are authorized to enforce federal laws against grantees and regulated parties who engage in discriminatory actions based on race, gender, and other identified characteristics. Recall, as well, that under the government speech doctrine the President and the Executive Branch can communicate their *own* ideas and viewpoints regarding race, gender, and other topics. However, the First Amendment limits governmental power to impose or coerce official *truths* or *orthodoxies* through regulation. Consider these boundaries as you examine the relevant Orders.

DOCTRINAL SYNOPSIS I: GOVERNMENT SPEECH

- The First Amendment limits governmental regulation of private speech but does not limit the government's own speech.
- When the government acts as a speaker, it is entitled to determine what it wishes to say.

DOCTRINAL SYNOPSIS II: VIEWPOINT NEUTRALITY

- "If there is any fixed star in our constitutional constellation, it is that no official, high or petty, can prescribe what shall be orthodox in politics, nationalism, religion, or other matters of opinion or force citizens to confess by word or act their faith therein." *West Virginia Bd. of Education v. Barnette* (1943)
- Speech regulations that suppress disfavored viewpoints are *presumptively* invalid: they are valid only if narrowly tailored to further compelling governmental interests.

A. RACE, GENDER, HISTORY, AND PATRIOTISM

President Trump's Executive Orders regarding race, gender, history, and patriotism apply broadly to the enforcement of federal anti-discrimination laws and the regulation of federal funding programs. As we will see in subsequent chapters, the Orders have affected expression in a wide range of areas including university operations, immigration enforcement, broadcast, arts funding, K-12 school libraries and curricula, access to data, scientific research, and displays at national museums and parks. Because they cut across many topics addressed in subsequent chapters, this Part begins with a general overview of the Executive Orders.

1. Race

President Trump has signed two Executive Orders concerning "Diversity, Equity, and Inclusion" (DEI) and race discrimination.[1] While both Orders prohibit "DEI" neither provides a definition or explanation of "DEI" or related concepts.

One of the President's Orders, *Ending Radical And Wasteful Government DEI Programs And Preferencing*, proclaimed that "radical DEI" must be replaced by "individual dignity, hard work, and excellence," which the Order asserts are "fundamental to American greatness."[2] Accordingly, the President instructed federal agencies to coordinate the *termination* of "all discriminatory programs, including illegal DEI and 'diversity, equity, inclusion, and accessibility' (DEIA) mandates, policies, programs, preferences, and activities in the Federal Government, under whatever name they appear."[3]

President Trump further ordered that all federal agencies and commissions provide the Director of the Office of Management and Budget with lists of "[f]ederal contractors who have provided DEI training or DEI training materials to agency or department employees" and "[f]ederal grantees who received Federal funding to provide or advance DEI, DEIA, or 'environmental justice' programs, services, or activities since January 20, 2021."[4] The President also directed the Department of Labor to "immediately cease . . . [p]romoting diversity."[5]

The DEI Orders also addressed the *private* sector. In *Ending Illegal Discrimination and Restoring Merit-Based Opportunity*, the President ordered federal agencies to "[e]xcise references to DEI and DEIA principles, under whatever name they may appear, from Federal acquisition, contracting, grants, and financial assistance procedures."[6] President Trump directed federal agencies to root out DEI and, in its place, "advance in the private sector the policy of individual initiative, excellence, and hard work."[7]

The "head of each agency" was directed to (1) include "term[s]" in "every contract or grant award" requiring the counterparty or grant recipient to agree to "its compliance in all respects with all applicable Federal antidiscrimination laws is material to the government's payment decisions for purposes of [the False Claims Act]" and (2) to "*certify* that it does not operate any programs promoting DEI that violate any applicable Federal anti-discrimination laws."[8] President Trump also ordered federal agencies to identify the "most egregious and discriminatory DEI practitioners" within their jurisdictions and propose investigations of private sector companies to investigate their use of "DEI."[9] He directed the Attorney General to "deter DEI programs or principles (whether specifically denominated 'DEI' or otherwise) that constitute illegal discrimination or preferences" and to "identify . . . potential civil compliance investigations" to accomplish such "deter[rence]."[10]

In sum, the President's Orders directed that "DEI" and related concepts be removed from all federal grant materials, directed that all "DEI" grants be terminated, required grantees to certify they were not engaged in "DEI" activities, and encouraged the Attorney General to investigate and sanction "DEI" practices. However, the President's Executive Orders did not define or explain "DEI" for these or other purposes.

2. Gender and Gender Identity

President Trump also addressed the concept of gender in Executive Orders. In an Order entitled *Defending Women From Gender Ideology Extremism and Restoring Biological Truth to the Federal Government*, he criticized "ideologues who deny the biological reality of sex."[11] The Order proclaimed: "It is the policy of the United States to recognize two sexes, male and female. These sexes are not changeable and are grounded in fundamental and incontrovertible reality. Under my direction, the Executive Branch will enforce all sex-protective laws to promote this reality[.]"[12]

The Executive Order expressly rejected all understandings of sex or gender that are not based solely on biological sex because they "[i]nvalidat[e] the true and biological category of 'woman.'"[13] "Basing Federal policy on truth," the Order proclaimed, "is critical to scientific inquiry, public safety, morale, and trust in government itself."[14] President Trump's Order rejected "the false claim that males can identify as and thus become women and vice versa" and proclaimed the administration's intent not to "regard this false claim as true."[15]

The *Defending Women* Order directed that "[f]ederal funds shall not be used to promote gender ideology. Each agency shall assess grant conditions and grantee preferences and ensure grant funds do not promote gender ideology."[16] Further, it directed that "every agency and all Federal employees acting in an official capacity on behalf of their agency shall use the term 'sex' and not 'gender' in all applicable Federal policies and documents."[17] The Order also directed agency heads to "implement changes to require that government-issued identification documents, including passports, visas, and Global Entry cards, accurately reflect the holder's sex," as defined in the Order.[18] Finally, President Trump directed that "[a]gencies shall remove all statements, policies, regulations, forms, communications, or other internal and external messages that promote or otherwise inculcate gender ideology."[19]

In a second Order, *Prioritizing Military Excellence and Readiness*, the President characterized service in the Armed Forces by transgender individuals as a form of "radical gender ideology" that harms the military.[20] The Order declared that "adoption of a gender identity inconsistent with an individual's sex conflicts with a soldier's commitment to an honorable, truthful, and disciplined lifestyle, even in one's personal life."[21] It further declared that "a man's assertion that he is a woman, and his requirement that others honor this falsehood, is not consistent with the humility and selflessness required of a service member."[22] The Order directed the Secretary of Defense to end all pronoun use in the U.S. Armed Forces and take steps to ban transgender individuals from entering or remaining in service.[23]

Finally, President Trump addressed gender and gender identity in an Executive Order concerning K-12 schools. The Order, *Ending Radical Indoctrination in K-12 Schooling*, directed federal agencies to recommend ways to "rescind Federal funds, to the maximum extent consistent with applicable law" that "directly or indirectly support or subsidize the instruction, advancement, or promotion of gender ideology or discriminatory equity ideology."[24]

3. American History and Patriotism

President Trump has also issued Executive Orders addressing how American history and patriotism are to be discussed, depicted, and taught to schoolchildren. In general, the Orders directed federal agencies and grantee institutions to ensure American history is presented using only positive, encouraging, and uplifting narratives.

In *Restoring Truth and Sanity to American History*, President Trump declared:

> It is the policy of my Administration to restore Federal sites dedicated to history, including parks and museums, to solemn and uplifting public monuments that remind Americans of our extraordinary heritage, consistent progress toward becoming a more perfect Union, and unmatched record of advancing liberty, prosperity, and human flourishing.[25]

The Order further decreed: "Museums in our Nation's capital should be places where individuals go to learn—not to be subjected to ideological indoctrination or divisive narratives that distort our shared history."[26]

The *Restoring Truth and Sanity* Executive Order directed the Vice President and other administration officials to "seek[] to remove improper ideology from such properties."[27] Section 4 of the Order, entitled "Restoring Truth in American History," directed the Secretary of the Interior to purge any monuments, memorials, statutes, or similar properties of images that "perpetuate a false reconstruction of American history, inappropriately minimize the value of certain historical events or figures, or include any other improper partisan ideology."[28] An accompanying "Fact Sheet" boasted that the President had ordered his administration "to work to eliminate improper, divisive, or anti-American ideology from the Smithsonian and its museums, education and research centers, and the National Zoo."[29]

Another Executive Order, *Ending Radical Indoctrination in K-12 Schooling*, purported to condition federal education funding on the adoption by K-12 schools of "patriotic" curricula.[30] The Order defined "patriotic education" as "a presentation of the history of America" that is "inspiring" and "ennobling," emphasizing "how the United States has admirably grown closer to its noble principles, and embracing "the concept that celebration of America's greatness and history is proper."[31] The Order threatened to withhold federal funding from any K-12 schools teaching that the United States is "fundamentally racist, sexist or otherwise discriminatory."[32]

Finally, President Trump addressed patriotism and American values in the context of enforcement of federal immigration law. An Executive Order, *Protecting the United States from Foreign Terrorists and Other National Security and Public Safety Threats*, declared that lawful resident aliens who "espouse hateful ideology" or "bear hostile attitudes toward [American] citizens, culture, government, institutions, or founding principles" are thereby subject to deportation.[33] The Order instructed the Secretary of State and federal agencies to "recommend any additional measures to be taken that promote a unified American identity and attachment to the Constitution, laws, and founding principles of the United States."[34]

DISCUSSION

1. *Government as Speaker or Regulator?* The Executive Orders communicate the Executive Branch's views concerning race, gender, American history, and patriotism. To the extent the Orders constitute government speech, the First Amendment does not restrict their content. For instance, the First Amendment does not constrain the government's choice of monuments to display at national parks. However, the Orders also direct agencies to take regulatory actions, including eliminating "DEI," which will affect private speech. Which aspects of the Orders are best viewed as government speech, and which as the regulation of private speech?

2. *Targeting Actions or Ideologies?* Executive Orders frequently adopt and announce the Executive Branch's interpretations of federal laws and set the administration's enforcement priorities. Provisions in the Executive Orders focusing on enforcement of federal anti-discrimination law, for example, are exercises of core executive power. However, some of these same provisions refer to "radical ideology," the promotion and inculcation of ideas, and biological "truths." In that respect, the Orders can be characterized as efforts to use executive power to impose official orthodoxies or viewpoints on private speakers—including universities, employers, scientists, and other federal grantees.

3. *Official Truths and Narratives.* President Trump's Executive Orders on race and other topics raise First Amendment and other legal issues, some of which are discussed below. Apart from legalities, are there reasons to be concerned about the federal government's efforts to eliminate certain ideas relating to race, establish the "truth" or falsity of gender, and insist that only "positive" narratives about American history be depicted in museums or school curricula?

4. *Ambiguities.* As noted, the Executive Orders relating to "DEI" nowhere define the term. "Gender ideology" is defined, but what constitutes prohibited "promotion" and "inculcation" of such ideas is not clear. The Orders do not define which depictions of American culture and history are "uplifting" and which are not. Can you tell from the text of the Orders which activities the Trump Administration views as falling on the wrong side of the line?

B. VAGUENESS AND PRE-ENFORCEMENT CHALLENGES

Various organizations and individuals subject to President Trump's Executive Orders on "DEI" and "gender ideology" have filed pre-enforcement challenges. A prevalent claim has been that the Executive Orders are unconstitutionally vague and thus chill expression. Consider how the district court and federal appeals cort analyzed such claims in the following challenge.

DOCTRINAL SYNOPSIS: VAGUENESS

- It is a basic principle of due process that an enactment is void for vagueness if its prohibitions are not clearly defined.
- Standards of permissible vagueness are *strict* in the area of free expression. Vague laws chill expression and risk sweeping and improper applications.

National Association of Diversity Officers v. Donald J. Trump

767 F. Supp. 3d 243 (D. Md. 2025)

ABELSON, D.J.

. . . Among the executive orders the President issued on the first two days of the administration were orders that (1) directed all executive agencies to "terminate . . . 'equity-related' grants or contracts" (the "*Termination Provision*"), (2) directed all executive agencies to "include in every contract or grant award" a certification, enforceable through the False Claims Act, that the contractor and grantee "does not operate any programs promoting DEI that violate any applicable Federal anti-discrimination laws" (the "*Certification Provision*"), and (3) directing the Attorney General to take "appropriate measures to encourage the private sector to end illegal discrimination and preferences, including DEI," to "deter" such "programs or principles," and to "identify . . . potential civil compliance investigations" to accomplish such "deter[rence]" (the "*Enforcement Threat Provision*") (collectively, the "Challenged Provisions").

The term "DEI," of course, is shorthand for "diversity, equity, and inclusion." And ensuring equity, diversity, and inclusion has long been a goal, and at least in some contexts arguably a requirement, of federal anti-discrimination law. But the administration has declared "DEI" to be henceforth "illegal," has announced it will be terminating all "'equity-related' grants or contracts"—whatever the administration might decide that means—and has made "practitioners" of what the government considers "DEI" the targets of a "strategic enforcement plan." The Challenged Provisions do not define any of the operative terms, such as "DEI," "equity-related," "promoting DEI," "illegal DEI," "illegal DEI and DEIA policies," or "illegal discrimination or preferences,"—let alone identify the types of programs or policies the administration considers "illegal."

According to a recent case, "approximately 20% of the nation's labor force works for a federal contractor." *Kentucky v. Biden*, 57 F.4th 545, 548 (6th Cir. 2023). The Termination Provision leaves those contractors and their employees, plus any other recipients of federal grants, with no idea whether the administration will deem their contracts or grants, or work they are doing, or speech they are engaged in, to be "equity-related." And the Order leaves the private sector at a loss for whether the administration will deem a particular policy, program, discussion, announcement, etc. to be among the "preferences, mandates, policies, programs, and activities" the administration now deems "illegal." Plaintiffs, who have easily established their standing to bring this case and irreparable harm, have shown they are likely to prove the Termination and Enforcement Threat Provisions are unconstitutionally vague on their face.

. . . One of the primary rationales of the void-for-vagueness doctrine is the importance of preventing arbitrary and discriminatory enforcement. Here, the very real possibility of arbitrary and discriminatory enforcement—both between and within executive agencies—is rooted in the vagueness of the term "'equity-related' grants or contracts."

The vagueness of the Termination Provision leaves current grant recipients and contractual counterparts unsure about what activities are prohibited under the Order. Specifically, these individuals and organizations have no reasonable way to know what, if anything, they can do to bring their grants into compliance such that they are not considered "equity-related."

The possibilities are almost endless, and many are pernicious. If an elementary school receives Department of Education funding for technology access, and a teacher uses a computer to teach the history of Jim Crow laws, does that risk the grant being deemed "equity-related" and the school being stripped of funding? If a road construction grant is used to fill potholes in a low-income neighborhood instead of a wealthy neighborhood, does that render it "equity-related"? If a university grant helps fund the salary of a staff person who then helps teach college students about sexual harassment and the language of consent, would the funding for that person's salary be stripped as "equity-related"? If a business with a grant from the Small Business Administration conducts a recruiting session at a historically Black college or university, could the business be stripped of the grant on that basis?

The due process clause of the Fifth Amendment requires that prohibitions on conduct be clearly defined. That is especially the case where the law interferes with the right of free speech. Vague laws invite arbitrary power. And Plaintiffs here have shown substantial evidence of the risks of such arbitrariness. By threatening the "private sector" with enforcement actions based on those vague, undefined standards, the Enforcement Threat Provision is facially unconstitutional under the due process clause of the Fifth Amendment.

Plaintiffs are also likely to succeed on their claim that [the Certification Provision] violates the First Amendment. On its face, this provision constitutes a content-based restriction on the speech rights of federal contractors and grantees. It also expands [the restriction on DEI] to all those contractors' and grantees work, whether funded by the government or not.

Because even the government does not know what constitutes DEI-related speech that violates federal anti-discrimination laws, Plaintiffs have easily shown a likelihood that they will prevail in proving that the Certification Provision operates as a content-based prior restraint on their speech, and likely will also prevail in showing that the Certification operates as a facially viewpoint-discriminatory order as well. The speech-chilling effect of the Certification Provision is particularly obvious given the vagueness of the [provisions].

Plaintiffs are also likely to succeed on their claim that the Enforcement Threat Provision violates the First Amendment, because it threatens to initiate enforcement actions against Plaintiffs (in the form of civil compliance investigations) for engaging in protected speech. The government's threat of enforcement is not just targeted towards enforcement of federal law. Rather, the provision expressly targets, and threatens, the expression of views supportive of equity, diversity and inclusion—a particular view taken by speakers.

Defendants contend that all they are threatening is to target non-compliance with existing federal anti-discrimination law, and that the Enforcement Threat Provision does not target a First Amendment right to begin with because Plaintiffs have no First Amendment right to engage in illegal discrimination. But, as explained, the Order offers no guidance or notice of what the government now considers "illegal" DEI.

National Association of Diversity Officers v. Donald J. Trump

Case No. 25-1189
(4th Cir., Feb. 27, 2025)

[The district court entered an injunction against enforcement of the DEI Orders on vagueness and First Amendment grounds. The Government appealed the district court's order and requested that the U.S. Court of Appeals for the Fourth Circuit issue a stay. The appeals court did so in a unanimous order. The following are excerpts from two concurring opinions.]

PAMELA HARRIS, Circuit Judge, concurring:

As the government explains, the challenged Executive Orders, on their face, are of distinctly limited scope. The Executive Orders do not purport to establish the illegality of all efforts to advance diversity, equity or inclusion, and they should not be so understood. Instead, the so-called "Certification" and "Enforcement Threat" provisions apply only to conduct that violates existing federal anti-discrimination law. . . . On this understanding, the government has shown the requisite likelihood that the challenged provisions do not on their face violate the First or Fifth Amendment.

But my vote to grant the stay comes with a caveat. What the Orders say on their face and how they are enforced are two different things. Agency enforcement actions that go beyond the Orders' narrow scope may well raise serious First Amendment and Due Process concerns, for the reasons cogently explained by the district court. This case, however, does not directly challenge any such action, and I therefore concur.

RUSHING, Circuit Judge, concurring:

I concur in the order granting the government's motion for a stay pending appeal. The government has made a strong showing that it is likely to succeed on the merits and that the district court erred in concluding otherwise. In other words, the government is likely to succeed in demonstrating that the challenged provisions of the Executive Orders—all of which are directives from the President to his officers—do not violate the First or Fifth Amendments.

In addition, as Judge Harris rightly points out, this case does not challenge any particular agency action implementing the Executive Orders.

Yet, in finding the Orders themselves unconstitutional, the district court relied on evidence of how various agencies are implementing, or may implement, the Executive Orders. That highlights serious questions about the ripeness of this lawsuit and plaintiffs' standing to bring it as an initial matter. Ripeness and standing doctrines prevent the judicial process from being used to usurp the powers of the political branches, by keeping courts within their "province"—deciding "the rights of individuals" in actual controversies, *Marbury v. Madison*, 5 U.S. (1 Cranch) 137, 170 (1983). Ignoring these limits on judicial power results in courts becoming virtually continuing monitors of the wisdom and soundness of Executive action.

We must not lose sight of the boundaries of our constitutional role and the imperative of judicial impartiality. Any individual judge's view on whether certain Executive action is good policy is not only irrelevant to fulfilling our duty to adjudicate cases and controversies according to the law, it is an impermissible consideration.

DISCUSSION

1. *Too Soon?* The concurring judges essentially concluded plaintiffs had gone to court prematurely. However, as the district court observed, the Trump Administration had taken various actions to *enforce* the provisions of the Executive Orders, including issuance of memos by the Department of Labor and Department of Defense instructing contracting officers in those agencies to "cancel" contracts that contained "DEI requirements." Judges Harris and Rushing responded that plaintiffs were not challenging any *specific* enforcement action. Rather, they were challenging policy directives to executive agencies and actors to enforce federal law. In a footnote, Chief Judge Diaz, the third member of the panel, observed: "Like [Judge Harris], I too reserve judgment on how the administration enforces these executive orders, which may well implicate cognizable First and Fifth Amendment concerns." Which position do you find more persuasive on this issue—the district court's, or the concurrences, and why? What problem(s) do you perceive in terms of waiting to file suit?

2. *Standing and Facial Challenges.* Another district court rejected pre-enforcement challenges to the "DEI" and "gender ideology" Executive Orders in part because the challengers lacked "standing" to sue.

The court held that plaintiffs failed to demonstrate the provisions of the Orders inflicted any concrete personal harm on them. *See National Urban League v. Donald J. Trump*, 783 F. Supp. 3d 61 (D.D.C. 2025). The court also rejected "facial" challenges to the Executive Orders because enforcement of the Executive Orders would not violate the First Amendment in all or nearly all circumstances. *See United States v. Salerno*, 481 U.S. 739, 745 (1987) (holding "facial" claims fail unless the plaintiff shows "that no set of circumstances exists under which the [law] would be valid" or "that the law lacks a "plainly legitimate sweep'"). In contrast, in so-called "as-applied" challenges, plaintiffs must only show that the law or policy is invalid as applied to their specific activities.

3. *The Judicial Role and Separation of Powers.* Judge Rushing warned that courts should not decide challenges to executive policy directives prematurely. On the one hand, perhaps federal judges ought to exercise restraint where it is not clear how the government will enforce laws or policies. On the other hand, a lack of certainty may make it even more important that courts guard against the suppression and chilling of expression. In response to judicial orders enjoining its policies, the Trump Administration has asserted that judges have "abused" their powers and interfered with the valid prerogatives of the Executive Branch. As the next Part discusses, Trump 2.0 has raised significant questions about how courts should balance concerns about limits on their power with protecting the First Amendment rights of regulated parties.

C. INFORMAL COERCION AND ANTICIPATORY COMPLIANCE

In *National Association of Diversity Officers*, the district court, invoking vagueness doctrine, expressed concerns that the lack of clarity in the Executive Orders would lead to self-censorship and arbitrary enforcement. By contrast, the Fourth Circuit judges declined to engage in what they perceived as pre-enforcement speculation about the effects of the Orders.

Even absent specific enforcement, the Executive Orders may substantially affect expression. Regulated parties may curb their expressive activities to avoid investigations and devastating sanctions—even if what they are doing and saying does not violate federal law. Indeed, ambiguity, informal coercion, and anticipatory compliance may be part of a governmental strategy to restrict expression without ever initiating formal agency action. Consider the following comments by Professor Genevieve Lakier:

> At this point in the Trump presidency, it is quite clear that a central way in which the administration wields power is by threatening those who speak and associate in ways that it dislikes with economic or legal harm if they do not stop. These threats and promises of payback are obviously intended to ensure compliance with the President's ideological agenda; or, at least, to ensure that those who oppose that agenda shut up. They pose, as such, a serious threat to the First Amendment. After all, the core idea underlying the modern First Amendment is that the government may not as Justice Jackson put it in *West Virginia v. Barnette*, "coerce uniformity of sentiment in support of [an] end [it believes to be] essential"; that in this democratic state, "[a]uthority is . . . to be controlled by public opinion, not public opinion by authority."
>
> At the same time, however, courts—particularly in recent decades—have recognized a rather expansive right to "freedom of government speech" (to use Judge Posner's useful phrase). They have recognized that government officials have broad freedom not only to express their point of view on contested matters of public concern but to criticize private citizens when they express opposing views and to cajole them into better behavior. The central question that courts must answer then, when deciding when and which of the administration's threats violate the First Amendment, is whether those threats work to coerce silence, or merely speak.
>
> . . . One would hope that . . . courts would be sensitive to the ways in which promises to do something—even if what that something is not clearly spelled out—can chill speech, even absent the realization of that promise. This is certainly something that six decades of First Amendment informal coercion, or "jawboning," cases recognize. In those cases, courts—including the Supreme Court—have made clear that threats to use the powers of the state to punish those who engage in disfavored expression violate the First Amendment even when those threats never come to fruition, so long as they are reasonably understood as serious expressions of intent. . . .

Of course, executive orders aren't the kinds of informal speech acts to which the jawboning precedents typically apply. They are laws, albeit laws that are produced without the ordinary processes of bicameralism and presentment (or even notice and comment). Nevertheless, one would think that the same First Amendment principles govern their constitutional analysis. In all cases, after all, the question is whether the promise to exercise government power is likely to lead to the suppression of private speech. . . .

[T]he concurrences in the Fourth Circuit's decision in *National Association of Diversity Officers*] suggest that the members of the panel granted the government's motion for a stay because they believed that, however problematic they may be, the executive orders themselves do not impact plaintiffs' rights in the absence of what Judge Harris described as specific "agency enforcement actions": that it is only when agencies cut off funds, or issue certification demands, or enforce the executive orders in other ways that constitutional rights are imperiled—and that it is these enforcement actions, not the orders themselves, that plaintiffs should challenge. The concurrences suggest that the members of the panel view the executive orders, in other words, as something akin to government speech.

This is a deeply troubling conclusion for the court to reach—if, as seems likely, it is what led the panel to stay the district court injunction—because it fails to take seriously what the jawboning cases indicate courts should take very seriously: namely, the powerful chilling effect that governmental speech acts like the anti-DEI executive orders can have on the willingness of private persons to engage in speech and association even absent specific enforcement actions. . . .

[W]hile Judges Harris and Rushing are entirely correct that those impacted by the specific enforcement actions that agencies undertake to enforce the anti-DEI orders can always challenge the constitutionality of those actions on First and Fifth Amendment grounds, it is very likely that many will not do so but will instead simply comply out of belief of the harms that they are likely to suffer from challenging the government's actions in court outweigh the benefits they are likely to receive from doing so, even if they succeed. Such a belief would be, after all, eminently rational. Going to court to defend one's free speech interests is often a perilous business. Plaintiffs can experience significant reputational harm by publicly defending their right to engage in disfavored expression. More relevant here, perhaps, businesses that regularly interact with the governmental entities they are suing risk injuring that relationship, with long-term consequences.

Given all these risks—risks that are surely magnified enormously by the retributive and tribal character of the Trump administration—the list of plaintiffs available to challenge any given enforcement action may be small indeed. Consider for example the certification requirement: surely any contractor who challenges the requirement to certify will do so knowing that they are now alerting the administration that they engage in problematic DEI practices or, at the very least, that they want to protect those who do. If they are a repeat player, how will they be certain—even if they win their case—that officials will not deny them a contract or a grant the next time around as a result? Officials generally possess broad discretion to decide with whom to contract, or to award grants—discretion that can easily be used to secretly punish disfavored actors.

For similar reasons, businesses targeted by investigation may not wish to rouse the administrator's ire by challenging the constitutionality of those investigations. Even if the lawsuit succeeds in ending the investigation, the ongoing nature of their relationship with the administration, and the many tools administrators possess to make life hard for the corporations they oversee, may make the victory a pyrrhic one. Companies know this, which is why, so far at least, they have tended not to challenge this kind of anti-DEI "deterrence." For example, after FCC Commissioner Brendan Carr sent a letter to the cable company Comcast warning it that he had ordered the agency's Enforcement Bureau to investigate whether it "promot[ed] invidious forms of DEI in a manner that does not comply with FCC regulations" the company—rather than challenging the agency's actions—promised to "cooperate with the FCC to address any questions."

It is also very unlikely that the Trump administration will take steps to clarify the scope of the challenged provisions and therefore cure whatever vagueness they may possess, as members of the panel may have hoped they would do (and for that reason, stayed the judicial firepower). This is because the administration clearly profits from the lack of clarity that plagues this like many other of

Trump's executive orders. This is certainly what the argument before the district court in this case suggests. As the district court judge, Judge Abelson, noted in his opinion, when pressed during oral arguments, the government's lawyer adamantly refused to provide any further clarity on the meaning of the key terms but "merely reiterated that promoting DEI can be unlawful and that there is uncertainty about whether programs or policies that are sometimes referred to as "DEI" are lawful after the Supreme Court's decision in *Students for Fair Admission*." This uncertainty is useful, of course, because it encourages precisely the harm that the void-for-vagueness doctrine is meant to prevent: namely, it leads even those whose speech is far from the "forbidden zone" to stop speaking.

By assuming that whatever problems are presented by the anti-DEI executive orders can be cured at a later stage in the game, the Fourth Circuit failed entirely to recognize the very serious harms that the orders are doing right now by promising uncertain but nevertheless serious harm to those who wish to talk about equity or diversity or inclusion. The order reflects, as such, a deeply problematic effort to maintain a minimalist role for the courts at a time when the Trump administration has made no bones about its willingness to wield its power expansively and aggressively.

Genevieve Lakier, *Chilling Effects, Trump's Anti-DEI Executive Orders, and the Role of the Courts (or why the Fourth Circuit Decision in National Association of Diversity Officers v. Trump is wrong)*, Balkinization (Mar. 19, 2025).

DISCUSSION

1. *The Government's Messages.* Professor Lakier suggests the Fourth Circuit judges might have viewed the Executive Orders as statements of governmental policy regarding federal anti-discrimination laws—in other words, as government speech. If that is so, are the President and Executive Branch communicating that (1) the federal government intends to enforce anti-discrimination laws to their full extent or (2) "DEI" and "radical gender ideology" are disfavored ideas that federal grantees can no longer advocate or discuss? Do the First Amendment implications of those two statements differ?

2. *The Problem of Anticipatory Compliance.* Several characteristics of President Trump's Executive Orders raise the prospect of self-censorship. Professor Lakier observes that the Executive Branch can make federal grantees' lives financially and otherwise difficult. She also focuses in part on the lack of clarity in the Orders, which leads to self-censorship. Consider also that the Trump Administration has terminated university and other funding without complying with procedural safeguards set forth in federal laws, which provide pre-enforcement opportunities to defend against allegations of discrimination. Thus, grantees must decide how to respond quickly, often without the benefit of these procedural protections. Finally, consider the *scope* of the Executive Orders, which affect businesses, broadcasters, schools, scientists, museums, nonprofits, and a host of others. Anticipatory compliance is a concern across wide swaths of American society.

D. DEI, GENDER IDEOLOGY, AND CONDITIONAL FUNDING

The First Amendment imposes limits on the government's power to condition receipt of federal funding. The following materials examine "unconstitutional conditions" challenges to President Trump's Executive Orders relating to DEI and gender.

DOCTRINAL SYNOPSIS I: UNCONSTITUTIONAL CONDITIONS

- Government is not required to provide funding or other support for expressive activities. However, it may not deny a benefit to a person on a basis that infringes their constitutionally protected interests.
- Government may not leverage funding to regulate speech outside the contours of the funded program.
- Nor may the Government rely on the threat of terminated funding or invocation of legal sanctions to achieve the suppression of disfavored viewpoints.

DOCTRINAL SYNOPSIS II: GOVERNMENT SPEECH

- The First Amendment limits governmental regulation of private speech but does not limit the government's own speech.
- When the government acts as a speaker, it is entitled to determine what it wishes to say.

Chicago Women in Trades v. Trump

779 F. Supp. 3d 959 (N.D. Ill. 2025)

KENNELLY, D.J.

[Plaintiffs challenged a provision in one of President Trump's DEI Orders, the Certification Provision, that requires a grant recipient to agree that their "compliance with all applicable Federal antidiscrimination laws is material to the government's payment decisions for purposes of [the False Claims Act]" and to "*certify* that it does not operate *any* programs promoting DEI that violate any applicable Federal anti-discrimination laws."[35]]

The government conceded at oral argument that the Certification Provision attempts to regulate grantees' speech outside of their federally-funded programs. The provision on its face makes clear that a counterparty must certify that it does not operate any program that promotes DEI, irrespective of whether the program is federally funded.

The government contends that the Certification Provision is permissible, as it simply requires certification that the grantee is not breaking the law. Because a grantee has no constitutional right to violate the law, the government argues, its receipt of funds may appropriately be conditioned upon its certification that it abides by antidiscrimination laws. In this regard, the government emphasizes that the Certification Provision requires acknowledging only that the grantee does not operate any DEI programs that "violate any applicable Federal antidiscrimination laws."

The problem, however, is that the meaning of this is left entirely to the grantee's imagination. The Order that contains the Certification Provision does not define the term "DEI" itself, and it does not refer to any other source indicating what the term means as used in the Order—let alone what might make any given "DEI" program violate Federal anti-discrimination laws. And although the government emphasized, both in its briefing and at oral argument, that the Certification Provision implicates only illegal DEI programs, it has studiously declined to shed any light on what this means. The answer is anything but obvious. Indeed, the thrust of the Orders is that the government's view of what is illegal in this regard has changed significantly with the new administration—even though the government has not (in the Orders) and has been unwilling to (in its briefs or at argument) define how it has changed.

Against this backdrop, the Certification Provision puts CWIT and other grantees in a difficult and perhaps impossible position. They have received multiple communications from [the Department of Labor] directing them to ensure compliance with the Orders. The Certification Provision's application to grantees' activities that are not federally funded means that CWIT and other grantees must either take steps now to revise their programmatic activity so that none of it "promote[s] DEI" (whatever that is deemed to mean), decline to make a certification and thus lose their grants, or risk making a certification that will be deemed false and thus subject them to liability under the False Claims Act.

The Order's reference to "programs promoting DEI," moreover, is fairly read as an express reference to First Amendment-protected speech and advocacy. Even if the Certification Provision is limited to promoting whatever the government may now contend is "illegal DEI," it is a bedrock First Amendment principle that advocating for violation of the law cannot be proscribed unless it rises to incitement.

[Plaintiffs also challenged the DEI Order's "Termination Provision," which instructed federal agencies to coordinate the *termination* of "all discriminatory programs, including illegal DEI and 'diversity, equity, inclusion, and accessibility' (DEIA) mandates, policies, programs, preferences, and activities in the Federal Government, under whatever name they appear."[36]]

[T]he Court concludes that CWIT is *not* likely to succeed on the merits of its First Amendment claim relating to the Termination Provision. The Court begins with a basic premise: The government can say what it wishes and select the views that it wants to express. The government must be able to pursue its policy priorities—it could barely function otherwise. To that end, the government has more leeway when funding activities than it does when regulating them. Although the government cannot favor one speaker over another when regulating activities, it may pick and choose what activities to fund.

Still, the government is not altogether unrestrained when funding. As discussed earlier with regard to the Certification Provision, the government may not impose a condition on its funding that affects protected conduct outside the scope of the federally funded program. The government may not attempt to use its funding power to regulate beyond the scope of the funded program and avoid First Amendment scrutiny in the process.

The question regarding the Termination Provision, then, is whether it reflects a funding decision or an impermissible attempt to regulate. The Court is persuaded at this juncture that the provision concerns funding. The Termination Provision requires agencies to terminate all "equity-related" federal grants; it does not prohibit equity-related activities outside of funded programs. The government has made a policy choice that it no longer wishes to support equity-related programs—a choice that it may make when funding. Grantees who find their grants threatened by termination remain able to pursue equity-related activities on their own time and dime.

National Rifle Association of America v. Vullo does not suggest a different conclusion. *Vullo* and the cases it cites concern situations in which the government attempts to use coercive threats to punish or suppress disfavored speech. At first glance, *Vullo*'s analysis would appear to apply here. CWIT has described how the Executive Order's denunciation of "illegal and immoral" DEI supports a conclusion that the Termination Provision is aimed at "disfavored speech." And although the government argues otherwise, coercive threats are not limited to threats of government investigations or prosecutions—as the Court repeated in *Vullo*, "[t]he First Amendment prohibits government officials from relying on the 'threat of invoking legal sanctions and other means of coercion . . . to achieve the suppression' of disfavored speech." *Vullo*, 602 U.S. at 197 (emphasis added) (quoting *Bantam Books, Inc. v. Sullivan*, 372 U.S. 58, 67 (1963)).

Yet even if coercion encompasses more than investigation and prosecution, it likely does not encompass the termination of government funding. As discussed above, the government must be able to make funding decisions. A finding that the government acts coercively, for purposes of the *Vullo* line of cases, when it terminates grants would essentially force the government to continue to support activities that conflict with its current policy determinations. This result cannot be squared with the government's power to selectively fund some programs and not others.

Because the Court has concluded that the Termination Provision simply involves the government engaging in funding, as opposed to regulating, the vagueness concerns fall away as well. *National Endowment for the Arts v. Finley* is analogous. In *Finley*, the plaintiff brought a facial challenge to language in the National Foundation on the Arts and Humanities Act directing the grantor to "tak[e] into consideration general standards of decency and respect for the diverse beliefs and values of the American public" when issuing a grant. *Finley*, 524 U.S. at 572 (quoting 20 U.S.C. § 954(d)(1)). The Supreme Court noted that "[t]he terms of the provision are undeniably opaque, and if they appeared in a criminal statute or regulatory scheme, they could raise substantial vagueness concerns." *Id.* at 588. But it went on to state that it was unlikely "that speakers will be compelled to steer too far clear of any 'forbidden area' in the context of grants of this nature" and thus that any concerns over chilled speech due to vagueness were "not constitutionally severe." *Id.* at 589; *see id.* at 590 (finding that the challenged language "merely adds some imprecise considerations to an already subjective selection process").

National Urban League v. Donald J. Trump

783 F. Supp. 3d 61 (D.D.C. 2025)

KELLY, D.J.

[In this case Plaintiffs challenged provisions in Executive Order No. 14,151, *Ending Radical And Wasteful Government DEI Programs And Preferencing* and Executive Order No. 14,168, *Defending Women From Gender Ideology Extremism and Restoring Biological Truth to the Federal Government.*]

Plaintiffs argue that the Challenged Provisions violate the First Amendment's free-speech guarantee. Only four provisions remain live for this challenge: the Certification Provision, the Equity Termination Provision, the Gender Funding Termination Provision, and the Promoting Gender Ideology Provision. Of those, Plaintiffs say the Certification Provision amounts to unlawful viewpoint discrimination. And all four provisions, Plaintiffs add, chill speech by penalizing disfavored views.

The First Amendment prohibits governments from "abridging the freedom of speech." Sometimes that right requires the government to accommodate expression. But the Supreme Court has rejected the notion that First Amendment rights are somehow not fully realized unless they are subsidized by the State. Put slightly differently, even where the Constitution prohibits coercive governmental interference with specific individual rights, it does not confer an entitlement to such funds as may be necessary to realize all the advantages of that freedom. That is why the refusal to fund protected activity, without more, cannot be equated with the imposition of a penalty on that activity. And for that reason, the typical recourse for a party that objects to a condition on the receipt of federal funding is to decline the funds.

At the same time, though, a funding condition can result in an unconstitutional burden on First Amendment rights. That line is hardly clear. But the key consideration—or at least one of them—is whether the condition specifies the activities the government wants to subsidize or if it seeks to leverage funding to regulate speech outside the contours of the program itself.

Begin with the Equity Termination, Promoting Gender Ideology, and Gender Funding Termination Provisions. By their terms, these provisions tell agencies what to do with federal funds and contracts. Under the first, agencies must terminate equity-related grants and contracts in accordance with the law. And the latter two target the federal funding of gender ideology. These provisions, then, do not reach beyond the scope of the grant or fund at issue. The directives do not tell agencies to cancel contracts with entities doing equity-related work outside their contracts or to ensure that federal funds do not support grantees promoting gender ideology with non-federal funds. In this way, the provisions do not prohibit the recipient from engaging in the protected conduct outside the scope of the federally funded program or contract. The provisions, in other words, are part of a government effort to fund one activity to the exclusion of another—or to contract for certain purposes to the exclusion of others—which does not amount to discrimination on the basis of viewpoint. That result follows from the principle that refusing to fund protected activity, without more, does not penalize the activity.

Because these provisions do not on their face restrict speech outside the scope of the federal funds or contract, they do not run afoul of the First Amendment. Or more specifically, most of their applications will not. Consider an entity that receives four federal grants. It uses one to fund a program advancing the idea that transgender women should be able to participate in women's sports. The other three grants, though, support projects far afield from transgender rights or gender ideology more generally. Directed to "end the Federal funding of gender ideology" as "permitted by law" and ensure that such funds do not "promote gender ideology," an agency would presumably terminate the first grant or tell the recipient that it will do so unless the recipient stops using the funds for that purpose. But because the other grants are not advancing gender ideology in any way, the gender-ideology provisions are no basis—at least in most of their applications—to cut those grants. Said another way, because the provisions do not effectively prohibit or otherwise restrict the recipient from engaging in the protected conduct outside the scope of the federal funds, they do not place a constitutionally problematic condition on the recipient of the subsidy. And the same result holds for the Equity Termination Provision: its text does not say that a contractor with four contracts, only one of which is equity-related, will lose the other three by advocating for equity principles outside the scope of those contracts.

Because the government is not constitutionally obligated to fund Plaintiffs' preferred speech or to contract with them for certain purposes, the decision to stop funding that speech or contracting for those ends is not an example of the government doing indirectly what it is barred from doing directly.

[T]he Equity Termination Provision and gender-ideology provisions do not on their face require Plaintiffs to profess a specific belief or disclose anything. They just tell agencies to cut some kinds of funding and cancel certain contracts as permitted by law. And because the Supreme Court has rejected the notion that First Amendment rights are somehow not fully realized unless they are subsidized by the State, any chill that Plaintiffs feel from these provisions is not the sort that can support a First Amendment claim.

The Certification Provision is not facially invalid either despite Plaintiffs' three-pronged attack on it. First, they claim that it imposes unconstitutional funding conditions based on viewpoint. Next, Plaintiffs say that this provision, like the others, chills protected speech.

As Defendants acknowledge, the Certification Provision does cover conduct outside the scope of federal grants and funds. It requires grant recipients and contractual counterparties to certify that they do "not operate any programs"—rather than just federally funded ones—"promoting DEI that violate" federal antidiscrimination law. So Plaintiffs have cleared a hurdle here that they did not for the other provisions.

But that victory is partial and short-lived. For the Certification Provision to violate the First Amendment, Plaintiffs must show that the certification requirement impermissibly restricts their ability to engage in protected speech. Yet neither Plaintiffs nor anyone else have a First Amendment right to violate federal antidiscrimination law. To the contrary, the Supreme Court has clearly held that the First Amendment does not protect the very act of discriminating on the basis of race. More generally, the right to speak freely provides no shield for private individuals or institutions that engage in discrimination that violates federal law. So Plaintiffs cannot assert an alleged first amendment right to be free of the strictures of federal antidiscrimination law and also claim the right to continued federal funding" and contracts.

Resisting that conclusion, Plaintiffs insist that the Certification Provision does not really mean what it says. On their reading, the provision purports to make organizations that promote DEI ineligible for government contracts and grants. But Plaintiffs offer no reason to disregard the Certification Provision's text for their preferred reading. On its face, all the provision requires is a certification that the grant recipient or contractual counterparty will not violate the federal antidiscrimination laws that they had to comply with long before President Trump issued the executive orders. It does not purport to establish the illegality of all efforts to advance DEI, and it "should not be so understood." *Nat'l Ass'n of Diversity Officers v. Trump*, No. 25-1189 (4th Cir. 2025), at 7 (Harris, J., concurring). And according to Plaintiffs, they do not engage in any unlawful discrimination.

If Plaintiffs worry that this administration takes a broader view of what counts as illegal discrimination, that is a concern with the interpretation of the underlying federal antidiscrimination law—which Plaintiffs do not challenge—rather than the Certification Provision. True, the provision incorporates that federal law. But Plaintiffs may contest whether their DEI programs fall within the scope of that law if they ever face an enforcement action connected to the Certification Provision.

Plaintiffs' second argument about the Certification Provision falters for reasons already discussed. A provision requiring counterparties to certify that they do not violate federal laws that they are otherwise obligated to comply with does not chill protected speech. Again, the First Amendment does not give Plaintiffs a right to disregard federal antidiscrimination law.... To reiterate: if Plaintiffs believe that the Executive Branch has wrongly interpreted federal antidiscrimination law, they can challenge that interpretation in a specific enforcement action. But Plaintiffs have not carried their burden of showing that the Court should presume that Defendants will, in most cases, apply the Certification Provision in a way that violates the First Amendment.

DISCUSSION

1. *Applying Unconstitutional Conditions Doctrine.* As the excerpted decisions suggest, the government has wide latitude in terms of deciding what activities—including speech activities—to fund. It is also authorized to enforce federal anti-discrimination laws. However, as the courts also recognized, government cannot leverage funding to limit what grantees say about race and gender *outside* funded programs. In *Chicago Women in Trades*, the court concluded the Certification Provision violated this limit, while in *National Urban League* the court acknowledged the limit but held the Certification Provision did not regulate expression. Unconstitutional conditions doctrine also prohibits government from using its funding authority to suppress disfavored viewpoints. However, both courts viewed the Termination and other provisions as regulations of discriminatory *conduct* rather than expression. Do you agree with that interpretation?

2. *Vagueness and Chill.* The two district courts also responded to Plaintiffs' vagueness claims. In *Chicago Women in Trades*, the court concluded the Certification Provision's ambiguity regarding "DEI" and "equity-related" activities put grantees in a "difficult and perhaps impossible position." However, it concluded the Orders' other provisions were sufficiently clear statements of governmental policy and limitations on funding. In *National Urban League* the court concluded "the Orders speak for themselves" and limit only discriminatory conduct. Consider, again, the concerns raised by Professor Lakier, *supra*, Part C., regarding informal coercion and self-censorship. Should the judges *at least* have required the federal government to define "DEI" and other regulatory terms in the Executive Orders?

3. *Arts Funding.* The President's DEI and gender Executive Orders have affected expressive activity in a variety of contexts. For example, a district court in Rhode Island granted summary judgment to a group of artists who challenged application of President Trump's "gender ideology" Executive Order on First Amendment grounds. *See Rhode Island Latino Arts v. National Endowment for the Arts*, 2025 WL

2689296 (D. R.I., Sept. 19, 2025). The court distinguished *NEA v. Finley*, 524 U.S. 569 (1998), which was discussed earlier by the court in *Chicago Women in Trades*. In *Finley*, the Supreme Court upheld regulations and procedures for funding artistic projects and productions, which "ensure that . . . artistic excellence and artistic merit are the criteria by which applications are judged, taking into consideration general standards of decency and respect for the diverse beliefs and values of the American public." *Id.* at 576. Although it upheld the "decency and respect" clause, the Court noted it "would confront a different case" if the NEA were to deny, or disfavor, grants to projects or productions *expressing disfavored viewpoints*. *Id.* at 587 (emphasis added). The Rhode Island court concluded plaintiffs had brought such a case. *See also Thakur v. Donald J. Trump*, 148 F. 4th 1096 (9th Cir. 2025) (denying a stay of a district court order enjoining the federal government from terminating research grants based on "DEI" and "gender ideology" provisions in Executive Orders).

E. PROBLEM EXERCISE: REPRESENTING A FEDERAL CONTRACTOR

Initech Corp., a private business that frequently contracts with the federal government, states on its company website that "promoting racial and gender diversity are core values of our business." The website boasts that Initech has "a proven track record of retaining and promoting a diverse workforce." The company also conducts an annual employee training, which covers the substance of workplace sexual harassment and anti-discrimination laws. A portion of that training addresses discrimination against transgender employees. As part of its enforcement of President Trump's "DEI" and "gender ideology" Executive Orders, the Department of Labor (DOL) recently sent Initech a Notice demanding that the company *certify* in writing that it "does not have any Diversity, Equity, and Inclusion programs or initiatives and does not promote gender ideology in violation of applicable Federal anti-discrimination laws." Your law firm represents Initech, whose Chief Executive Officer has come to the firm seeking legal advice concerning the DOL notice. What legal and other options does Initech have? What advice would you give the CEO?

4

HIGHER EDUCATION

The Trump Administration has taken a variety of actions against public and private universities. As recipients of federal education and other funding, universities are required to comply with Title VI, which prohibits funding recipients from discriminating based on race, national origin, and other characteristics. Early in President Trump's second term in office, the Education Department issued guidance to universities informing them that "Diversity, Equity, and Inclusion" (DEI) is a form of racial discrimination that violates Title VI. President Trump has also issued two Executive Orders directing federal agencies to deny federal funds to grantees, including universities, which engage in DEI practices.[1] Finally, the Trump Administration has alleged that universities, including Harvard University and Columbia University, have discriminated against Jewish students in violation of Title VI. As a result, it has conditioned universities' access to federal funding on their compliance not just with Title VI but also with requirements relating to admissions, campus protests, and viewpoint diversity. The Trump Administration has also taken other actions against universities, including prohibiting them from admitting international students and threatening to terminate federal funding if they allow transgender women to participate in sports.

A. FEDERAL ANTI-DISCRIMINATION LAW AND "DEI"

On February 14, 2025, the United States Department of Education, Office of Civil Rights (OCR), issued the following "Dear Colleague" Letter to universities and K-12 educational institutions. "Dear Colleague" Letters address executive branch interpretations of federal anti-discrimination and other laws and provide guidance to universities regarding compliance. Following the doctrinal synopsis, the portions of the OCR Letter addressing "DEI" and raising potential First Amendment issues are highlighted below.

DOCTRINAL SYNOPSIS: VAGUENESS

- It is a basic principle of due process that an enactment is void for vagueness if its prohibitions are not clearly defined.
- Standards of permissible vagueness are *strict* in the area of free expression. Vague laws chill expression and risk sweeping and improper applications.

UNITED STATES DEPARTMENT OF EDUCATION
OFFICE FOR CIVIL RIGHTS

February 14, 2025

Dear Colleague:

Discrimination on the basis of race, color, or national origin is illegal and morally reprehensible. Accordingly, I write to clarify and reaffirm the nondiscrimination obligations of schools and other entities that receive federal financial assistance from the United States Department of Education (Department). This letter explains and reiterates existing legal requirements under Title VI of the Civil Rights Act of 1964, the Equal Protection Clause of the United States Constitution, and other relevant authorities.

In recent years, American educational institutions have discriminated against students on the basis of race, including white and Asian students, many of whom come from disadvantaged backgrounds and low-income families. These institutions' embrace of pervasive and repugnant race-based preferences and other forms of racial discrimination have emanated throughout every facet of academia. For example, colleges, universities, and K-12 schools have routinely used race as a factor in admissions, financial aid, hiring, training, and other institutional programming. In a shameful echo of a darker period in this country's history, many American schools and universities even encourage segregation by race at graduation ceremonies and in dormitories and other facilities.

Educational institutions have toxically indoctrinated students with the false premise that the United States is built upon "systemic and structural racism" and advanced discriminatory policies and practices. Proponents of these discriminatory practices have attempted to further justify them—particularly during the last four years—under the banner of "diversity, equity, and inclusion" ("DEI"), smuggling racial stereotypes and explicit race-consciousness into everyday training, programming, and discipline. But under any banner, discrimination on the basis of race, color, or national origin is, has been, and will continue to be illegal.

The Supreme Court's 2023 decision in *Students for Fair Admissions v. Harvard* (SFFA), which clarified that the use of racial preferences in college admissions is unlawful, sets forth a framework for evaluating the use of race by state actors and entities covered by Title VI. The Court explained that "[c]lassifying and assigning students based on their race" is lawful only if it satisfies "strict scrutiny," which means that any use of race must be narrowly tailored—that is, "necessary"—to achieve a compelling interest. To date, the Supreme Court has recognized only two interests as compelling in the context of race-based action: (1) "remediating specific, identified instances of past discrimination that violated the Constitution or a statute"; and (2) "avoiding imminent and serious risks to human safety in prisons, such as a race riot." Nebulous concepts like racial balancing and diversity are not compelling interests. As the Court explained in *SFFA*, "an individual's race may never be used against him" and "may not operate as a stereotype" in governmental decision-making.

Although SFFA addressed admissions decisions, the Supreme Court's holding applies more broadly. At its core, the test is simple: If an educational institution treats a person of one race differently than it treats another person because of that person's race, the educational institution violates the law. Federal law thus prohibits covered entities from using race in decisions pertaining to admissions, hiring, promotion, compensation, financial aid, scholarships, prizes, administrative support, discipline, housing, graduation ceremonies, and all other aspects of student, academic, and campus life. Put simply, educational institutions may neither separate or segregate students based on race, nor distribute benefits or burdens based on race.

Although some programs may appear neutral on their face, a closer look reveals that they are, in fact, motivated by racial considerations. And race-based decision-making, no matter the form, remains impermissible. For example, a school may not use students' personal essays, writing samples, participation in extracurriculars, or other cues as a means of determining or predicting a student's race and favoring or disfavoring such students.

Relying on non-racial information as a proxy for race, and making decisions based on that information, violates the law. That is true whether the proxies are used to grant preferences on an individual basis or a systematic one. It would, for instance, be unlawful for an educational institution to eliminate standardized testing to achieve a desired racial balance or to increase racial diversity.

Other programs discriminate in less direct, but equally insidious, ways. DEI programs, for example, frequently preference certain racial groups and teach students that certain racial groups bear unique moral burdens that others do not. Such programs stigmatize students who belong to particular racial groups based on crude racial stereotypes. Consequently, they deny students the ability to participate fully in the life of a school.

The Department will no longer tolerate the overt and covert racial discrimination that has become widespread in this Nation's educational institutions. The law is clear: treating students differently on the basis of race to achieve nebulous goals such as diversity, racial balancing, social justice, or equity is illegal under controlling Supreme Court precedent.

All students are entitled to a school environment free from discrimination. The Department is committed to ensuring those principles are a reality.

This letter provides notice of the Department's existing interpretation of federal law. Additional legal guidance will follow in due course. The Department will vigorously enforce the law on equal terms as to all preschool, elementary, secondary, and post-secondary educational institutions, as well as state educational agencies, that receive financial assistance.

The Department intends to take appropriate measures to assess compliance with the applicable statutes and regulations based on the understanding embodied in this letter beginning no later than 14 days from today's date, including antidiscrimination requirements that are a condition of receiving federal funding.

All educational institutions are advised to: (1) ensure that their policies and actions comply with existing civil rights law; (2) cease all efforts to circumvent prohibitions on the use of race by relying on proxies or other indirect means to accomplish such ends; and (3) cease all reliance on third-party contractors, clearinghouses, or aggregators that are being used by institutions in an effort to circumvent prohibited uses of race. Institutions that fail to comply with federal civil rights law may, consistent with applicable law, face potential loss of federal funding.

Anyone who believes that a covered entity has unlawfully discriminated may file a complaint with OCR. Information about filing a complaint with OCR, including a link to the online complaint form, is available here [link omitted].

Thank you in advance for your commitment to providing our Nation's students with an educational environment that is free of race, color, or national origin discrimination.

Sincerely,

/s/ Craig Trainor
Acting Assistant Secretary for Civil Rights
United States Department of Education

DISCUSSION

1. *Void for Vagueness.* Educational associations and school districts successfully challenged the "Dear Colleague Letter," in part on the ground that it is unconstitutionally vague. *See Nat'l Education Ass'n v. United States Department of Education*, 779 F. Supp. 3d 149, 187 (D.N.H. 2025) (concluding that the Letter is vague because it does not say "what the Department believes constitutes a DEI program, or the circumstances in which the Department believes DEI programs run afoul of Title VI. The Letter does not even define what a 'DEI program' is."); *American Federation of Teachers v. Dept. of Education*, ___ F. Supp.3d ___, 2025 WL 2374697 (D. Md., Aug. 14, 2025) (observing that "[t]he Letter leaves it entirely within DOE's discretion to decide what conduct counts as DEI at all, and what conduct is unlawful DEI"). *See also Nat'l Ass'n for the Advancement of Colored People v. Dep't of Educ.*, 779 F. Supp. 3d 53, 66 (D.D.C. 2025) (concluding that asking whether an action treats a person differently than another person because of their race "hardly provides sufficient guidance.")

2. *Viewpoint Discrimination.* Lower courts also enjoined or invalidated the Letter because it targets speech based on its viewpoint. *See Nat'l Education Ass'n*, 779 F. Supp. 3d at 194 (observing that "[a] professor runs afoul of the [OCR] Letter if she expresses the view in her teaching that structural racism exists in America, but does not do so if she denies structural racism's existence. That is textbook viewpoint discrimination."); *American Fed. of Teachers*, ___ F. Supp.3d at ___ (noting the Letter expressly singles out "[p]roponents" of diversity, equity, inclusion, and social justice."). After courts enjoined enforcement of the Letter, the Department of Education issued a notice that it would not enforce the challenged requirements "until further notice."

3. *Interpreting the Letter.* The Education Department argued that the Letter merely reminded fund recipients that they were required to follow existing civil rights laws and judicial decisions. Imagine you are a university or law school instructor or administrator who has just received OCR's Letter. What do you understand to be the limits on course materials or instruction according to OCR's interpretation of Title VI?

- Would the OCR Letter prohibit a history teacher from leading a class discussion on the economic development of the antebellum south?
- Would it prohibit an English teacher from assigning students to write a paper comparing the persecution of Tom Robinson—whom Atticus Finch championed in *To Kill a Mockingbird*—to that of Emmett Till?
- Would the decision to host events featuring black scholars (open to all students) constitute an impermissible advantaging of black students over students of other races?
- Would courses taught by professors who promote the view that systemic racism exists, and race can be central to one's experiences and identity, be unlawful?

4. *Academic Freedom*. Academic freedom consists of a longstanding set of principles designed to preserve the independence of universities and faculty regarding core aspects of education. Among other things, academic freedom is generally understood to protect the rights of universities to decide what subject matters to offer as part of their curricula, the freedom of individual faculty to decide what materials to cover in the classroom and how to teach them, and the right of students to learn. The Supreme Court has described academic freedom as "a special concern of the First Amendment, which does not tolerate laws that cast a pall of orthodoxy over the classroom." *Keyishian v. Bd. of Regents of Univ. of N.Y.*, 385 U.S. 589, 603 (1967). And it has observed that ours is a Nation "deeply committed to safeguarding academic freedom, which is of transcendent value to all of us and not merely to the teachers concerned." *Id.* at 603. Academic freedom is a complicated concept, and its specific relationship to the First Amendment remains uncertain. However, as you consider Trump 2.0 actions involving universities and faculty, in particular, keep in mind they may implicate not just the First Amendment but also related academic freedom principles and rights.

B. PROBLEM EXERCISE: REPRESENTING A UNIVERSITY

Shortly after the Dear Colleague Letter was issued, the Education Department announced it had opened investigations into forty-five universities for potential violations of Title VI. Imagine you are a lawyer advising one of those universities. Which, if any, of the following courses of action would you recommend to university leadership? You may choose one, a combination, or some other option, but whatever option(s) you choose make sure to explain your reasoning.

1. Reach out to DOE for further clarification.
2. Consult with other universities regarding their compliance strategies.
3. Recommend the university remove all references to "DEI" or race from its website and other public-facing materials.
4. Recommend the university remove all references to "DEI" or race from course descriptions, course syllabi, and other materials. To facilitate this recommendation, have an academic dean review all course descriptions and syllabi and recommend deletions.
5. Advise faculty not to discuss controversial topics relating to race or racial discrimination in their classes.
6. File or join a lawsuit challenging the "Dear Colleague Letter."

C. PROSECUTORIAL INQUIRIES

Ed Martin, who was at the time Interim United States Attorney for the District of Columbia (and currently serves as the head of President Trump's "Weaponization Working Group") sent the following letter to the Dean of the Georgetown University Law Center. Consider how you might respond if you were its recipient. [The Dean's response follows.]

U.S. Department of Justice

Edward R. Martin, Jr.
United States Attorney

District of Columbia

Patrick Henry Building
601 D Street, NW
Washington D.C. 20530

February 17, 2025

Mr. William M. Treanor
Dean, Georgetown Law
600 New Jersey Avenue, NW Suite 508
Washington, DC 20001

Dear Sir,

As United States Attorney for the District of Columbia, I receive requests for information and clarification. I take these requests seriously and act on them with letters like this one you are receiving.

It has come to my attention reliably that Georgetown Law School continues to teach and promote DEI. This is unacceptable. I have begun an inquiry into this and would welcome your response to the following questions:

First, have you eliminated all DEI from your school and its curriculum?

Second, if DEI is found in your courses or teaching in anyway[sic], will you move swiftly to remove it?

At this time, you should know that no applicant for our fellows program, our summer internship, or employment in our office who is a student or affiliated with a law school or university that continues to teach and utilize DEI will be considered.

I look forward to your cooperation with my letter of inquiry after request. Thank you in advance for your assistance. Please respond by Monday, February 24, 2025. Should you have further questions regarding this matter, please do not hesitate to call my office or schedule a time to meet in person.

Sincerely,

Edward R. Martin, Jr.

17 89

GEORGETOWN LAW

March 6, 2025

William M. Treanor
Dean and Executive Vice President
Paul Regis Dean Leadership Chair

Edward R. Martin, Jr.
Interim United States Attorney
District of Columbia
Judiciary Center
555 4th Street, N.W.
Washington, D.C. 20001

Dear Interim United States Attorney Martin:

I write in response to your letter dated February 17, 2025, which you sent to me via email on March 3, 2025. As a Catholic and Jesuit institution, Georgetown University was founded on the principle that serious and sustained discourse among people of different faiths, cultures, and beliefs promotes intellectual, ethical, and spiritual understanding. For us at Georgetown, this principle is a moral and educational imperative. It is a principle that defines our mission as a Catholic and Jesuit institution. Georgetown University also prohibits discrimination and harassment in its programs and activities and takes seriously its obligations to comply with all federal and local laws.

Your letter challenges Georgetown's ability to define our mission as an educational institution. It inquires about Georgetown Law's curriculum and classroom teaching, asks whether diversity, equity, and inclusion is part of the curriculum, and asserts that your office will not hire individuals from schools where you find the curriculum "unacceptable." The First Amendment, however, guarantees that the government cannot direct what Georgetown and its faculty teach and how to teach it. The Supreme Court has continually affirmed that among the freedoms central to a university's First Amendment rights are its abilities to determine, on academic grounds, who may teach, what to teach, and how to teach it.

This is a bedrock principle of constitutional law—recognized not only by the courts, but by the administration in which you serve. The Department of Education confirmed last week that it cannot restrict First Amendment rights and that it is statutorily prohibited from "exercising control over the content of school curricula."

Your letter informs me that your office will deny our students and graduates government employment opportunities until you, as Interim United States Attorney for the District of Columbia, approve of our curriculum. Given the First Amendment's protection of a university's freedom to determine its own curriculum and how to deliver it, the constitutional violation behind this threat is clear, as is the attack on the University's mission as a Jesuit and Catholic institution.

Georgetown Law has one of the preeminent faculties in the country, fostering groundbreaking scholarship, educating students in a wide variety of perspectives, and thriving on the robust exchange of ideas. Georgetown Law faculty have educated world leaders, members of Congress, and Justice Department officials, from diverse backgrounds and perspectives. We pride ourselves on providing an excellent graduate and professional education, built upon the Catholic and Jesuit tradition. Georgetown-educated attorneys have, for decades, served this country capably and selflessly in offices such as yours, and we have confidence that tradition will continue. We look forward to your confirming that any Georgetown-affiliated candidates for employment with your office will receive full and fair consideration.

Sincerely,

William M. Treanor
Dean and Executive Vice President
Paul Regis Dean Leadership Chair

DISCUSSION

1. *The First Amendment Rights of Universities.* Georgetown University has a First Amendment right to express its views on race and other matters. When the federal government threatens adverse consequences, including the potential loss of students for engaging in disfavored expression, it engages in coercive action that violates the First Amendment. *See Nat'l Rifle Ass'n v. Vullo*, 602 U.S. 175 (2024).

2. *The First Amendment Rights of Job Candidates.* Mr. Martin's threat not to consider students from Georgetown Law for positions in his office also violates the First Amendment rights of putative job candidates. Like other government employees, prosecutors are protected by the First Amendment and cannot be excluded from employment based on the communication of personal viewpoints, coursework they have done that adopts a disfavored point of view, or attendance at universities that support disfavored views. *See, e.g., Chrzanowski v. Bianchi* (7th Cir. 2013). Even interns and volunteers have these rights. *See LeFande v. District of Columbia*, 613 F.3d 1155 (2010).

3. *Illegal Conduct v. Protected Expression.* Suppose Mr. Martin's letter had relied on allegations or information that the law school had engaged in discriminatory *conduct*, including violations of Title VI in admissions and other facets of university operations. Framed to address such concerns, would the letter raise any First Amendment issues?

D. AGENCY INVESTIGATIONS: FUNDING DENIALS AND OTHER SANCTIONS

At one point, the Department of Education's Office of Civil Rights (OCR) informed *sixty* universities that it was preparing to investigate them for violations of Title VI. OCR premised the investigations primarily on the universities' alleged failure to address harassment of Jewish students and other anti-Semitic acts committed during 2023–24 on-campus demonstrations relating to the Hamas-Israel war. It also cited alleged race discrimination by universities in admissions and programs. Although the Trump Administration has cast a wide net, it focused most intently on

Harvard University, which has been the subject of at least *ten* investigations by six separate federal agencies. The following are excerpts from (1) a letter sent by the Department of Education, the General Services Administration, and the Department of Health and Human Services to Alan Garber, the President of Harvard University, setting forth the administration's "demands," and (2) Dr. Garber's response, entitled "The Promise of American Higher Education." The letter and response are reproduced in full, to provide a sense of the scope and substance of the government's investigations and demands.

Dr. Alan M. Garber
President
Harvard University
Office of the President
Massachusetts Hall
Cambridge, MA 02138

Penny Pritzker
Lead Member, Harvard Corporation
Harvard Corporation
Massachusetts Hall
Cambridge, MA 02138

April 11, 2025

Dear Dr. Garber:

The United States has invested in Harvard University's operations because of the value to the country of scholarly discovery and academic excellence. But an investment is not an entitlement. It depends on Harvard upholding federal civil rights laws, and it only makes sense if Harvard fosters the kind of environment that produces intellectual creativity and scholarly rigor, both of which are antithetical to ideological capture.

Harvard has in recent years failed to live up to both the intellectual and civil rights conditions that justify federal investment. But we appreciate your expression of commitment to repairing those failures and welcome your collaboration in restoring the University to its promise. We therefore present the below provisions as the basis for an agreement in principle that will maintain Harvard's financial relationship with the federal government.

If acceptable to Harvard, this document will constitute an agreement in principle, which the parties will work in good faith to translate into a more thorough, binding settlement agreement.

- **Governance and leadership reforms.** By August 2025, Harvard must make meaningful governance reform and restructuring to make possible major change consistent with this letter, including: fostering clear lines of authority and accountability; empowering tenured professors and senior leadership, and, from among the tenured professoriate and senior leadership, exclusively those most devoted to the scholarly mission of the University and committed to the changes indicated in this letter; reducing the power held by students and untenured faculty; reducing the power held by faculty (whether tenured or untenured) and administrators more committed to activism than scholarship; and reducing forms of governance bloat, duplication, or decentralization that interfere with the possibility of the reforms indicated in this letter.
- **Merit-Based Hiring Reform.** By August 2025, the University must adopt and implement merit-based hiring policies, and cease all preferences based on race, color, religion, sex, or national origin throughout its hiring, promotion, compensation, and related practices among faculty, staff, and leadership. Such adoption and implementation must be durable and demonstrated through structural and personnel changes. All existing and prospective faculty shall be reviewed for plagiarism and Harvard's plagiarism policy consistently enforced. All hiring and related data shall be shared with the federal government and subjected to a comprehensive audit by the federal government during the period in which reforms are being implemented, which shall be at least until the end of 2028.
- **Merit-Based Admissions Reform.** By August 2025, the University must adopt and implement merit-based admissions poli-

cies and cease all preferences based on race, color, national origin, or proxies thereof, throughout its undergraduate program, each graduate program individually, each of its professional schools, and other programs. Such adoption and implementation must be durable and demonstrated through structural and personnel changes. All admissions data shall be shared with the federal government and subjected to a comprehensive audit by the federal government—and non-individualized, statistical information regarding admissions shall be made available to the public, including information about rejected and admitted students broken down by race, color, national origin, grade point average, and performance on standardized tests—during the period in which reforms are being implemented, which shall be at least until the end of 2028. During this same period, the dean of admissions for each program or school must sign a public statement after each admissions cycle certifying that these rules have been upheld.

- **International Admissions Reform.** By August 2025, the University must reform its recruitment, screening, and admissions of international students to prevent admitting students hostile to the American values and institutions inscribed in the U.S. Constitution and Declaration of Independence, including students supportive of terrorism or anti-Semitism. Harvard will immediately report to federal authorities, including the Department of Homeland Security and State Department, any foreign student, including those on visas and with green cards, who commits a conduct violation. As above, these reforms must be durable and demonstrated through structural and personnel changes; comprehensive throughout all of Harvard's programs; and, during the reform period, shared with the federal government for audit, shared on a non-individualized basis with the public, and certified by deans of admissions.
- **Viewpoint Diversity in Admissions and Hiring.** By August 2025, the University shall commission an external party, which shall satisfy the federal government as to its competence and good faith, to audit the student body, faculty, staff, and leadership for viewpoint diversity, such that each department, field, or teaching unit must be individually viewpoint diverse. This audit shall begin no later than the summer of 2025 and shall proceed on a department-by-department, field-by-field, or

teaching-unit-by-teaching-unit basis as appropriate. The report of the external party shall be submitted to University leadership and the federal government no later than the end of 2025. Harvard must abolish all criteria, preferences, and practices, whether mandatory or optional, throughout its admissions and hiring practices, that function as ideological litmus tests. Every department or field found to lack viewpoint diversity must be reformed by hiring a critical mass of new faculty within that department or field who will provide viewpoint diversity; every teaching unit found to lack viewpoint diversity must be reformed by admitting a critical mass of students who will provide viewpoint diversity. If the review finds that the existing faculty in the relevant department or field are not capable of hiring for viewpoint diversity, or that the relevant teaching unit is not capable of admitting a critical mass of students with diverse viewpoints, hiring or admissions within that department, field, or teaching unit shall be transferred to the closest cognate department, field, or teaching unit that is capable of achieving viewpoint diversity. This audit shall be performed and the same steps taken to establish viewpoint diversity every year during the period in which reforms are being implemented, which shall be at least until the end of 2028.

- **Reforming Programs with Egregious Records of Antisemitism or Other Bias.** By August 2025, the University shall commission an external party, which shall satisfy the federal government as to its competence and good faith, to audit those programs and departments that most fuel antisemitic harassment or reflect ideological capture.
    - The programs, schools, and centers of concern include but are not limited to the Divinity School, Graduate School of Education, School of Public Health, Medical School, Religion and Public Life Program, FXB Center for Health & Human Rights, Center for Middle Eastern Studies, Carr Center for Human Rights at the Harvard Kennedy School, Department of Near Eastern Languages and Cultures, and the Harvard Law School International Human Rights Clinic.
    - The report of the external party shall include information as to individual faculty members who discriminated against Jewish or Israeli students or incited students to violate Harvard's rules following October 7, and the University and fed-

eral government will cooperate to determine appropriate sanctions for those faculty members within the bounds of academic freedom and the First Amendment.

- The report of the external party shall be submitted to University leadership and the federal government no later than the end of 2025 and reforms undertaken to repair the problems. This audit shall be performed and the same steps taken to make repairs every year during the period in which reforms are being implemented, which shall be at least until the end of 2028.

- **Discontinuation of DEI.** The University must immediately shutter all diversity, equity, and inclusion (DEI) programs, offices, committees, positions, and initiatives, under whatever name, and stop all DEI-based policies, including DEI-based disciplinary or speech control policies, under whatever name; demonstrate that it has done so to the satisfaction of the federal government; and demonstrate to the satisfaction of the federal government that these reforms are durable and effective through structural and personnel changes. By August 2025, the University must submit to the government a report—certified for accuracy—that confirms these reforms.
- **Student Discipline Reform and Accountability.** Harvard must immediately reform its student discipline policies and procedures so as to swiftly and transparently enforce its existing disciplinary policies with consistency and impartiality, and without double standards based on identity or ideology. Where those policies are insufficient to prevent the disruption of scholarship, classroom learning and teaching, or other aspects of normal campus life, Harvard must develop and implement disciplinary policies sufficient to prevent those disruptions. This includes but is not limited to the following:
  - Discipline at Harvard must include immediate intervention and stoppage of disruptions or deplatforming, including by the Harvard police when necessary to stop a disruption or deplatforming; robust enforcement and reinstatement of existing time, place, and manner rules on campus, including ordering the Harvard police to stop incidents that violate time, place, and manner rules when necessary; a disciplinary process housed in one body that is accountable to Harvard's president or other capstone official; and removing or reform-

ing institutional bodies and practices that delay and obstruct enforcement, including the relevant Administrative Boards and FAS Faculty Council.

- Harvard must adopt a new policy on student groups or clubs that forbids the recognition and funding of, or provision of accommodations to, any student group or club that endorses or promotes criminal activity, illegal violence, or illegal harassment; invites non-students onto campus who regularly violate campus rules; or acts as a front for a student club that has been banned from campus. The leaders or organizers of recognized and unrecognized student groups that violate these policies must be held accountable as a matter of student discipline and made ineligible to serve as officers in other recognized student organizations. In the future, funding decisions for student groups or clubs must be made exclusively by a body of University faculty accountable to senior University leadership. In particular, Harvard must end support and recognition of those student groups or clubs that engaged in anti-Semitic activity since October 7th, 2023, including the Harvard Palestine Solidarity Committee, Harvard Graduates Students 4 Palestine, Law Students 4 Palestine, Students for Justice in Palestine, and the National Lawyers Guild, and discipline and render ineligible the officers and active members of those student organizations.
- Harvard must implement a comprehensive mask ban with serious and immediate penalties for violation, not less than suspension.
- Harvard must investigate and carry out meaningful discipline for all violations that occurred during the 2023–2024 and 2024–2025 academic years, including the Harvard Business School protest of October 2023, the University Hall sit-in of November 2023, and the spring encampment of 2024. This must include permanently expelling the students involved in the October 18 assault of an Israeli Harvard Business School student, and suspending students involved in occupying university buildings, as warranted by the facts of individual cases.
- The Harvard president and police chief must publicly clarify that the Harvard University Police Department will enforce University rules and the law. Harvard must also commit to cooperating in good faith with law enforcement.

- **Whistleblower Reporting and Protections.** The University must immediately establish procedures by which any Harvard affiliate can report noncompliance with the reforms detailed in this letter to both university leadership and the federal government. Any such reporter shall be fully protected from any adverse actions for so reporting.
- **Transparency and Monitoring.** The University shall make organizational changes to ensure full transparency and cooperation with all federal regulators. No later than June 30, 2025, and every quarter thereafter during the period in which reforms are being implemented, which shall be at least until the end of 2028, the University shall submit to the federal government a report—certified for accuracy—that documents its progress on the implementation of the reforms detailed in this letter. The University must also, to the satisfaction of the federal government, disclose the source and purpose of all foreign funds; cooperate with the federal government in a forensic audit of foreign funding sources and uses, including how that money was used by Harvard, its agents, and, to the extent available, third parties acting on Harvard's campus; report all requested immigration and related information to the United States Department of Homeland Security; and comply with all requirements relating to the SEVIS system.
- We expect your immediate cooperation in implementing these critical reforms that will enable Harvard to return to its original mission of innovative research and academic excellence.

Sincerely,

Josh Gruenbaum
Comm'r of the Fed. Acquisition Serv.
General Services Administration

Thomas E. Wheeler
Acting General Counsel
U.S. Dept. of Education

Sean R. Keveney
Acting General Counsel
U.S. Dep't Health & Human Servs.

HARVARD
Office of the President

April 14, 2025

Dear Members of the Harvard Community,

For three-quarters of a century, the federal government has awarded grants and contracts to Harvard and other universities to help pay for work that, along with investments by the universities themselves, has led to groundbreaking innovations across a wide range of medical, engineering, and scientific fields. These innovations have made countless people in our country and throughout the world healthier and safer.

In recent weeks, the federal government has threatened its partnerships with several universities, including Harvard, over accusations of antisemitism on our campuses. These partnerships are among the most productive and beneficial in American history. New frontiers beckon us with the prospect of life-changing advances—from treatments for diseases such as Alzheimer's, Parkinson's, and diabetes, to breakthroughs in artificial intelligence, quantum science and engineering, and numerous other areas of possibility. For the government to retreat from these partnerships now risks not only the health and well-being of millions of individuals but also the economic security and vitality of our nation.

Late Friday night, the administration issued an updated and expanded list of demands, warning that Harvard must comply if we intend to "maintain [our] financial relationship with the federal government." It makes clear that the intention is not to work with us to address antisemitism in a cooperative and constructive manner. Although some of the demands outlined by the government are aimed at combating antisemitism, the majority represent direct governmental regulation of the "intellectual conditions" at Harvard.

I encourage you to read the letter to gain a fuller understanding of the unprecedented demands being made by the federal government to control the Harvard community. They include requirements to "audit" the viewpoints of our student body, faculty, staff, and to "reduc[e] the power" of certain students, faculty, and administrators targeted because of their ideological views. We have informed the administration through our legal counsel that we will not accept their proposed agreement. The University will not surrender its independence or relinquish its constitutional rights.

The administration's prescription goes beyond the power of the federal government. It violates Harvard's First Amendment rights and exceeds the statutory limits of the government's authority under Title VI. And it threatens our values as a private institution devoted to the pursuit, production, and dissemination of knowledge. No government—regardless of which party is in power—should dictate what private universities can teach, whom they can admit and hire, and which areas of study and inquiry they can pursue.

Our motto—Veritas, or truth—guides us as we navigate the challenging path ahead. Seeking truth is a journey without end. It requires us to be open to new information and different perspectives, to subject our beliefs to ongoing scrutiny, and to be ready to change our minds. It compels us to take up the difficult work of acknowledging our flaws so that we might realize the full promise of the University, especially when that promise is threatened.

We have made it abundantly clear that we do not take lightly our moral duty to fight antisemitism. Over the past fifteen months, we have taken many steps to address antisemitism on our campus. We plan to do much more. As we defend Harvard, we will continue to:

- nurture a thriving culture of open inquiry on our campus; develop the tools, skills, and practices needed to engage constructively with one another; and broaden the intellectual and viewpoint diversity within our community;
- affirm the rights and responsibilities we share; respect free speech and dissent while also ensuring that protest occurs in a time, place, and manner that does not interfere with teaching, learning, and research; and enhance the consistency and fairness of disciplinary processes; and
- work together to find ways, consistent with law, to foster and support a vibrant community that exemplifies, respects, and embraces difference. As we do, we will also continue to comply with *Students For Fair Admissions v. Harvard*, which ruled that Title VI of the Civil Rights Act makes it unlawful for universities to make decisions "on the basis of race."

These ends will not be achieved by assertions of power, unmoored from the law, to control teaching and learning at Harvard and to dictate how we operate. The work of addressing our shortcomings, fulfilling our commitments, and embodying our values is ours to define and undertake as a community. Freedom of thought and inquiry, along with the government's longstanding commitment to respect and protect it, has enabled universities to contribute in vital ways to a free society and to healthier, more prosperous lives for people everywhere. All of us share a stake in safeguarding that freedom. We proceed now, as always, with the conviction that the fearless and unfettered pursuit of truth liberates humanity—and with faith in the enduring promise that America's colleges and universities hold for our country and our world.

Sincerely,

Alan M. Garber

As indicated in President Garber's letter, unlike other universities Harvard University chose not to comply with the Trump Administration's list of demands. Instead, it filed a federal lawsuit against various federal agencies, challenging the administration's Title VI investigation and denial of federal funding on First Amendment and other grounds. Excerpts from Harvard's Memorandum in Support of Motion for Summary Judgment in *Presidents and Fellows of Harvard College v. U.S. Dept. of Health and Human Services* (D. Mass.) follow the doctrinal synopses.

DOCTRINAL SYNOPSIS I: FIRST AMENDMENT RETALIATION

- The First Amendment prohibits government officials from subjecting an individual to retaliatory actions for speaking out or engaging in protected expression.
- To prevail on a First Amendment retaliation claim, Plaintiff must show (1) they engaged in conduct protected under the First Amendment; (2) Defendants took some retaliatory action sufficient to deter a person of ordinary firmness in Plaintiff's position from speaking again; and (3) there is a causal link between the exercise of a constitutional right and the adverse action.

DOCTRINAL SYNOPSIS II: UNCONSTITUTIONAL CONDITIONS

- Government is not required to provide funding or other support for expressive activities. However, it may not deny a benefit to a person on a basis that infringes their constitutionally protected interests.
- Government may not leverage funding to regulate speech outside the contours of the funded program.
- Nor may the Government rely on the threat of terminated funding or invocation of legal sanctions to achieve the suppression of disfavored viewpoints.

Plaintiff's Memorandum in Support of Motion for Summary Judgment

INTRODUCTION

Since Harvard's founding nearly 400 years ago, its students, faculty, and researchers have worked to identify and solve some of society's most pressing problems. They have developed novel drugs to fight Parkinson's and Alzheimer's diseases, engineered nanofibers to protect American military servicemembers and first responders, supported American astronauts in space, and designed an artificial intelligence system that can be used to diagnose and treat cancer. These pathbreaking and lifesaving advancements are due in part to the longstanding collaboration between the Government and research universities such as Harvard. Generations of Americans are healthier and safer as a result.

Over the last two months, the Government has abruptly—without any process or reasoned explanation—ended that longstanding partnership in a manner that flagrantly violates the First Amendment multiple times over. On April 11, 2025, citing concerns about alleged antisemitism and ideological bias at Harvard, the Government identified a list of "conditions" that Harvard must satisfy to continue receiving federal funding. Those demands included hiring a third party to conduct an "audit" of the viewpoints of Harvard's student body, faculty, and staff; depending on the audit's results, hiring a "critical mass" of new faculty and admitting a "critical mass" of new students to achieve "viewpoint diversity" in "each department, field, or teaching unit"; and "reducing the power" of certain faculty and students on campus. All told, the tradeoff put to Harvard was clear: Allow the Government to micromanage your viewpoints and your academic institution or jeopardize your ability to pursue medical breakthroughs, scientific discoveries, and innovative solutions.

Because Harvard would not allow itself to be taken over by the Government, Harvard rejected the Government's demands on April 14, 2025. [*See* Alan M. Garber, *The Promise of American Higher Education.*] Within hours, the Government retaliated by freezing billions of dollars in federal funding to Harvard. One week later, Harvard again acted to protect its First Amendment freedoms by bringing this lawsuit. The Government again retaliated, announcing an end of all new grants to the University, followed by a slew of letters from various agencies formally terminating existing grants with Harvard. Leaving no doubt that the Government's actions were retaliation for Harvard filing suit, the President contrasted Harvard with schools that have not sued, making clear that Harvard is "hurting [itself]" by "fighting." In his words, "every time [Harvard] fight[s], they lose another $250 million." The Secretary of Education echoed that sentiment, announcing that Harvard must "answer to" the filing of this "lawsuit."

The Government's across-the-board freeze and terminations are unreasonable and unreasoned. The Government asserts antisemitism concerns as the basis for its actions but fails to explain how the termination of funding for research to treat cancer, support veterans, and improve national security addresses antisemitism. The Government further fails to acknowledge, let alone engage with, the dozens of steps Harvard has taken and committed to take to address antisemitism and bias. The administrative record, although heavily redacted, nevertheless makes clear that the directive to freeze and terminate every dollar of Harvard's research funds came directly from the White House, which dictated the form that such terminations would take and set arbitrary deadlines for particular terminations. That blunt force punishment is the antithesis of reasoned agency decisionmaking.

The Government's actions violate the First Amendment. They are unconstitutional retaliation against Harvard for exercising its First Amendment rights to decide what to teach, to express certain views, and to petition the courts to defend itself. The Government's actions also impose unconstitutional conditions that seek to "interfere with private actors' speech to advance [the Government's] own vision of ideological balance," *Moody v. NetChoice*, 603 U.S. 707, 741 (2024), and "'to achieve the suppression' of disfavored speech," *Nat'l Rifle Ass'n v. Vullo*, 602 U.S. 175, 189 (2024) (citation omitted). The Government's content- and viewpoint-based attempt to coerce and control Harvard is blatantly unconstitutional.

ARGUMENT

I. The Government's Actions Violate the First Amendment.

This case is about the Government's attempt to control the balance of viewpoints at Harvard and commandeer Harvard's autonomous decisionmaking by offering the University an impermissible choice: submit to federal control over its viewpoints, governance, academic programs, students, faculty, and staff or lose every dollar in federal funding. After Harvard exercised its well-established First Amendment rights to reject the Government's unconstitutional demands and to sue to protect its constitutional freedoms, the Government made good on its unconstitutional ultimatum, freezing and terminating billions of dollars in funding and foreclosing Harvard's ability to seek future federal grants.

A. The Government's Targeted Coercion of Harvard Is Unlawful Retaliation for Harvard's Protected Expression.

First, Harvard engaged in constitutionally protected conduct (1) when it refused the Government's demands, which sought to control viewpoints at Harvard, and (2) when it filed this lawsuit. Harvard's First Amendment rights establish a zone of First Amendment protection for the educational process itself and encompass not only the independent and uninhibited exchange of ideas among teachers and students, but Harvard's "autonomous decisionmaking," *Regents of Univ. of Mich. v. Ewing*, 474 U.S. 214, 226 n.12 (1985). Those rights include the ability to manage an academic community and evaluate teaching and scholarship free from governmental interference. They also include Harvard's prerogative to determine for itself on academic grounds who may teach, as well as what is taught in the college classroom, *Healy v. James*, 408 U.S. 169, 180 (1972). The First Amendment also protects the right "to petition the Government for a redress of grievances," U.S. Const. amend. I, meaning "the right of individuals to appeal to courts and other forums established by the government for resolution of legal disputes." *Borough of Duryea v. Guarnieri*, 564 U.S. 379, 387 (2011). Put simply, filing and pursuing lawsuits are forms of protected petitioning that are integral to the democratic process.

Harvard exercised both of these critical First Amendment freedoms here, and each drew a swift retaliatory response from the Government. In its April 3 and April 11 Letters, the Government demanded that Harvard overhaul its governance, hiring, and academic programs to the Government's liking—including adopting a balance of ideological diversity and viewpoint that the Government preferred. These extraordinary demands sought to substitute the Government's own judgment for Harvard's. And when Harvard exercised its First Amendment rights by rejecting the Government's unlawful demands and protecting the University's academic freedom, the Government took no time in striking back. Within hours, the Government froze billions of dollars in federal funding to the University. When Harvard again engaged in First Amendment-protected activity by filing the present lawsuit, the Government again retaliated, announcing a complete and total ban on Harvard's ever again obtaining federal grant funding and terminating billions of dollars of Harvard's federal funding.

Second, the Government's actions are patently adverse. Viewed objectively, they would have a chilling effect on Plaintiff's exercise of First Amendment rights or would deter a reasonably hardy individual in the exercise of his or her constitutional rights. The Government threatened to withhold federal funding unless Harvard surrendered its academic freedom to government control. When Harvard refused, the Government made true on its threat and froze the funds. When Harvard then sued to protect its rights, the Government began terminating the frozen funds and foreclosed all future funding to Harvard.

The message from the Government is clear: Fight, and you will suffer. The Freeze Orders and Termination Letters were the chosen means. And the termination of research funding would deter most any university from exercising its First Amendment rights to avoid jeopardizing its research and educational missions and the livelihoods of its faculty and researchers.

Third, the causal link between Harvard's constitutionally protected conduct and the Government's decision to issue its demands and to sanction Harvard for exercising its right not to accept them is abundantly clear. The Government has been strikingly forthcoming about its motivation. The Termination Letters articulate no individualized grounds for terminating specific grants but instead refer back to the

Government's earlier demands and not only state but stress that the impetus for the terminations was Harvard's refusal to accede to the Government's demands.

The Government has made no secret that Harvard's suit is the reason for reprisal. Just last week, President Trump contrasted the Government's comparatively more favorable treatment of Columbia—which "has been . . . very, very bad" but, importantly to the Government, has not sued—with its treatment of Harvard, which the President perceives as "want[ing] to fight." As the President explicitly stated, "every time [Harvard] fight[s], they lose another $250 million." The Secretary of Education likewise connected the dots on the Government's retaliatory motive: "[W]hen the response out of the box is a lawsuit, then you've got to answer that." As did a White House spokesperson: "Mr. Garber's public outbursts only fuel the push to shut off the taxpayer money propping up their institution." After a multi-agency meeting just last Wednesday, May 28, 2025, reportedly convened by the White House to "brainstorm additional punitive measures" against Harvard, the same White House spokesperson suggested that if Harvard had not sued, it "would have saved [itself] from [its] self-inflicted demise." The Government has made its retaliatory motive painfully clear.

Although any governmental retaliation based on protected speech is an affront to the First Amendment, the retaliation here was especially unconstitutional because it was based on Harvard's particular views—the balance of speech on its campus and its refusal to accede to the Government's unlawful demands. The Government's actions against Harvard target not just subject matter, but particular views taken by speakers on a subject. The Supreme Court has many times held that "on the spectrum of dangers to free expression, there are few greater than allowing the government to change the speech of private actors in order to achieve its own conception of speech nirvana." *Moody*, 603 U.S. at 719, 741–42.

The Government's demand that Harvard achieve the Government's conception of "viewpoint diversity" in faculty hiring and student admissions is expressly viewpoint-based. It requires Harvard to hire certain faculty and admit certain students based on (1) the current balance of viewpoints at Harvard and (2) the expressed viewpoints of the faculty to be hired and students to be admitted. Such viewpoint-based demands are pernicious. They coerce Harvard to host and promote more of the Government's favored views and less of its disfavored views. Although the First Amendment promotes an expressive realm in which the public has access to a wide range of views, it does so "by preventing the government from 'tilt[ing] public debate in a preferred direction'" and "decid[ing] what counts as the right balance of private expression." *Moody*, 603 U.S. at 719, 741–42.

B. The Government's Demands Imposed Unconstitutional Conditions on Harvard's Funding.

Even if the Government's actions were not retaliatory, they would independently violate the First Amendment because they condition federal funding on the Government's content- and viewpoint-based restrictions on Harvard's speech and views. For the reasons above, the Government's demands target Harvard's exercise of its First Amendment rights to make decisions that affect the balance of viewpoints on its campus. Those viewpoint-based demands seek to replace the balance of private expression at Harvard with the Government's preferred balance of expression.

It would unquestionably violate the First Amendment if the Government sought to directly regulate Harvard's governance, admissions, and hiring decisions to "un-bias" what it thinks biased. Because it would be unconstitutional for the Government to impose its demands on Harvard directly, it is also unconstitutional to impose those same speech restrictions indirectly, through conditions on Harvard's receipt of federal funding. It is blackletter law that the Government may not deny a benefit to a person on a basis that infringes his constitutionally protected interests, because such a denial would penalize and inhibit the exercise of constitutional rights to produce a result which the Government could not command directly. Even if the Government could deny funding for some other reason, that authority does not imply a lesser power to condition funding on a person's forfeiture of his constitutional rights.

The Government threatened to—and the Freeze Orders and Termination Letters in fact did—deny Harvard the valuable benefit of federal funding due to Harvard's unwillingness to relinquish its First Amendment rights. Specifically, as a condition of a continued financial relationship with the federal government, the Government demanded, among other measures, that Harvard increase "viewpoint diversity" in faculty hiring and admissions to achieve the Government's preferred balance of views and shutter academic programs associated with viewpoints the Government disfavors. The Government thus threatened and terminated funding to produce a result—government control over Harvard's academic freedom and speech—that it could not command directly.

These conditions went far beyond any permissible regulation of speech in the context of the programs funded by the Government at Harvard. The Government did not attach germane restrictions that define the limits of the government spending program to individual research grants; it required Harvard to fundamentally reshape all aspects of its operations as an institution of higher education in order to achieve the Government's preferred ideological balance. By demanding that funding recipients adopt—as their own—the Government's view on an issue of public concern, the condition by its very nature affects protected conduct outside the scope of the federally funded program. If it had accepted the Government's demands, Harvard would have had no ability to make academic decisions about the expression of ideas on its campus without government oversight. The demands thus would not leave Harvard free to exercise its First Amendment rights outside the scope of the federal programs and are therefore unconstitutional.

DISCUSSION

1. *The Government's Principal Responses.* In its responsive pleadings the Government argued as follows:
   a. *Retaliation*: The Government argued that, as a "contractor," Harvard University's First Amendment rights are "circumscribed" and hence the government has wide authority to terminate its funding. It also argued that it was doubtful the "breakdown of a settlement negotiation" could be the basis for a retaliation claim. In any event, the Government contended, the agencies decided to terminate the grants *prior to* Harvard's rejection of the offer letter or its lawsuit. Finally, the Government argued that the reason for the termination—Harvard's inadequate response to campus anti-Semitism—is non-retaliatory and breaks any casual connection between Harvard's alleged expression and the termination of funding.
   b. *Unconstitutional Conditions*: The Government argued that its "offer" letter to Harvard was a non-binding proposal and, as such, Harvard could not challenge it as an unconstitutional condition. Even if the unconstitutional condition doctrine applied, it argued, "The Government is entitled to discern between programs of higher education and to fund only those that effectively deal with the problem of antisemitic discrimination. This is not condition-

ing funding on viewpoints articulated by a contracting party, but on actions taken by that party."

2. *Summary Judgment.* The district court granted Harvard and the other plaintiffs summary judgment on their First Amendment retaliation and unconstitutional condition claims. *See President and Fellows of Harvard College, et al. v. U.S. Department of Health and Human Services*, __ F. Supp. 3d __, 2025 WL 2528380 9 (D. Mass., Sept. 3, 2025). The court wrote that "a review of the administrative record makes it difficult to conclude anything other than that Defendants used antisemitism as a smokescreen for a targeted, ideologically-motivated assault on this country's premier universities." The court also concluded that Defendants' actions "have jeopardized decades of research and the welfare of all those who could stand to benefit from that research, as well as reflect a disregard for the rights protected by the Constitution and federal statutes."

3. *Title VI and Process.* In Title VI, Congress set forth detailed procedures that the Government "shall" satisfy before revoking or refusing to grant or continue federal funding based on discrimination concerns. *See* 42 U.S.C. § 2000d-1. Those procedures include advising the institution of any failure to comply with Title VI and determining that compliance cannot be secured by voluntary means. If voluntary compliance cannot be secured, there must be "an express finding on the record, after opportunity for hearing, of a failure to comply with such requirement" and the termination must be "limited to the particular . . . recipient as to whom such a finding has been made," as well as "the particular program, or part thereof, in which such non-compliance has been so found." *Id.* The agency must also inform Congress of the investigation and file a report. Harvard argued that these provisions demonstrated Congress's intent that "termination of or refusal to grant or to continue" federal financial assistance should be a remedy of last resort. *Id.* The district court agreed, concluding "[i]t is undisputed that Defendants did not comply with these requirements." In June 2025, after the funding terminations, the Trump Administration informed Harvard that after a "thorough investigation" it had concluded the university violated Title VI.

4. *Executive Power and Universities.* What is the scope and nature of authority of the Executive Branch regarding universities that receive federal funding?

- Does the Executive have the authority, under Title VI and other federal laws, to deny funding based on discriminatory conduct?
- Does it have the authority to impose conditions relating to faculty hiring, including that such hiring not violate anti-discrimination laws and the constitutional guarantee of equal protection?
- Does it have the power to regulate specific courses of study or to require classroom discussions be "balanced" in terms of viewpoint?
- Can the Executive Branch place a university under an effective form of federal receivership, until it is satisfied the institution has complied with federal laws? Is that what the Trump Administration was effectively proposing in its letter to Harvard?

5. *A Proposed "Compact."* The Trump Administration has proposed a "compact" under which assenting universities would receive "multiple positive benefits," including access to federal funding, if they (1) limit admission of international students, (2) "revise governance structures" to ensure ideological diversity and abolish units that "purposefully punish, belittle and even spark violence against conservative ideas," (3) "maintain institutional neutrality," (4) freeze tuition rates for five years, and agree to other conditions. Several universities, including Brown University, which had previously entered into a "deal" with the administration to restore its funding, have rejected the compact's terms based on academic freedom and institutional autonomy concerns. Other universities have indicated they will likely accept the terms of the compact. As a reminder, in general, academic freedom protects "the four essential freedoms of a university[:] . . . to determine for itself on academic grounds who may teach, what may be taught, how it shall be taught, and who may be admitted to study." *Sweezy v. New Hampshire*, 354 U.S. 234, 263 (1957) (Frankfurter, J., concurring).
6. *First Amendment Institutions.* Because they play such a vital role in public discourse, some have described universities (along with libraries and the institutional press) as "First Amendment Institutions." *See generally* Paul Horwitz, First Amendment Institutions (Harv. Univ. Press, 2013). The primary functions of universities are to produce and disseminate knowledge. To perform these functions, it is important that governments not interfere with universities' core operations.

Why do you suppose the Trump Administration has focused so much investigative and other attention on universities? Is there any connection between or among Trump 2.0 (a) demands made to universities, (b) Executive Orders targeting law firms, and (c) actions against the institutional press?

7. *Subsequent Actions Against Harvard.* The Trump Administration has initiated at least *ten* separate investigations of various aspects of Harvard University's operations. In addition to directing all federal aid to the university be terminated, the administration threatened to remove Harvard's tax-exempt status and prohibited Harvard from admitting foreign students. In response to the ban on admitting foreign students, Harvard filed a second federal lawsuit raising statutory and constitutional claims—including, again, that the administration had violated the First Amendment by retaliating against it based on protected expression. A district court ruled in Harvard's favor. *See President and Fellows of Harvard College v. U.S. Dept. of Homeland Security*, 788 F. Supp. 3d 182 (D. Mass. 2025)

8. *Suing v. Settling.* Like targeted law firms, universities must choose whether to take legal action or adopt a more conciliatory approach. So far, Harvard is the *only* university that has decided to litigate. Many other universities, including Columbia University and Brown University, have decided to "settle" or negotiate with the administration rather than file suit. Among other things, Columbia University agreed to (1) pay a $221 million "fine," (2) overhaul its disciplinary process in ways that reduce faculty authority, (3) ban masks on campus, (4) add three dozen security officers, and (5) appoint a new senior vice provost to oversee academic programs on the Middle East. Some view the agreement as a form of capitulation and the surrender of fundamental academic freedom rights, while others believe Columbia and other universities have little choice but to make a deal. According to its terms, none of the agreement's provisions give the federal government "the authority to dictate faculty hiring, university hiring, admissions decisions or the content of academic speech" at Columbia.

    - In the *long term*, is the better course of action for universities to settle and cooperate or to resist? Universities may have strong First Amendment claims regarding threats to *current* funding but may have weaker or no such claims regarding *future* federal funding. Is it possible a university could successfully win the current battle only to lose the longer war?

- On the other hand, as the proposed "Compact" shows, deals like the one Columbia entered into do not *guarantee* the university will avoid future funding denials. The Columbia University agreement provides, "Nothing in this Agreement prohibits the United States from bringing actions against Columbia for future violations of Title VI or Columbia's violations of any other provision of federal law on the same basis it would bring similar actions against other institutions."
- If you were a university president, how would you balance the following considerations: (a) institutional financial viability, (b) the need to address campus discrimination, and (c) the preservation of academic freedom?

5

IMMIGRATION ENFORCEMENT

In an Executive Order, *Protecting the United States from Foreign Terrorists and Other National Security and Public Safety Threats*, President Trump directed federal agencies to arrest and deport lawfully admitted aliens who "bear hostile attitudes toward [American] citizens, culture, government, institutions, or founding principles" or "advocate for, aid, or support designated foreign terrorists and other threats to our national security."[1] A second Executive Order, *Additional Measures to Combat Anti-Semitism*, stated that the Hamas terrorist attacks against Israel in 2023 "unleashed an unprecedented wave of vile anti-Semitic discrimination, vandalism, and violence against our citizens, especially in our schools and on our campuses."[2] The Order announced it "shall be the policy of the United States to combat anti-Semitism vigorously, using all available and appropriate legal tools, to prosecute, remove, or otherwise hold to account the perpetrators of unlawful anti-Semitic harassment and violence."[3] The Order further called on immigration authorities to encourage universities to "monitor for and report activities by alien students and staff" relevant to their possible deportation.[4] The President also issued a Fact Sheet announcing the administration would revoke the visas of and deport "Hamas sympathizers." It stated, "To all the resident aliens who joined in the pro-jihadist protests, we put you on notice: come 2025, we will find you, and we will deport you. I will also quickly cancel the student visas of all Hamas sympathizers on college campuses, which have been infested with radicalism like never before."[5] Based on these orders, the Department of Homeland Security and Department of State arrested, detained, and sought to deport students and scholars who were in the U.S. lawfully (either temporarily pursuant to a student visa or permanently based on a Green Card), for their political speech and activism. These actions raised important questions about the free expression rights of noncitizens and the relationship between federal immigration law and the First Amendment.

A. ARRESTING AND DETAINING INTERNATIONAL STUDENT ACTIVISTS

Based on President Trump's directives and pursuant to existing immigration laws, Department of Homeland Security officers arrested and detained several international students who participated in campus protests or other expressive activities relating to Israel and Palestine. Several students challenged their detentions in *habeas corpus* proceedings, in part on First Amendment grounds. Excerpts from two district court decisions relating to these proceedings follow the doctrinal synopses.

DOCTRINAL SYNOPSIS I: THE FIRST AMENDMENT RIGHTS OF NONCITIZENS

- The Supreme Court has indicated that "[f]reedom of speech and of press is accorded aliens residing in this country." *Bridges v. Wixon*, 326 U.S. 135, 148 (1945).
- However, the Court has not addressed the precise relationship between immigration law and the First Amendment.
- Lower courts have reached different conclusions about the extent to which resident aliens can rely on First Amendment protections.

DOCTRINAL SYNOPSIS II: FIRST AMENDMENT RETALIATION

- The First Amendment prohibits government officials from subjecting an individual to retaliatory actions for speaking out or engaging in protected expression.
- To prevail on a First Amendment retaliation claim, Plaintiff must show (1) they engaged in conduct protected under the First Amendment; (2) Defendants took some retaliatory action sufficient to deter a person of ordinary firmness in Plaintiff's position from speaking again; and (3) there is a causal link between the exercise of a constitutional right and the adverse action.

Mahdawi v. Donald J. Trump

781 F. Supp. 3d 214 (D. Vt. 2025)

CRAWFORD, D.J.

Facts

Mr. Mahdawi is 34 years old. He was born and raised in the West Bank. He entered the United States legally in July 2014 and was married for some years to an American citizen. He has been a Legal Permanent Resident of the United States for ten years; his Permanent Resident Card ("green card") confirms that he has been a resident since January 2015. His permanent address is in White River Junction, Vermont. He also owns a small cabin that he built himself in nearby Vershire, Vermont.

Since 2021, Mr. Mahdawi has been an undergraduate student at Columbia University, majoring in philosophy. He hopes to graduate next month. He has been admitted to a master's degree program at Columbia's School of International and Public Affairs; that course of study would begin in September 2025.

As a student at Columbia, Mr. Mahdawi has dedicated himself to understanding how to achieve a lasting peace for Palestinians and Israelis, particularly through the study of conflict resolution. After Israel took military action in Gaza in fall 2023, Mr. Mahdawi was outspoken in opposition to the war. He took part in student demonstrations where he spoke publicly about the importance of respecting international law, human rights, and the need for a permanent ceasefire and a peaceful resolution. The letters submitted on Mr. Mahdawi's behalf describe him as a person who seeks common ground between students who support Israel's military response to the atrocities committed by Hamas and those who express outrage against the level of destruction and civilian casualties.

On March 27, 2025, Mr. Mahdawi received a notification from the United States Customs and Immigration Services (USCIS) portal that his naturalization interview had been scheduled for April 14, 2025, in Colchester, Vermont. The interview was the last stage of Mr. Mahdawi' s naturalization process before the formal naturalization ceremony. Mr. Mahdawi suspected that the Trump administration would use the interview as an opportunity to target and detain him for his speech. He nevertheless made arrangements to attend the interview in person.

Mr. Mahdawi traveled to Colchester, Vermont on the morning of April 14, 2025, to attend his naturalization interview. Upon entering the interview room, he recognized the interviewer as the official who interviewed him for his green card. The entire interview was recorded on video. Mr. Mahdawi answered all the interviewer's questions and passed the citizenship test. He also signed a document affirming that he was willing to take the Oath of Allegiance to the United States.

After Mr. Mahdawi signed that document, the official said he needed to check on some information and would be right back. Once the official left the room, three masked agents wearing Homeland Security Investigations ("HSI") jackets and their supervisor entered the room. They showed Mr. Mahdawi their badges and told him that he was under arrest. They did not show him a warrant or any documents. The agents separated Mr. Mahdawi from his attorney, brought him to a hallway where two more masked agents were waiting, and then shackled him and escorted him to a black van. They transported him to another USCIS office building approximately 10 or 15 minutes away from the Colchester office.

As he was being processed at the USCIS office, agents shoved a Notice to Appear ("NTA") document into his jacket. The NTA stated that Mr. Mahdawi was removable because "[t]he Secretary of State has determined that your presence and activities in the United States would have serious adverse foreign policy consequences and would compromise a compelling U.S. foreign policy interest." The NTA ordered Mr. Mahdawi to appear before an immigration judge at the South Louisiana Correctional Center on May 1, 2025.

Shortly before 2:00 p.m., the agents transported Mr. Mahdawi to the Burlington, Vermont airport. At the airport, two other agents took charge of him; one of the agents had a gun visible in a holster. Mr. Mahdawi repeatedly asked where he was being taken, and the agents finally told him that he was being sent to Louisiana. The flight left before the agents and Mr. Mahdawi were able to board it; the agents appeared to Mr. Mahdawi to be visibly upset that we had missed the flight. Mr. Mahdawi was then transported to the ICE field office in St. Albans, Vermont. After seeing his attorney at the St. Albans office, Mr. Mahdawi was re-shackled and transported to the Northwest State Correctional Facility in Swanton, Vermont.

Counsel for Mr. Mahdawi filed a Petition for Writ of Habeas Corpus in this court on April 14, 2025—the same day that Mr. Mahdawi was detained. Through counsel, Mr. Mahdawi filed a Motion for Release on April 22, 2025. That motion is supported by over 125 letters of support from professors, neighbors, fellow students, and others who know him well. All attest to his mild and peaceful nature, his deep intelligence, and his commitment to principles of non-violence and political activism. A striking number of these letters come from Jewish colleagues and professors involved in the study of the history and culture of Israel and Judaism.

Analysis

The Supreme Court has been unambiguous that executive detention orders, which occur without the procedural protections required in courts of law, call for the most searching review. Both sides agree in a general way that the arrest was prompted by Mr. Mahdawi's statements during protests on the Columbia campus. The Government describes these statements as harmful to the conduct of its foreign policy; Mr. Mahdawi alleges that the administration seeks to shut down criticism of the conduct of the war in Gaza.

Noncitizen residents like Mr. Mahdawi enjoy First Amendment rights in this country to the same extent as United States citizens. *See, e.g., Bridges v. Wixon*, 326 U.S. 135, 148 (1945) (holding that a noncitizen who published communist literature was protected by First Amendment); *Kwong Hai Chew v. Colding*, 344 U.S. 590, 596 n.5 (1953) (noting that the First Amendment does not distinguish "between citizens and resident [noncitizens]"); *United States v. Verdugo-Urquidez*, 494 U.S. 259,270 (1990) (confirming that resident noncitizens "enjoy certain constitutional rights," including "First Amendment rights"); *Rafeedie v. INS*, 795 F. Supp. 13 (D.D.C. 1992) ("Plaintiff is entitled to the same First Amendment protections as United States citizens, including the limitations imposed by the overbreadth and vagueness doctrines."); *OPAWL—Building*

AAPI Feminist Leadership v. Yost, 747 F. Supp. 3d 1065, 1080 (S.D. Ohio 2024) ("[T]he Supreme Court has never held that the First Amendment fails to protect [noncitizens'] political speech to the same extent it protects citizens' political speech."). That includes the right to be free from retaliation for the exercise of his First Amendment rights.

Official reprisal for protected speech offends the Constitution because it threatens to inhibit exercise of the protected right, and the law is settled that as a general matter the First Amendment prohibits government officials from subjecting an individual to retaliatory actions for speaking out. The Second Circuit has specifically recognized that retaliation for protected political speech is a cognizable ground for habeas relief in the immigration context.

Mr. Mahdawi has presented sufficient evidence that his speech was protected under the First Amendment. Speech on a matter of public concern is at the heart of First Amendment protection and occupies the highest rung of the hierarchy of First Amendment values. Here, Mr. Mahdawi's speech concerned an issue of great public interest. His speech, which advocated for a peaceful resolution of the conflict in Gaza and opposed Israel's military campaign, is at the heart of an ongoing political debate among the American people. Because Mr. Mahdawi's speech concerns political change, it is also core political speech and thus trenches upon an area in which the importance of First Amendment protections is at its zenith.

Mr. Mahdawi' s speech does not appear to fall within any areas in which the First Amendment permits restrictions based on the content of speech [the court described several categories of unprotected expression: incitement, true threats, defamation, and obscenity]. In a memorandum written by Secretary of State Marco Rubio, the government accused Mr. Madawi of "engag[ing] in threatening rhetoric and intimidation of pro-Israeli bystanders" at a protest. A bail hearing is not the time to make detailed findings on the merits of the First Amendment claim. On the limited record available, Mr. Mahdawi has provided enough information to show that his speech was protected.

There is also record evidence that Mr. Mahdawi' s arrest and detention constitutes adverse action for the purposes of his First Amendment retaliation claim. He was removed from his community and his family and cannot currently make progress toward completing his undergraduate degree. The threat of such conduct would chill a person of ordinary firmness from continuing to engage in the protected activity.

Mr. Mahdawi bears the burden of proving that the Government detained him in retaliation for his protected speech or to chill the speech of others. A bail hearing is not the time to rule on the merits of the evidence or the methods of inferring retaliatory motive. It is sufficient at this juncture to consider the Government's public statements as evidence of retaliatory intent. [The court described statements in the Executive Orders and Fact Sheet.] Before his election, President Trump reportedly promised donors, in reference to pro-Palestinian activism, that he would "set that movement back 25 or 30 years" if elected. Robert Tait, *Trump Tells Donors He Will Crush Pro-Palestinian Protests if Re-Elected*, The Guardian (May 27, 2024).

Together, this evidence is sufficient for Mr. Mahdawi' s present purpose of raising a substantial claim of First Amendment retaliation.

Ozturk v. Donald J. Trump

779 F. Supp. 3d 462 (D. Vt. 2025)

SESSIONS, D.J.

The instant matter concerns the government's motion to dismiss this case. For the reasons set forth below, the Court finds that Ms. Ozturk has raised significant constitutional concerns with her arrest and detention which merit full and fair consideration in this forum. [The court later ordered Ozturk released from detention based on the following analysis.]

Factual Background

Ms. Ozturk and three other students coauthored a March 26, 2024, editorial in the Tufts University school newspaper, *The Tufts Daily*. The editorial, which to date still appears on the *Tufts Daily* website, criticized the university administration's dismissal of several resolutions passed by the student senate that demanded the university acknowledge the existence of an ongoing genocide in Palestine, apologize for statements made by the university president, and disclose its investments in and divest from companies with ties to Israel.

The editorial criticized the university for "mischaracterizing" the student senate's stances as divisive and stated, "[w]e, as graduate students, affirm the equal dignity and humanity of all people[.]" Rumeysa Ozturk et al., *Op-ed: Try again, President Kumar: Renewing calls for Tufts to adopt March 4 TCU Senate resolutions*, The Tufts Daily (Mar. 26, 2024). It urged the university administration "to meaningfully engage with and actualize the resolutions passed by the Senate." The op-ed expresses agreement between Graduate Students for Palestine and three other campus groups, including Tufts Students for Justice in Palestine, about the university's response to the Senate resolutions. In the fall of 2024, Tufts University temporarily suspended Tufts Students for Justice in Palestine. Ms. Ozturk has not been alleged to be a member of that group, and the suspension occurred several months after the op-ed was published.

In an April 1, 2025, declaration, Sunil Kumar, the Tufts University president, attested that the opinion piece coauthored by Ms. Ozturk "was not in violation of any Tufts policies" and that "no complaints were filed with the University or, to our knowledge, outside of the University about this op-ed." The declaration noted that the newspaper also published other "op-eds on multiple sides of the issue with opinions that were shared just as strongly as the op-ed Ms. Ozturk co-authored."

Ms. Ozturk is a Turkish national and doctoral candidate in Child Study and Human Development at Tufts University. On June 28, 2024, she entered the United States pursuant to a validly issued F-1 student visa. On March 21, 2025, the government revoked Ms. Ozturk's visa, potentially subjecting her to removal from the United States. Pursuant to 8 U.S.C. § 1227(a)(1)(B), "[a]ny alien who is present in the United States . . . whose nonimmigrant visa (or other documentation authorizing admission into the United States as a nonimmigrant) has been revoked . . . is deportable."

Prior to her arrest, ICE determined that it would take Ms. Ozturk to a detention facility in Louisiana. According to ICE, there was no available bedspace for her at a facility where she could appear for a hearing in New England and transfers out of state are routinely conducted after arrest, due to operational necessity and considerations. Ms. Ozturk has submitted affidavits from several experienced New England immigration attorneys stating that immigration detainees are typically booked and processed at the ICE Boston Field Office in Burlington, Massachusetts, before being sent to a detention facility. She also submitted an affidavit from an experienced Maine immigration attorney stating that based on the attorney's review of records from the Cumberland County Jail, the facility had at least sixteen open beds to house female detainees on March 25 and 26, 2025.

Ms. Ozturk was not notified promptly of her student visa's revocation. On March 25, 2025, at approximately 5:25 p.m., Ms. Ozturk was near her residence in Somerville, Massachusetts when a hooded and masked officer in plainclothes approached her and grabbed her wrists. Five additional officers then surrounded her, took her cell phone, and handcuffed her. Ms. Ozturk was driven away in an unmarked vehicle.

ICE agents took Ms. Ozturk to Methuen, Massachusetts, arriving at 6:22 p.m. that day. Shortly thereafter, the agents and Ms. Ozturk departed for Lebanon, New Hampshire. At approximately 9:03 p.m., ICE agents began transporting Ms. Ozturk to the ICE Field Office in St. Albans, Vermont. At approximately 10:02 p.m. on March 25, 2025, having been unable to speak to Ms. Ozturk or otherwise ascertain her location after attempting to do so, Ms. Ozturk's counsel filed a habeas petition in the District of Massachusetts. At that time, Ms. Ozturk was in Vermont en route to the St. Albans Field Office.

Ms. Ozturk arrived at the St. Albans Field Office at 10:28 p.m. on March 25, 2025 and was kept in custody there overnight. On the morning of March 26, 2025, at approximately 4:00 a.m., ICE agents transported Ms. Ozturk to the Burlington, Vermont airport and placed her on a plane to Louisiana. Ms. Ozturk arrived in Alexandria, Louisiana at 2:35 p.m. and was taken to the South Louisiana Correctional Facility, where she is presently detained.

Between the evening of March 25, 2025 and the afternoon of March 26, 2025, Ms. Ozturk's counsel repeatedly attempted to ascertain her location, to no avail. Although Ms. Ozturk's attorney checked ICE's Detainee Locator System online several times, the "current detention facility" section was blank. Counsel's inquiries about Ms. Ozturk's location to ICE's Enforcement and Removal Operations ("ERO") division in Burlington, Massachusetts and Homeland Security Investigations ("HSI") in Boston, Massachusetts went unanswered.

According to a memorandum by John L. Armstrong (hereinafter "Armstrong Memorandum"), a senior bureau official of the Bureau of Consular Affairs, the Bureau of Consular Affairs had approved revocation of Ms. Ozturk's F-1 visa pursuant to a request from ICE and the Department of Homeland Security ("DHS") on March 21, 2025. According to the memo, ICE and DHS had made an assessment that Ms. Ozturk "had been involved in associations that 'may undermine U.S. foreign policy by creating a hostile environment for Jewish students and indicating support for a designated terrorist organization' including co-authoring an op-ed that found common cause with an organization that was later temporarily banned from campus."

Discussion—First Amendment

Ms. Ozturk argues that her detention is in retaliation for her political speech, thus violating her rights under the First and Fifth Amendments. Her evidence supports her argument that the government's motivation or purpose for her detention is to punish her for co-authoring an op-ed in a campus newspaper which criticized the Tufts University administration, and to chill the political speech of others. The government has so far offered no evidence to support an alternative, lawful motivation or purpose for Ms. Ozturk's detention.

Ms. Ozturk supports her claim that her adverse treatment from the government is improperly motivated by pointing to several statements made by high-level government officials. On May 14, 2024, then-candidate Donald Trump reportedly said, "any student that protests, I throw them out of the country. You know, there are a lot of foreign students. As soon as they hear that, they're going to behave." On March 28, 2025, Secretary of State Marco Rubio delivered remarks to the press regarding Ms. Ozturk's detention. Secretary Rubio stated in response to a question about Ms. Ozturk, "The activities presented to me meet the standard of what I've just described to you: people that are supportive of movements that run counter to the foreign policy of the United States." Secretary Rubio further indicated that Ms. Ozturk's detention was the government "basically asking them to leave the country." He explicitly noted that "that's why they've been detained."

Secretary Rubio, however, alluded that the government had more evidence than the op-ed to support Ms. Ozturk's detention, stating: "I would caution you against solely going off of what the media has been able to identify, and those presentations, if necessary, will be made in court."

The First Amendment's protection of the right to free speech is often considered the cornerstone of our vibrant American democracy. As Benjamin Franklin famously wrote in 1737, "Freedom of speech is a principal pillar of a free government; when this support is taken away, the constitution of a free society is dissolved."

It is against this backdrop that Ms. Ozturk alleges that her detention is retaliation for political speech which is core First Amendment protected conduct. The only specific act cited by the government so far as justification for any of their adverse actions towards Ms. Ozturk is her co-authored op-ed. The Supreme Court has repeatedly reaffirmed that speech on public issues occupies the highest rung of the hierarchy of

First Amendment values, and is entitled to special protection because political speech is at the core of what the First Amendment is designed to protect.

As a general rule, the First Amendment means that government has no power to restrict expression because of its message, its ideas, its subject matter, or its content. Furthermore, First Amendment protections have long extended to noncitizens residing within the country.

The Court hesitates to characterize the content of Ms. Ozturk's speech, which is obviously about public issues, but it is necessary to clarify that Ms. Ozturk's op-ed does not readily fall into one of the established exemptions to the First Amendment's protection from government speech regulation. The op-ed focuses largely on the authors' belief that the Tufts University administration erred by not affording sufficient deference to resolutions adopted by the Tufts undergraduate student senate. The op-ed quotes school documents to argue that the school administrators are not upholding their stated values of supporting critical thinking and debate in the community. The authors express their belief regarding violations of international law that have motivated the student senate's resolutions.

Tufts University has confirmed that the op-ed did not violate any Tufts policy, that no complaints were filed about the op-ed, that the speech in the op-ed was consistent with University guidelines, and indeed that it was just one of many op-eds discussing the issue published in the school newspaper.

The First Amendment protects individuals from government action that is based on improper motives, namely silencing disfavored speech. The Second Circuit has specifically recognized potential retaliation for protected political speech as a cognizable ground for habeas relief in the immigration context, noting that "to allow this retaliatory conduct to proceed would broadly chill protected speech, among not only activists subject to final orders of deportation but also those citizens and other residents who would fear retaliation against others." *Ragbir [v. Homan*, 923 F.3d 53 (2d Cir. 2019)].

Ms. Ozturk has presented evidence to support her argument that she may qualify for a retaliation claim. Administration officials have identified her speech as the reason her visa was revoked. If this Court were evaluating the question of motivation for Ms. Ozturk's visa revocation, this inquiry could likely conclude now. It may well be that Ms. Ozturk's detention shares common motivation with her visa revocation. But as this Court has found that visa revocation and detention proceedings are not inextricably linked, the Court seeks additional evidence of the connection between Ms. Ozturk's speech and her detention. For present purposes it is sufficient to find that Ms. Ozturk's First Amendment claims are serious and worthy of further exploration in this Court.

Secretary Rubio has argued publicly that there are additional justifications for the government's actions adverse to Ms. Ozturk and that these justifications may be filed in court if necessary. The Court invites an immediate submission any such evidence in this case. In the absence of additional information from the government, the Court's habeas review is likely to conclude that Ms. Ozturk has presented a substantial claim. [Secretary Rubio did not submit any additional evidence.]

DISCUSSION

1. *Detention, Removal, and Exclusion of Noncitizens.* Thus far, all district courts that have addressed the issue have concluded that the Trump Administration's arrest and detention of individuals studying on foreign visas or pursuant to Green Cards based on political expression likely violated the First Amendment. Note these decisions addressed *detention* rather than *removal* or *deportation.* At least in the detention context, courts have concluded First Amendment retaliation doctrine applies. The administration has also increased scrutiny of visa applications and reportedly denied entry based on the expression of political viewpoints. The Supreme Court has held that aliens can be excluded from the U.S. based on disfavored viewpoints. *See Kleindienst v. Mandel*, 408 U.S. 753, 767–69 (1972) (rejecting First Amendment challenge to journalist's denial of entry based on ideology). The Trump Administration has also asserted that it has the authority to revoke the visas of, and deport, individuals based on political expression. These actions are addressed in Part B.

2. *A Page of History.* Throughout American history, fear of foreign persons and ideologies have led to suppression of political expression. The district court in *Mahdawi* addressed this historical context:

   > The court also considers the extraordinary setting of this case and others like it. Legal residents—not charged with crimes or misconduct—are being arrested and threatened with deportation for stating their views on the political

issues of the day. Our nation has seen times like this before, especially during the Red Scare and Palmer Raids of 1919–1920 that led to the deportation of hundreds of people suspected of anarchist or communist views. In *Colyer v. Skeffington*, 265 F. 17 (1920), Judge Anderson of the District of Massachusetts granted habeas relief to multiple immigrants detained for their political beliefs. His decision was instrumental in bringing an end to the moral panic that gripped the nation and its officials. Similar themes were sounded during the McCarthy period in the 1950s when thousands of non-citizens were targeted for deportation due to their political views. Ellen Schrecker, *Immigration and Internal Security: Political Deportations During the McCarthy Era*, Vol. 60 Sci. & Soc 'y 393 (1996).

3. *Democracy and Dissent.* After his release from detention, Mohsen Mahdawi published an op-ed in the *New York Times* about his ordeal. Here is an excerpt:

> On April 14, 2025, I was detained during what should have been my citizenship naturalization interview. After more than two weeks of unjust imprisonment, a federal judge ruled in favor of releasing me. In a major victory for democracy, I may be the first of the many student activists who have been detained by the Trump administration to be freed from detention.
>
> . . . The American government accuses me of undermining U.S. foreign policy, a patently absurd pretext for deportation for political speech that the Trump administration dislikes. The government is scraping the bottom of the barrel in its attempts to smear me. My only "crime" is refusing to accept the slaughter of Palestinians, opposing war and promoting peace. I have simply insisted that international law must be respected. I believe the way to a just and long-lasting peace for Palestinians and Israelis is through diplomacy and restorative justice.
>
> . . . By seeking to deport me, the Trump administration is sending a clear message: There is no room for dissent, free speech be damned. It seems willing to shield an extremist Israeli government from criticism at the expense of consti-

> tutional rights, all while suppressing the possibility of a peaceful future for both Palestinians and Israelis, a future free of trauma and fear.
>
> ... Once the repression of dissent, in the name of security, becomes a key objective of a government, authoritarian rule and even martial law are not far off. When they look at my case, all Americans should ask themselves: What is left of our democracy, and who will be targeted next?

Mohsen Mahdawi, *I Was Detained For My Beliefs. Who Will Be Next?*, N.Y. Times (May 2, 2025)

4. *Other Immigration-Related Issues.* Although arrests of international students have grabbed headlines, the Trump Administration's immigration enforcement actions have raised other First Amendment concerns. For example, its effort to ban Harvard University from enrolling international students, which was mentioned in Chapter 4, raised free speech and academic freedom concerns. Immigration lawyers and advocates have also challenged restrictions that have affected their ability to engage in legal advocacy on behalf of detained clients.

B. DEPORTING NONCITIZENS BASED ON POLITICAL EXPRESSION

The decisions in Part A addressed the government's power to arrest and detain international students based on political expression. The Trump Administration claims that these noncitizens are subject to removal or deportation based on their support for Palestine or criticism of Israel. Federal immigration laws grant broad authority to the executive to revoke visas and remove aliens. One statutory provision authorizes the Secretary of state to revoke the "visa or other documentation" of any noncitizen "at *any* time" for *any* reason.[6] Another provision states that an alien's visa can be revoked based on otherwise lawful expression "*if the Secretary of State has reasonable grounds to believe that the alien's presence or activities in the United States would have potentially serious adverse foreign policy consequences for the United States.*" The following Memorandum, filed by Secretary of State Marco Rubio in a case involving two international students, invoked the latter provision.

THE SECRETARY OF STATE
WASHINGTON

SENSITIVE BUT UNCLASSIFIED//LAW ENFORCEMENT SENSITIVE

MEMORANDUM FOR THE SECRETARY OF HOMELAND SECURITY

FROM: Marco Rubio

SUBJECT: Notification of Removability Determinations under Section 237(a)(4)(C) of the Immigration and Nationality Act (INA)

I am writing to inform you that upon notification from the Department of Homeland Security's Homeland Security Investigations (DHS/ICE/HSI) on March 7, 2025, I have determined that [REDACTED] and Mahmoud Khalil[7] (DOB: 01-JAN-1995; POB: Algeria), both U.S. Lawful Permanent Residents (LPR), are deportable aliens under INA section 237(a)(4)(C). I understand that ICE now intends to initiate removal charges against them, based on assurances from DHS/ICE/HSI.

Under INA section 237(a)(4)(C)(i), an alien is deportable from the United States if the Secretary of State has reasonable ground to believe that the alien's presence or activities in the United States would have potentially serious adverse foreign policy consequences for the United States. Under INA section 237(a)(4)(C)(ii), for cases in which the basis for this determination is the alien's past, current, or expected beliefs, statements, or associations that are otherwise lawful, the Secretary of State must personally determine that the alien's presence or activities would compromise a compelling U.S. foreign policy interest.

Pursuant to these authorities, I have determined that the activities and presence of these aliens in the United States would have potentially serious adverse foreign policy consequences and would compromise a compelling U.S. foreign policy interest. These determinations are based on information provided by the DHS / ICE / HSI regarding the participation and roles of [REDACTED] and Khalil in antisemitic protests and disruptive activities, which fosters a hostile environment for Jewish students in the United States. My determination for [REDACTED] is also based on citations for unlawful activity during these protests. The public actions and continued presence of [REDACTED] and Khalil in the United States undermine U.S. policy to combat anti-Semitism around the world and in the United States, in addition to efforts to protect Jewish students from harassment and violence in the United States. Consistent with E.O. 14150, *America First Policy Directive to the Secretary of State*, the foreign policy of the United States champions core American interests and American citizens and condoning anti-Semitic conduct and disruptive protests in the United States would severely undermine that significant foreign policy objective.

DISCUSSION

1. *Vagueness.* Mahmoud Khalil, a Columbia student mentioned in Secretary Rubio's memorandum, organized pro-Palestine protests at Columbia University. As the memo indicates, based on that political activism Secretary Rubio concluded Khalil was deportable because his presence in the U.S. compromised a compelling U.S. foreign policy interest—combatting anti-Semitism across the globe. Given the variable and often *unknown* foreign policy objectives of the U.S., is the federal law Secretary Rubio relied upon in Khalil's case void for vagueness? How would an alien, or anyone else, know *ex ante* how to conform their expression or expressive activities to the requirements of U.S. foreign policy? A district court invalidated the provision cited in the Rubio memo on vagueness grounds. *See Massieu v. Reno*, 915 F. Supp. 681 (D.N.J. 1996). The decision in *Massieu*, which was reversed on appeal on other grounds, was issued by the late Judge Maryanne Trump Barry—President Trump's sister.

2. *Viewpoint Discrimination.* Assuming Khalil and other noncitizens have the *same* First Amendment rights as citizens, or at least the core right to engage in political expression, revocation of their visas based on participation in "*antisemitic protests and disruptive activities, which fosters a hostile environment for Jewish students in the United States*" would likely constitute a presumptively invalid viewpoint-based restriction on speech. Even if the federal government has a compelling interest in combatting anti-Semitism, arresting and deporting aliens based on their political viewpoints is likely neither a necessary nor narrowly tailored way to further that interest.

3. *Support for Hamas.* Whatever their scope, noncitizens' First Amendment rights do not extend to communications or expressive activity that is unlawful. In some of the proceedings against international

students and scholars, the government has argued that pro-Palestine or anti-Israel expression constitutes the unlawful provision of "material support" to Hamas, a designated foreign terrorist organization. *See Holder v. Humanitarian Law Project*, 561 U.S. 1, 36 (2010) (upholding federal law prohibiting the provision of "material support," including coordinated expression, to designated foreign terrorist organizations). However, the federal "material support" law requires *coordination* between the speaker and the foreign terrorist organization. Merely organizing and participating in campus protests on behalf of, or in support of, Palestine or its people would not constitute a violation of federal law. In the detention cases, the administration did not provide any evidence that international students or scholars had coordinated with Hamas or any other foreign terrorist organization. As the district court in the following case concluded, administration officials falsely equated support for Palestine and support for Hamas.

American Association of University Professors v. Rubio,

___ F. Supp. 3d ___, 2025 WL 2777659
(D. Mass., Sept. 30, 2025)

[Two educational associations, along with their chapters and members, filed a lawsuit in which they challenged, on First Amendment and other grounds, what they characterized as the Trump Administration's "ideological deportation policy." Plaintiffs alleged that under this policy the administration arrested, detained, and subjected to deportation lawfully present international students and foreign scholars based solely on their political expression. The district court denied the government's motion to dismiss the lawsuit. After holding a bench trial, the court issued the following excerpted Findings of Fact and Rulings of Law.]

FINDINGS OF FACT AND RULINGS OF LAW

YOUNG, D.J.

I. Introduction

On January 20, 2025, the first day of President Donald Trump's second term in office, he promulgated 26 Executive Orders. Executive Order 14149, entitled "Restoring Freedom of Speech and Ending Federal Censorship" ostensibly issued to reverse conduct of his predecessor, barred federal officials from "any conduct that would unconstitutionally abridge the free speech of any American citizen." Id. at § 2(b). President Trump here makes clear that, in his view, the First Amendment's protection of freedom of speech applies to American citizens alone, and to an unconstitutionally narrow view of citizenship at that.

This case—perhaps the most important ever to fall within the jurisdiction of this district court—squarely presents the issue whether non-citizens lawfully present here in United States actually have the same free speech rights as the rest of us. The Court answers this Constitutional question unequivocally "yes, they do." "No law" means "no law." The First Amendment does not draw President Trump's invidious distinction and it is not to be found in our history or jurisprudence. *See* Section III.A *infra*. No one's freedom of speech is unlimited, of course, but these limits are the same for both citizens and non-citizens alike.

With this constitutional ruling firmly undergirding its approach, the Court here held a full hearing and a nine-day bench trial on the issue of whether the rights of these plaintiffs to constitutional freedom of speech have been unconstitutionally chilled by the deliberate conduct of any or all of the Public Official defendants. The Court heard 15 witnesses and admitted 250 exhibits consisting of documents, photographs, and video clips.

Having carefully considered the entirety of the record, this Court finds by clear and convincing evidence that the Secretary of Homeland Security Kristi Noem and the Secretary of State Marco Rubio, together with the subordinate officials and agents of each of them, deliberately and with purposeful aforethought, did so concert their actions and those of their two departments intentionally to chill the rights to freedom of speech and peacefully to assemble of the non-citizen plaintiff members of the plaintiff associations.

II. Findings of Fact

[The following is a distillation of some of the district court's key findings of fact, based on the trial record.]

- According to a 2023 State Department Report, on October 7, 2023, Hamas, Palestinian Islamic Jihad, and other Palestinian terrorists launched a large-scale attack on Israel from the Gaza Strip, killing an estimated 1,200 individuals, injuring more than

5,400, and abducting 253 hostages. Israel responded with a sustained, wide-scale military operation in Gaza, which had killed more than 21,000 Palestinians and injured more than 56,000 by the end of the year, displaced the vast majority of Palestinians in Gaza, and resulted in a severe humanitarian crisis.

- Demonstrations on college campuses across the United States ensued, many of which were pro-Palestine/anti-Israel. Many protesters were non-citizens, many here on non-immigrant visas or lawful permanent resident status.
- On February 3, 2025, the Department of Justice announced the creation of the Task Force to Combat Anti-Semitism ("Task Force"), coordinated through its Civil Rights Division. The Task Force's first priority was to root out anti-Semitic harassment in schools and on college campuses.
- On February 28, 2025, Secretary Rubio issued a diplomatic cable entitled "Catch and Revoke: National Security Through Timely Processing of Visa Systems Messages." That cable implements Executive Order 14161, explaining in its summary that because "the Department is directed to ensure maximum screening and vetting throughout the visa process," consular officers must "use the whole-of-government law enforcement systems to vigilantly monitor the activities of aliens—whether they are inside the United States or not."
- The Homeland Security Council is an executive branch council under the Executive Office of the President. Throughout March 2025, the Homeland Security Council held interagency meetings to discuss, among other things, student visa revocations.
- The Department of Homeland Security (DHS) Office of Intelligence focused on non-citizens and was charged "[t]o look at the protesters, to develop reports of analysis on the protesters, specifically looking for violations of U.S. laws, including and specific to immigration and customs laws."
- DHS leadership instructed investigators to review the names of student protestors on the *Canary Mission* website, which contains a database of over 5,000 individuals. Canary Mission's website purports to "document[] individuals and organizations that promote hatred of the USA, Israel and Jews on North American college campuses and beyond."

- Public officials pursued student protestors using an elastic definition of "anti-Semitism." In several individual cases, investigators equated speech "critical of Israel" with speech supporting Hamas. They also cited participation in campus demonstrations and, in one case, publication of an op-ed as possible grounds for visa revocation.
- State Department and other officials involved in recommending visa actions did not receive any guidance concerning what constitutes "anti-Semitism." One high-level Consular Affairs official testified, "In my opinion, antisemitism is unjustified views, biases, or prejudices, or actions against Jewish people, or Israel, that are the result of hatred towards them." The same witness testified: "In my understanding antisemites will sometimes try to hide their views and say they're not against Jews, they're just against Israel, which is a farcical argument in my mind. It's just a dodge."
- Trump administration officials widely publicized the arrests of international students and scholars on social and other media outlets. Officials claimed that the arrested and detained students had "sided with terrorists" or engaged in anti-Semitic activities, although there was no evidence they were linked to any terrorist organization.
- Plaintiffs' members who became aware of the arrest and detention of international students by ICE were chilled in their expressive activities. For example, one faculty member testified she "has canceled overseas trips, shied away from writing on certain topics critical of Israeli policies, including ceasing development of a specific article that was to discuss Hamas and Israel, stopped engaging in protests as she previously did, and generally kept a low profile."

F. Inferences From the Factual Record

The great paradox of this case is that the government witnesses—to a person—are decent, credible, dedicated nonpartisan professionals. True patriots who, in order to do their duty, have been weaponized by their highest superiors to reach foregone conclusions for most ignoble ends.

There was no ideological deportation policy. It was never the Secretaries' immediate intention to deport all pro-Palestinian non-citizens for that obvious First Amendment violation, that could have raised a major outcry. Rather, the intent of the Secretaries was more invidious—to target a few for speaking out and then use the full rigor of the Immigration and Nationality Act (in ways it had never been used before) to have them publicly deported with the goal of tamping down pro-Palestinian student protests and terrorizing similarly situated non-citizen (and other) pro-Palestinians into silence because their views were unwelcome.

III. Rulings of Law

This Court rules that the Plaintiffs have shown by clear and convincing evidence that Secretaries Noem and Rubio have intentionally and in concert implemented Executive Orders 14161 and 14188 in a viewpoint-discriminatory way to chill protected speech. This conduct violated the First Amendment. The coercion line of case law bolsters this conclusion, and the Public Officials' threats to continue detaining, deporting, and revoking visas based on political speech serves as circumstantial evidence that such enforcement exists, is viewpoint discriminatory, and has objectively chilled the Plaintiffs' speech, but the campaign of threats itself, because not directed specifically at the Plaintiffs, does not separately violate the Constitution under this precise line of case law.

B. First Amendment Viewpoint Discrimination (Count I)

Two preliminary questions must be settled before the Plaintiffs' First Amendment viewpoint discrimination claim can be analyzed: (1) what First Amendment rights the noncitizens at issue here possess; and (2) what standard of review applies to the Plaintiffs' challenge to an "ideological deportation policy" implementing the President's Executive Orders. The first question is dealt with more easily, in part because the Court has already addressed it and ruled that noncitizens have at least the core First Amendment right to political speech without reprisal. Despite that ruling, the Court pauses to acknowledge the complexity of this issue, and to explain its reasoning.

1. The First Amendment Rights of Noncitizens

This Court appreciates, as the Plaintiffs have urged, that several courts to have addressed the issue of noncitizen speech in recent months have stated in no uncertain terms that noncitizens' speech rights are identical to those of citizens. *See, e.g., Mahdawi*, 781 F. Supp. 3d 214, 229 (D. Vt. 2025) (Crawford, Ch. J.). Although the Court broadly agrees with these analyses, the Public Officials are not wrong to suggest that the matter is complex.

Unlike with citizens, the question involves a collision between two doctrines that do not admit of easy compromise: plenary power doctrine in the immigration context and this nation's steadfast and foundational commitment to freedom of speech. *See Bustamante v. Mukasey*, 531 F.3d 1059, 1061–62 (9th Cir. 2008) (discussing *Kleindienst v. Mandel*, 408 U.S. 753 (1972), where the Supreme Court "acknowledged that First Amendment rights were implicated, but emphasized the longstanding principle that Congress has plenary power to make policies and rules for the exclusion of aliens"); *but see Bridges v. Wixon*, 326 U.S. 135, 162 (1945) (Murphy, J., concurring) ("[T]he First Amendment and other portions of the Bill of Rights make no exception in favor of deportation laws or laws enacted pursuant to a 'plenary' power of the Government.").

Judicial review of Executive Branch decision-making with respect to noncitizens is importantly limited in certain contexts, even where recognized rights may be implicated. *See, e.g., Trump v. Hawaii*, 138 S.Ct. 2392, 2419–20 (2018) (applying rational basis review, and citing *Mandel*'s more deferential "facially legitimate and bona fide" reason standard when evaluating Establishment Clause challenge to allegedly discriminatory admission policy affecting aliens abroad, which policy involved "matters of entry and national security"); *Reno v. American-Arab Anti-Discrim. Comm.*, 525 U.S. 471, 491–92 (1999) (holding that "[w]hen an alien's continuing presence in this country is in violation of the immigration laws, the Government does not offend the Constitution by deporting him for the additional reason that it believes him to be a member of an organization that supports terrorist activity," but not "ruling out the possibility of a rare case in which the alleged basis of discrimination is so outrageous" that this rule might be overcome); *Kandamar v. Gonzalez*, 464 F.3d 65, 72 (1st Cir. 2006) ("The Supreme Court has long held that judicial review of line-drawing in the immigration context is deferential.").

Broadly speaking, however, the Supreme Court has applied to aliens the same First Amendment test then applicable to citizens, with the significant exception that citizens generally cannot be deported. This makes sense of the cases from the early Cold War era relied on by the Public Officials, where Anarchist and Communist speech and association were sometimes penalized as to citizens and noncitizens alike, although the penalties differed. *See, e.g., Harisiades v. Shaughnessy*, 342 U.S. 580, 587–92 (1952) (upholding statute allowing deportation of former Communist Party members based on "[c]ongressional apprehension of foreign or internal dangers short of war," *id.* at 587, including Congress' receiving "evidence that the Communist movement here has been heavily laden with aliens and that Soviet control of the American Communist Party has been largely through alien Communists," *id.* at 590, based on distinction between lawful advocacy and "advocating overthrow of government by force and violence," *id.* at 591–92); *Dennis v. United States*, 341 U.S. 494, 502–11 (1951) (upholding criminal conviction of citizens based on conspiracy to teach Communism against First Amendment challenge, applying same test later used in *Harisiades*, again citing potential "attempt to overthrow the Government by force and violence").

Furthermore, some of the most notorious Red Scare First Amendment Supreme Court cases were significantly cabined by the infamous "Red Monday" cases of 1957. *See e.g.*, *Yates v. United States*, 354 U.S. 298, 318 (1957) (distinguishing between "effort to instigate action to th[e] end" of "forcible overthrow" of the government, which was illegal under the Smith Act's advocacy or organizing provisions, and "advocacy and teaching . . . divorced from any [such] effort," which, even when done with "evil intent," was not). The Court therefore continues to assume that the best reading of the relevant First Amendment case law entitles noncitizens to the protection of the Court's post-Cold War development of an "incitement test" requiring "a likelihood of imminent harm" in order to render otherwise lawful political speech subject to adverse government action. *See Brandenburg v. Ohio*, 395 U.S. 444 (1969).

The Public Officials urge, and this Court acknowledges, that *Harisiades* has not been expressly overruled by the Supreme Court. Even assuming that the First Amendment law of the second Red Scare era still applies to noncitizens in its entirety, the Public Officials' reliance on these Red Scare era cases only accentuates two important distinctions between this case and the cases on which the Public Officials most rely.

First, *Harisiades* carefully examined a specific congressional determination that the organization of which the plaintiffs were former members advocated the "methodical but prudent incitement to violence," and ultimately "incitement to violent overthrow" of the United States government. *Harisiades*, 342 U.S. at 592. Here, there is no alleged membership of any organization and no congressional determination specific to it or to the targeted noncitizens, much less a determination that the targeted noncitizens are involved in advocating for the government's violent overthrow.

Second, *Mandel* and *Hawaii*, which the Public Officials cite for the proposition that all burdens on noncitizens' First Amendment rights are subject to only a "facially legitimate and bona fide" reason standard of review, are exclusion cases, and "[t]he distinction between an alien who has effected an entry into the United States and one who has never entered runs throughout immigration law," *Zadvydas v. Davis*, 533 U.S. 678, 693 (2001); *Gastelum-Quinones v. Kennedy*, 374 U.S. 469, 479 (1963) ("[D]eportation is a drastic sanction, one which can destroy lives and disrupt families, and . . . a holding of deportability must therefore be premised upon [meaningful evidence of the relevant violation]."). In any case, political speech is not, on its own, a facially legitimate reason for expelling persons from this country, *see Abourezk v. Reagan*, 592 F. Supp. 880, 887 & n.23 (D.D.C. 1984) (Greene, J.) ("[A]lthough the government may deny entry to aliens altogether, for any number of specific reasons, it may not, consistent with the First Amendment, deny entry solely on account of the content of speech."), vacated and remanded on other grounds, 785 F.2d 1043 (D.C. Cir. 1986).

Indeed, even at the height of the second Red Scare, and even when examining loyalty oaths required to obtain union leadership rather than the far more serious consequence of deportation, the Supreme Court stressed the need for some connection to intended, concrete violent action in order to attach any negative consequences to political speech and association: "The congressional purpose is therefore served if we construe the [challenged statutory language requiring an anti-Communist loyalty oath] to apply to persons and organizations who believe in violent overthrow of the Government as it presently exists under the Constitution as an objective, not merely a prophecy. . . . Of course we agree that one may not be imprisoned . . . because he holds particular beliefs." *American Commc'ns Ass'n, C.I.O. v. Douds*, 339 U.S. 382, 407–08 (1950) (emphasis added). And again, in the deportation case *Harisiades*, the Supreme Court specifically rejected the proposition "that the First Amendment allows Congress to make no distinction between advocating change in the existing order by lawful elective processes and advocating change by force and violence," and observed that "Communist Governments avoid the inquiry by suppressing everything distasteful." 342 U.S. at 592. The Supreme Court "apprehend[ed] that the Constitution enjoins upon [courts] the duty, however difficult, of distinguishing between" pure political speech and incitement to violence. *Id.*

For these reasons, this Court rules that here the Plaintiffs have shown that Secretaries Noem and Rubio are engaged in a mode of enforcement leading to detaining, deporting, and revoking noncitizens' visas solely on the basis of political speech, and with the intent of chilling such speech and that of others similarly situated. Such conduct is not only unconstitutional, but a thing virtually unknown to our constitutional tradition.

Lastly, as is relevant to its analysis below, this Court observes that, on its face, the First Amendment does not distinguish between citizens and noncitizens; rather, it states simply, "Congress shall make no law . . . abridging the freedom of speech[.]" U.S. Const. amend. I. As the Supreme Court's now frequently cited statement in *Bridges v. Wixon* confirmed, this text at least arguably implies that "[f]reedom of speech . . . is accorded aliens residing in this country." 326 U.S. 135, 148 (1945). It also suggests something a little less obvious, but still worth saying, which is that its chief concern is with the character and quality of the "speech" that occurs on American soil, in what Justice Holmes called "free trade in ideas," which is "the best test of truth," *Abrams v. United States*, 250 U.S. 616, 630 (1919), and ensuring that Congress may not twist that speech in the federal government's preferred direction.

In other words, as Professor Zechariah Chafee Jr. put it, the First Amendment declares a "national policy in favor of the public discussion of all public questions." *Freedom of Speech in War Time*, 32 Harv. L. Rev. 932, 934, 956 (1919); *see also Mandel*, 408 U.S. at 775 (Marshall, J., dissenting) ("The freedom to speak and the freedom to hear are inseparable; they are two sides of the same coin. But the coin itself is the process of thought and discussion. The activity of speakers becoming listeners and listeners becoming speakers in the vital interchange of thought is the 'means indispensable to the discovery and spread of political truth.' Its protection is 'a fundamental principle of the American government.' The First Amendment means that Government has no power to thwart the process of free discussion[.]" (citations omitted)). Although this Court rejected the Plaintiffs' arguments that their citizen members had standing to sue on the basis of chilled listening and association as such, it nevertheless takes seriously their concern that their own speech rights and rights to hear and to associate are implicated in this case.

2. The Standard of Review

As for the second question, that is, what standard of review ought apply to the Plaintiffs' First Amendment viewpoint discrimination challenge to the alleged procedures, this Court rules that it need not decide, because even under the "facially legitimate and bona fide" standard proposed by the Public Officials under Department of *State v. Munoz*, 602

U.S. 899, 908 (2024), or *Hartman v. Moore*, 547 U.S. 250 (2006), on this record, the Plaintiffs prevail.

The Plaintiffs have alleged, and here have proved, a discrete practice of targeting pro-Palestine and anti-Israel speech, which arose from a kind of intentional ratcheting-up of the Executive Orders' instruction to target antisemitic harassment and violence, while referencing a definition of antisemitism that includes protected speech such as comparing Israel's policies to those of the Nazis.

On this Court's understanding of the law, however, this is not enough: because some showing of intent on the part of government officials probably is necessary to make out an as-applied First Amendment viewpoint discrimination claim in this case. The Plaintiffs must show that the Public Officials' implementation of the Executive Orders through the challenged enforcement steps was targeted intentionally at specific viewpoints in order to chill speech.

This Court finds that the Plaintiffs have made this showing. The evidence presented at trial included the Public Officials' many public statements suggesting that they wished to staunch public protest related to Israel's treatment of Palestinians, including the President's campaign promise that he would put an end to the student protests on this issue by kicking out protestors and subsequent promise that the Public Officials would deport and cancel the visas of those "who joined in the pro-jihadist protests" and Secretary Rubio's plainspoken guarantee to deport "Hamas-supporters" and those who "participat[e] in pro-Hamas events."

Evidence introduced at trial also showed that the Public Officials consistently referred to campus protests related to Palestine as *per se* "pro-Hamas," key inter-agency meetings included discussion of whether protesting alone could be grounds for visa revocation, and the tasking of HSI with investigating protestors for violations of laws based on anonymous website lists targeted at protesters. The Plaintiffs have proved that, as the fruits of this investigation percolated up the chain of command, decisionmakers at every step of the challenged implementation interpreted the "support" for terrorists (a key term from Executive Order 14161) that they construed as potentially subject to the penalty of detention, deportation, and visa revocation to encompass, and indeed to be centered on, core First Amendment speech and expressive conduct, such as attending public protests, leading such protests, or even publishing op-eds.

This review process, such as it was, was essentially frictionless. Despite the apparent good intentions and professionalism of the Public Officials' subordinates, the Court saw virtually no evidence that anyone along the way seriously questioned whether pure political speech in support of Palestine or against Israel could be construed as support for terrorism, whether support for terrorism as such could be grounds for the adverse actions that were contemplated, or whether any targeted individual had met any circumscribed, ascertainable standard of speech or conduct that might be grounds for these actions. Trial produced no evidence that the challenged procedures contemplated the speech to have been as incitement to imminent violence or, per the terms of an older test, clear and present danger. Rather, the subordinates spoke the language of "violat[ing]" the Executive Orders, as if they were the law, and of "align[ing] with the executive order's focus on deporting 'Hamas sympathizers,'" as if "Hamas sympathizers" were a self-interpreting term. They appear to have treated "antisemitism," which, however heinous, is, without more, protected speech, as something that, in essence, one simply knows when one sees it. In short, if it looked like the Executive Orders might have disapproved of it, that was potential grounds for deportation.

This might seem a matter of recklessness or even indifference as to how the Executive Orders ought be interpreted or what the Constitution requires. But just as a general matter ignorance of the law is no excuse, the Secretary of State's and other high officials' apparent indifference as to whether support or sympathy for terrorism, as opposed to material support, could be grounds for adverse action by law, or whether such support could be construed to include the voicing of support for Palestine or objection to the policies of the State of Israel, is no defense to the charge that they have done what they have repeatedly said they were doing: intentionally targeted political speech in order to stop campus protests.

The Public Officials' selection of anonymously sourced lists of campus protestors to supply the thousands of names initially subject to investigation, moreover—despite their representations, which the Court credits, that HSI may at other times act on totally anonymous tips—belies any suggestion that whatever unnamed person who supplied the lists to HSI for review did not intend the policy to operate as it did. Due to the frictionless quality described above, once one was on the lists, one was potentially subject to adverse action so long as, it seems, there was any online mention of one's pro-Palestine activities.

The Public Officials' argument that few of the originally investigated names were targeted is little comfort. Those names that were passed up the chain of command by the investigating subordinates were almost universally approved for adverse action, and, again, the reasons for being passed up the chain of command included any form of online suggestion that one was "pro-Hamas." Watching the process at work, and not wishing to credit the Public Officials with incompetence, it would require a remarkable naivete not to conclude that this process worked as intended.

For these reasons, in addition to the reasons discussed below with respect to Count II—which this Court considers collapsed ultimately into Count I—the enforcement policy adopted by the Public Officials to implement the President's Executive Orders are intentionally viewpoint-discriminatory, and thus violate the First Amendment.

C. First Amendment Coercion Campaign (Count II)

This Court denied the motion to dismiss as to the Plaintiffs' claim of an unlawful coercion campaign in part because it judged that the essence of this claim overlapped somewhat with their claim on Count I. Given the substantiated allegations of generalized threats to noncitizen speech, the Plaintiffs had plausibly alleged a targeted campaign under the line of cases associated with *Bantam Books, Inc. v. Sullivan*, 372 U.S. 58 (1963). Ultimately, because the Plaintiffs have not produced evidence of threats targeted specifically at their members, but rather of threats targeted at noncitizens in a general way, the Court rules that the Plaintiffs have not proved a campaign of coercion as defined by this line of case law.

The Court notes, however, that the general principles underlying *Bantam Books*, and, more recently, *National Rifle Ass'n of America v. Vullo*, 144 S.Ct. 1316 (2024), have significantly informed its analysis of Count I. The Court considers evidence relevant to Plaintiffs' campaign of threats claim as further circumstantial evidence that the chilling of speech at issue here was intentional. Because "a government official cannot do indirectly what she is barred from doing directly," *Vullo*, 144 S. Ct. at 1328, the Public Officials may not in effect regulate speech by means of an unwritten enforcement procedure implementing a facially lawful Executive Order, as if speech codes were permissible so long as they were not written down. Again, an unwritten speech code seems, if anything, potentially more threatening to core constitutional values than a written one. The Plaintiffs' noncitizen members here have all been made to understand that there are certain things that it may be gravely dangerous for them to say or do, but have not been told precisely what those things are (or are not); the diffuseness and ambition of this coercion campaign do not render it less constitutionally suspect.

This understanding of danger has been conveyed, moreover, not just by means of the threatening statements and speech-targeted arrests, detentions, and visa revocations already discussed, but also by the manner in which these arrests, detentions, and revocations have been conducted: by often-masked agents, without prior notice of visa revocation or altered status, sometimes on the street or at immigration appointments, followed by conveyance quickly out of district and across the country.

This Court credits the testimony of the agents involved that at least some of these practices were not per se abnormal for HSI arrests and detentions; but this only begs the question, however, why special agents previously deployed for sensitive intelligence matters have been deployed to enforce this particular policy of, in essence, rounding up campus protestors and op-ed writers? Or why, having observed the first arrests that were made under this policy and seen that these arrests by these agents involved an obvious, highly publicized atmosphere of secrecy and fright, the Public Officials responsible for it did not adjust the policy to make the arrests less obviously chilling? Or why the members of the inter-agency advisory council whom the Public Officials will not name, did not adjust the policy to make the arrests less obviously chilling? Again, deprived of any real attempted explanation as to what the members of this council intended by the selected means of these arrests, this Court must draw the most reasonable inference: that the manner and method of their execution was adopted, or at least approved of once the first such arrest had been made, in part intentionally to chill the speech of other would be pro-Palestine and anti-Israel speakers, including Plaintiffs' noncitizen members.

The intended effect of the policy proved by a preponderance of the evidence on Count I is essentially the same as the aim that was held unconstitutional in the *Bantam Books* line of cases. The Plaintiffs' case on Count I is therefore strengthened by this line of case law with its emphasis on indicia of coercion and thus of intended chill, but this Court does not extend that particular doctrine here.

* * *

To conclude, and to be clear, this Court has no sympathy for terrorism, or for those who genuinely support it. It has proudly sentenced terrorists and understands its own role as one small part of a federal scheme that exists significantly to protect this Nation's national security. Nor does the Court take a position on any foreign conflict or express special sympathy for any side of any political debate, foreign or domestic. Rather, the judicial role is limited to safeguarding the rights of all persons lawfully present in this country. This includes the freedom of speech that allows those persons to understand each other and to debate. If "terrorist" is interpreted to mean "pro-Palestine" or "anti-Israel," and "support" encompasses pure political speech, then core free speech rights have been imperiled.

Throughout these proceedings, the Public Officials have emphasized that the noncitizens at issue are present at our grace. They describe their presence here as a privilege, which can be revoked for almost any reason, or at least when we begin to feel we would not have invited them here had we known what they were going to say to us. This Court in part must agree: non-citizens are, indeed, in a sense our guests. How we treat our guests is a question of constitutional scope, because who we are as a people and as a nation is an important part of how we must interpret the fundamental laws that constrain us. We are not, and we must not become, a nation that imprisons and deports people because we are afraid of what they have to tell us.

IV. Conclusion

For all these reasons, this Court finds as fact and concludes as matter of law that Secretaries Noem and Rubio and their several agents and subordinates acted in concert to misuse the sweeping powers of their respective offices to target noncitizen pro-Palestinians for deportation primarily on account of their First Amendment protected political speech. They did so in order to strike fear into similarly situated noncitizen pro-Palestinian individuals, pro-actively (and effectively) curbing lawful pro-Palestinian speech and intentionally denying such individuals (including the plaintiffs here) the freedom of speech that is their right. Moreover, the effect of these targeted deportation proceedings continues unconstitutionally to chill freedom of speech to this day.

DISCUSSION

1. *Remedial Issues.* After describing its factual conclusions and legal rulings, the district court stated, "What remains after issuing this opinion is to consider what, if anything, may be done to remedy these constitutional violations." The court indicated that it would hold a separate hearing regarding the appropriate remedy for the Public Of-

ficials' violations. What remedial issues may arise based on the court's findings and conclusions? How, if at all, can the court ensure that the unconstitutional actions it has identified do not recur?

2. *The First Amendment and Immigration Law.* In the detention cases discussed earlier in the chapter, district courts uniformly concluded the First Amendment applied to non-citizens as it would to citizens arrested and detained based on their viewpoints. However, as the district court acknowledged in *AAUP*, the scope of noncitizens' speech rights is a "complex" issue. As one scholar has observed, "For much of U.S. history, the federal courts have not laid down clear principles governing the relationship between the First Amendment's commitment to freedom of speech and the immigration laws." Jennifer Lee Koh, *Executive Discretion and First Amendment Constraints on the Deportation State*, 56 Ga. L. Rev. 1473, 1482 (2022). The United States has not generally relied on *ideological* grounds for deportation since the Red Scare of the 1950s. The district court discussed the Supreme Court's decisions from that era. Despite the expansion of First Amendment freedoms in the decades since the middle of the twentieth century, the Court has not expressly repudiated its older precedents and, as the district court noted, has suggested in subsequent cases that the government may rely to some extent on expression or association when exercising its broad authority to exclude and perhaps remove aliens.

3. *Chilling Expression.* In *AAUP*, the district court rejected plaintiffs' contention that the federal government had implemented a policy that targeted *all* non-citizens who engaged in pro-Palestine or anti-Israel expression. Rather, the court concluded, "the intent of the Secretaries was more invidious—to target a few for speaking out and then use the full rigor of the Immigration and Nationality Act (in ways it had never been used before) to have them publicly deported with the goal of tamping down pro-Palestinian student protests and terrorizing similarly situated non-citizen (and other) pro-Palestinians into silence because their views were unwelcome." If that was the administration's intent, has it been successful? Thinking again about remedies, what can the district court do to counteract the chilling of expression?

4. *Who Should Sue?* In *AAUP*, educational organizations and some of their members brought the legal challenge. Universities that admit foreign students and employ foreign scholars presumably have not

just financial but also academic reasons for objecting to the government actions challenged in *AAUP*. Should *universities* have filed lawsuits challenging those actions? What are the potential advantages and disadvantages, both to the institutions and their students, of universities doing so?

C. PROBLEM EXERCISE: A DETAINED STUDENT ACTIVIST

The family of Nisha Nawali, a foreign national studying at a public university pursuant to a visa, is worried and has reached out to you for legal counsel. According to news accounts, yesterday Nisha was arrested and detained by U.S. Immigration and Customs Enforcement (ICE) officers. Her family is unaware of her current whereabouts. In a public statement, an ICE spokesperson stated that Nisha has been arrested and will be deported because she is "a threat to national security and supports Hamas, a terrorist organization." Nisha is a member of Students for Justice in Palestine (SJP), a campus student organization that has been vocally opposed to Israel's actions in Gaza. She served as the Secretary of SJP and participated, with members of that group, in pro-Palestine campus protests. SJP was banned from campus last year, based on the university's claim that it failed to follow applicable procedures for obtaining a permit for a protest event. Nisha's family says she does not have a criminal record and has never been in any sort of legal trouble.

What *initial* steps will you take on Nisha's behalf? What First Amendment arguments will you make in seeking Nisha's release from detention? What advice will you give to Nisha's family concerning whether she will ultimately prevail on a First Amendment claim in future deportation proceedings?

6

FREEDOM OF THE PRESS

As a candidate and during his first presidential term, Donald Trump waged a persistent and public war on the institutional press. He frequently referred to the press as "the enemy of the people" and attacked individual reporters and networks.[1] As a candidate, Trump also talked about "opening up" the libel laws—presumably to make it easier to sue media defendants for unfavorable coverage.[2] During his first term, President Trump threatened to use executive power against the press but rarely followed through. During his second term, by contrast, President Trump has aggressively targeted the media. He has been a plaintiff in defamation and other civil actions filed against disfavored outlets. As president, Trump has excluded news outlets from White House events based on their expression. He has also relied on federal agencies, including the Federal Communications Commission and the Federal Trade Commission, to investigate and pressure broadcasters. Finally, President Trump signed an Executive Order that directed federal funding for public broadcast stations, including PBS and NPR, be terminated. Congress later terminated this funding. The following materials examine how these executive actions affect First Amendment free speech and free press rights.

A. LAWSUITS AGAINST THE PRESS

Donald Trump has long relied on civil lawsuits to attack and intimidate the press. Like any citizen, a candidate, president, or ex-president has the right to file lawsuits and seek redress for reputational or other harms. However, prior to Trump's presidencies, candidates and chief executives rarely filed lawsuits against the press. By contrast, Trump has used civil lawsuits as a potent political weapon and has promised to continue this practice.

1. All the President's Lawsuits

Both as a presidential candidate and officeholder, Trump has filed several defamation and other civil lawsuits against the media. Among other outlets, Trump has sued CNN, *The Washington Post*, *The New York Times*, and local media for critical coverage of his campaign and first term as president. For example, Trump brought a $475 million defamation lawsuit against CNN over the network's use of the term "the Big Lie" to describe his false claims that he won the 2020 election. The claim was dismissed.[3] Trump also sued *The New York Times* for unflattering (and Pulitzer Prize-winning) coverage of his personal and business dealings.[4] That claim was also dismissed, and the court ordered Trump to pay the newspaper $400,000 in legal fees.

Prior to his second term, Trump sued ABC News and George Stephanopoulos for allegedly defamatory statements that Trump had been found civilly liable for "rape" (a term the trial judge held was "substantially true" in another defamation lawsuit). He also brought a $20 billion civil action against *60 Minutes* and CBS for allegedly editing an interview with then-presidential candidate Kamala Harris, in ways Trump alleged obscured or improved Harris's answers to questions about Israel. As discussed below, both ABC and CBS settled these lawsuits for large sums and other concessions. Trump also sued the *Des Moines Register*, its parent company Gannett, and a pollster for publishing poll results showing Trump trailing Harris in the 2024 presidential election in Iowa (he eventually carried the state).

Trump and his lawyers have expanded their civil suit repertoire beyond defamation claims. The lawsuits against *60 Minutes* and the *Des Moines Register* allege that the media outlets engaged in "election interference" and consumer fraud.

Claiming these lawsuits are necessary to "straighten out the press," President Trump vowed to file many more civil lawsuits against media.[5] As president, he threatened to sue *The New York Times* and CNN over their coverage of the attack he ordered on Iran's nuclear facilities.[6] He filed a $10 billion defamation lawsuit against *The Wall Street Journal* based on its reporting that Trump had sent a bawdy birthday card to the infamous sexual predator Jeffrey Epstein.[7] And President Trump sued *The New York Times* (again), four of its reporters, and Penguin Random

House for defamation based on the publication of articles and a book that questioned Trump's purported business acumen. The lawsuit, which claims Trump's losses exceed $15 billion, also alleges that the publications were a form of "election interference."[8]

For all his litigation experience, Trump has a poor track record in civil lawsuits against the press. Indeed, he almost always *loses*—sometimes very badly. Some courts have even ordered Trump to pay media defendants substantial damages and attorneys' fees for filing harassing and frivolous defamation lawsuits.[9] Some states have enacted laws imposing liability on plaintiffs for bringing so-called "SLAPP" (Strategic Lawsuit Against Public Participation) lawsuits—essentially, defamation lawsuits intended to silence or intimidate critics. In the case described earlier against *The New York Times*, a court ordered Trump to pay damages under an anti-SLAPP law.[10]

2. The Political Purposes of Trump's Civil Lawsuits

This is one arena in which Trump may not mind being a loser and even paying substantial damages. Filing civil lawsuits is not about restoring Trump's damaged reputation, protecting consumers, or ensuring the integrity of elections. For example, he *won* the presidential contest in Iowa and the presidency—despite inaccurate polling, unflattering coverage, and media interviews of his opponent. For Trump, civil lawsuits serve several *political* purposes.

First, the lawsuits are political diatribes against what Trump and his supporters consider a common enemy. Win or lose, President Trump's supporters are likely to give him credit for suing the "dishonest" and "crooked" media. This is why his legal complaints have generally been so heavy on incendiary rhetoric against the press and so light on factual and legal substance. Some courts have pushed back. A district court recently dismissed one of President Trump's lawsuits, admonishing his counsel: "As every lawyer knows (or is presumed to know), a complaint is not a public forum for vituperation and invective—not a protected platform to rage against an adversary. A complaint is not a megaphone for public relations or a podium for a passionate oration at a political rally or the functional equivalent of the Hyde Park Speakers' Corner."[11] The court allowed the president's lawyers to refile a shorter complaint.

Second, for Trump, defamation and other civil lawsuits are a means of punishing critics and chilling, through expensive and often frivolous litigation, the publication of unfavorable or unflattering opinions and information. The strategy relies on the burden of defending against expensive and harassing lawsuits to convince defendants to settle, scale back critical reporting, or both. Civil damage lawsuits can be an effective means of intimidating, leveraging, and silencing the press. Moreover, as Trump likely understands, the ordinary demands and pressures of civil litigation are even more pronounced when the plaintiff is the *sitting President of the United States.* Judges may be reluctant to dismiss frivolous claims brought by the president. Juries may be inclined to side with the president against his critics, despite the evidence. As discussed later, media outlets with business before the administration risk additional adverse actions should they vigorously defend themselves and their reporters. Even if the lawsuits have little or no merit, media defendants must take all these exceptional risks into account.

Third, in a broader sense, like other aspects of Trump 2.0, civil lawsuits are part of a campaign to entrench executive power. The lawsuits are intended to undermine the standing and credibility of the press. Like attacks on lawyers, scientists, and universities, lawsuits against the media undermine institutions and actors that can expose governmental abuses of power and correct misinformation. Destroying the credibility of the press, harassing it into settlements, and declaring "wins" against the "fake media" neutralizes another important check on executive power.

3. The Chilling Effects of Civil Lawsuits

Using civil lawsuits as a cudgel against the media and other critics is an abusive practice that threatens to chill reporting and eliminate independent sources of information. Although unprecedented for a presidential candidate or president, weaponizing defamation and other civil lawsuits to achieve such goals is not a new tactic. During the Civil Rights Era, local southern officials relied on pro-plaintiff defamation standards to censor and intimidate both media outlets and civil rights activists. Through frequent and harassing lawsuits, local and state officials sought to suppress reporting about racial segregation.[12]

Recognizing the chilling effect of this litigation tactic, in its 1964 decision in *New York Times Co. v. Sullivan*, 376 U.S. 254 (1964), the Supreme Court adopted a demanding standard of proof applicable to public officials who sued for allegedly defamatory statements about the performance of their official duties.[13] Under that precedent, public officials must show such statements were made with "actual malice," *i.e.*, that the defendant knew they were false when published or published them with reckless disregard for their truth.[14] The Court later extended the actual malice standard to suits brought by public figures, including those, like Donald Trump, who have gained extensive public notoriety.[15]

Sullivan was a direct response to early SLAPP lawsuits. As the Court recognized, because no double jeopardy limit applied in the civil context, defamation lawsuits could be even more chilling to a free press than the threat of criminal prosecution.[16] Indeed, by 1964, southern officials had brought *$300 million* in libel claims against the press for truthfully reporting on civil rights abuses (about $3 billion in today's dollars). To put this in perspective, in recent civil actions Donald Trump has sued CBS for $20 billion and *The Wall Stret Journal* for $10 billion.

As the civil rights experience shows, weaponizing civil lawsuits raises serious First Amendment concerns. *Sullivan*'s protective standard—which Trump favors eliminating—provides critically important protection for media covering the president and his administration.[17] Without it, defendants would face sizable damage awards for publishing even *truthful* criticism of Trump or his administration. Some outlets, such as *The New York Times*, may have the resources to defend against presidential lawsuits. But smaller newspapers and media, such as the *Des Moines Register*, may struggle to respond and face considerable pressure to settle and/or alter their reporting. The current situation is even more precarious for the press, since lawyers will be deterred from representing media defendants *pro bono* if they fear being targeted by the Trump Administration.

To be sure, the press does not always act responsibly. As *Fox News* learned in connection with its $800 million settlement of a defamation lawsuit brought by Dominion Voting Systems, plaintiffs can hold media outlets and reporters liable—even under the demanding *Sullivan* standard.[18] At the same time, anti-SLAPP legislation exists precisely because harassing and vexatious litigation threatens to undermine the ability of the press and others to share vitally important information with the public. In the hands of powerful political officials including the President of the United States, civil lawsuits can significantly undermine efforts to check power, counter official narratives, and educate the public.

4. Executive Power and Press Capitulation

Despite their weak merits, Donald Trump has achieved a significant degree of success in recent civil lawsuits. As noted, ABC News settled with Trump. The network agreed to donate $15 million to Trump's presidential library and issue an apology for George Stephanopoulos's comments about the civil sexual assault verdict against Trump.[19] CBS's parent company, Paramount, agreed to give Trump's presidential library $16 million *and* henceforth to release written transcripts of all interviews with presidential candidates.[20] ABC settled even though its anchor's statement was substantially true. Paramount settled an even weaker lawsuit aimed directly at the broadcaster's First Amendment right to engage in editorial decision-making.[21]

The Paramount settlement has exposed the exceptional dangers to a free press of settling with a president-as-plaintiff. At the time of the settlement, Trump was serving as president. Paramount had a merger application with Skydance pending with the Federal Communications Commission. Paramount was also the subject of *another* FCC proceeding in which the agency was investigating whether CBS's Harris interview violated federal communications laws. (*see* discussion in Part D., below). Although the parties denied there was any connection between the civil settlement and the agency proceedings, it is hard to imagine Paramount did not factor in the risks to its merger of fighting the president in court.

The terms of the settlement suggest a connection. According to Trump, as part of the settlement Paramount's new owner, Skydance, agreed to provide another $20 million in free advertising and public service announcements to the president.[22] As well, shortly after entering the settlement with Trump, Paramount and CBS fired late night talk show host and frequent Trump critic Stephen Colbert. Critics viewed that move as further evidence of Paramount's capitulation to the president.[23] In a social media post, the president said of the Paramount settlement: "This is another in a long line of VICTORIES over the Fake News Media, who we are holding to account for their widespread fraud and deceit."

As the Paramount and other settlements show, President Trump is no ordinary civil plaintiff. The administration can make life very difficult for those seeking mergers or having other business before the federal government. The president's executive powers can be used to inflict significant financial harm or even destroy businesses he sues. As a civil litigant, the president can leverage the power of executive agencies to extract not just monetary but, as Trump has shown, other concessions from the media. Squeezed between the rock of a defamation or fraud lawsuit by the

President of the United States and the hard place of a merger or other regulatory review, corporate defendants may be willing to sacrifice press independence to further shareholder or financial interests.

Of course, there are legitimate reasons a media defendant might want to settle a civil lawsuit. Defendants often settle to avoid protracted and costly court proceedings, embarrassing discovery, or the risk of substantial jury verdicts. However, the settlements with President Trump involve exceptional concerns media defendants have not historically faced. Trump's leveraging of executive power has created a real danger that media capitulation to frivolous and harassing lawsuits will chill reporting and destroy the independence of the press.

DISCUSSION

1. *Calculating Risks.* Although the ideal response to a lawsuit threatening core press freedoms might be to resist, defending civil lawsuits is expensive, time-consuming, and increasingly perilous for media entities. The calculations may be somewhat different depending on the size and resources of a media defendant. What legal advice would you give to a small market newspaper faced with a defamation lawsuit by the President of the United States, in which the presidential plaintiff seeks multiple millions of dollars in damages based on allegedly "fraudulent" reporting? To what extent would you factor into your assessment that the plaintiff is the sitting president?

2. *Executive Leverage and Corruption.* As suggested, rather than defend core First Amendment press prerogatives and functions, large media corporations with regulatory or other business before the Trump Administration may be making balance sheet decisions. Worse, some have raised alarms that settlements like the ones entered by ABC and Paramount constitute a novel form of pay-to-play political corruption. Media companies must, of course, take their business and regulatory interests into account. Aware of this, an administration can extract substantial financial and other concessions.

3. *Limits on Abusive Civil Lawsuits.* There are ways to combat the strategic abuse of civil lawsuits, even by presidents. As noted, one way is for the media to vigorously defend its First Amendment interests. If

there is an "anti-SLAPP" law in the relevant jurisdiction, that could provide a means of dismissing harassing lawsuits at an early stage. Judges also have the power to dismiss baseless claims on their own and to sanction parties who file frivolous lawsuits. Courts could also refuse to approve media settlements of frivolous claims on the ground that they are the product of duress or fraud or are otherwise against public policy. Finally, shareholders of broadcast companies can sue to challenge the terms of monetary settlements.

4. *Suing—and Settling With—Social Media.* President Trump has also sued X, Meta, and YouTube based on these private platforms' enforcement of their own terms of service. Like the defamation lawsuits, Trump's actions against the platforms were legally weak. Nevertheless, YouTube paid $24.5 million to settle a lawsuit stemming from the suspension of then-President Trump's channel six days after the January 6 riot at the Capitol. According to YouTube, the account was suspended owing to concerns about the potential for more violence. Meta and X also settled lawsuits with Trump for $25 million and $10 million, respectively. What are the implications of these settlements for content moderation and free speech online?

B. LIMITS ON NEWSGATHERING

Presidents have wide discretion concerning whether and how to engage with the press. No reporter, newspaper, or network has a right to demand an interview with or access to the president. However, the First Amendment may limit certain kinds of selective exclusion. Consider the following decision. Since the court relies on a First Amendment doctrine—"public forum"—we have not yet encountered, the Part begins witha brief synopsis of its standards.

DOCTRINAL SYNOPSIS: PUBLIC FORUM

- For purposes of First Amendment analysis, properties owned or managed by government fall into three categories of fora: (1) traditional (public parks, streets, and sidewalks); (2) designated (places or resources intentionally opened for public use); and (3) non-public (neither by tradition nor intent available for expressive activities).
- The First Amendment standard of review differs depending on the type of forum plaintiff seeks to access.
  - In traditional and designated fora, all content based speech regulations are subject to strict scrutiny.
  - In non-public fora, speech regulations are valid so long as they are reasonable and neutral regarding the speaker's viewpoint.

Associated Press v. Budowich

___ F.4th ___, 2025 WL 1649265
(D.C. Cir., June 6, 2025)

[After the district court enjoined a White House decision to exclude the Associated Press from certain events because it declined to refer to the Gulf of Mexico as the "Gulf of America," as President Trump demanded, the government sought a stay from the District of Columbia Court of Appeals. The following excerpts are from the panel decision *granting* the stay, which was subsequently affirmed by the full D.C. Circuit.]

RAO, Circuit Judge

The Associated Press wants to be in the room where it happens. But in February 2025, White House officials excluded the AP from the Oval Office and other restricted spaces. Officials announced that access was denied because the AP continued to use the name Gulf of Mexico in its Stylebook, rather than the President's preferred Gulf of America. The AP sued, alleging that its exclusion violated the First Amendment. The district court held the AP was likely to succeed on its constitutional claims, and it issued a preliminary injunction prohibiting White House officials from denying, on the basis of viewpoint, access to press events held in the Oval Office, on Air Force One, and at the President's home in Mar-a-Lago.

We grant in part the government's motion for a stay pending appeal. The White House is likely to succeed on the merits because these restricted presidential spaces are not First Amendment fora opened for private speech and discussion. The White House therefore retains discretion to determine, including on the basis of viewpoint, which journalists will be admitted. Moreover, without a stay, the government will suffer irreparable harm because the injunction impinges on the President's independence and control over his private workspaces.

Reporters and photographers have long been permitted access to the White House complex to cover the President and his administration. The White House manages access by requiring journalists to obtain a press credential called a hard pass. More than one thousand journalists hold hard passes, through which they may access spaces such as the James S. Brady Briefing Room, where the White House Press Secretary delivers regular briefings.

Hard pass holders may also sign up via a reservation system to attend larger events hosted in the East Room, which is often used for meetings with foreign leaders, executive order signings, and press conferences. Because the White House has opened these press facilities "to all bona fide Washington-based journalists," hard passes may not be denied arbitrarily or based on the content of a journalist's speech. *Sherrill v. Knight* (D.C. Cir. 1977).

A small subset (around one percent) of hard pass holders is sometimes invited into even more restricted White House spaces, such as the Oval Office and the Cabinet Room. This group of privileged journalists, referred to as the "press pool," has historically been selected by the White House Correspondents' Association, a private organization of which the AP is a founding member. Since its inception, the press pool has had a relatively stable, although not fixed, membership. Journalists selected to be part of the press pool may travel with the President aboard Air Force One and attend small press events at the President's home in Mar-a-Lago, usually to observe presidential speeches and events. For many years, the Correspondents' Association offered the AP a standing invitation to send one reporter and one photographer to press pool events.

On February 11, 2025, White House Press Secretary Karoline Leavitt informed the AP that it would not be permitted in the Oval Office or press pool unless it revised its Stylebook to refer to the Gulf of America, which President Trump had recently renamed from the Gulf of Mexico. The President and other senior White House officials publicly stated that the reason for the AP's exclusion was its continued use of the name Gulf of Mexico. The AP was similarly excluded from events in the East Room, despite signing up in advance through the reservation process. On February 25, the White House announced it would select journalists for participation in press pool events, instead of deferring to the selection made by the Correspondents' Association. . . .

The district court held the Oval Office, Air Force One, and similar restricted spaces are nonpublic fora when members of the press pool are present, and therefore the AP's exclusion on the basis of viewpoint violates the First Amendment. We conclude the spaces to which the AP seeks access are not any type of forum. As such, the White House may consider journalists' viewpoints when deciding whether to grant access.

A.

1.

To determine the extent of any First Amendment protection, we must first identify the relevant government space or spaces to which the AP claims access. "The existence of a right of access to public property and the standard by which limitations upon such a right must be evaluated differ depending on the character of the property at issue." *Perry Educ. Ass'n v. Perry Loc. Educators' Ass'n*, 460 U.S. 37, 44 (1983). Forum analysis guides our assessment of whether and to what extent the government may restrict speech on its property. *Cornelius v. NAACP Legal Def. & Educ. Fund, Inc.*, 473 U.S. 788, 799–800 (1985).

The AP argues that it suffers harm through its viewpoint-based exclusion from press pool events. The district court identified the press pool as the relevant forum because the AP has "not been admitted in any form or fashion to the press pool since February 14" and therefore "seeks restored eligibility for . . . press pool events." Focusing on the press pool, however, distracts from the actual fora relevant to our analysis. The press pool is an historically privileged group of reporters that is at times given access to spaces like the Oval Office. Reporters and photographers within the pool gather news and speak to the public about what they have seen and heard, but the pool is not an instrumentality used for communication by the AP or other journalists. The press pool is simply a mechanism for granting a select group of reporters access to the most private spaces in the White House.

Although the AP emphasizes its storied place in the history of the press pool, the pool is relevant only because it is often granted access to spaces in which the President conducts business. If the press pool were not allowed in the Oval Office, membership in the pool would be irrelevant to the access that the AP seeks. The proper context for our First Amendment analysis is therefore the restricted spaces to which the AP seeks access, namely the Oval Office, Air Force One, Mar-a-Lago, and the East Room, when they are opened to a small group of journalists to observe presidential events.

2.

No one suggests the Oval Office is a traditional public forum such as a park or sidewalk held in trust for expressive activity. Nor is the Oval Office a designated public forum that the government has made generally available to the public for discourse and communication. The disagreement between the parties is whether the spaces at issue are nonpublic fora or not fora at all, and so we focus on this distinction.

A nonpublic forum is government property that is not by tradition or designation a forum for public communication. The government, no less than a private owner of property, has power to preserve the property under its control for the use to which it is lawfully dedicated. Government property does not become a nonpublic forum unless and until the government takes some affirmative step to open the space for private communication. While the government need not open up property that is not by tradition or designation a forum for public communication, the government creates a nonpublic forum when it provides selective access for individual speakers. Until the government opens a restricted space to private speech between private parties, such a space is not a First Amendment forum at all.

Our cases provide guideposts for applying forum analysis to spaces in the White House. When the White House opens its facilities to the press generally, as it does in the Brady Briefing Room, it cannot exclude journalists based on viewpoint. In *Sherrill*, we held that the White House press facilities having been made publicly available as a source of information for newsmen, the protection afforded newsgathering under the First Amendment guarantee of freedom of the press attached, requiring that access not be denied arbitrarily or for less than compelling reasons. We recently explained that although *Sherrill* predated modern forum analysis, its description of the Press Area fits the definition of a nonpublic First Amendment forum. Thus, access to the White House Press Area can be restricted as long as the restrictions are viewpoint neutral and reasonable.

On the other hand, we have never suggested that there are any First Amendment restrictions on the discretion of the President to grant interviews or briefings with selected journalists. In deciding which journalists to speak with, the President may of course take into account their viewpoint. If President Trump sits down for an interview with Laura Ingraham, he is not required to do the same with Rachel Maddow. The First Amendment does not control the President's discretion in choosing with whom to speak or to whom to provide personal access. It is a time honored and entirely mundane aspect of our competitive and free press that public officials regularly subject all reporters to some form of differential treatment based on whether they approve of the reporters' expression.

3.

To properly characterize the Oval Office and like spaces, we examine their history and the government's policy and practice with respect to allowing access. We also consider whether the tradition of activity in these spaces demonstrates that they have historically been made available for speech activity. The design and function of the space is also relevant when determining whether the government has created any type of forum for private speech.

The Oval Office is the President's office, over which he has absolute control and discretion to exclude the public or members of the press. The President uses the space for myriad purposes, including speeches, signing ceremonies, and meetings with senior officials or heads of state. When events in the Oval Office are broadcast to the public, they feature the President's speech and expressive activity.

It hardly needs to be said that the Oval Office, Air Force One, or even the East Room are not places traditionally open to assembly and debate, nor are they open to the public for expressive activity. The parties agree the White House could, consistent with the First Amendment, exclude press from these spaces entirely.

The AP's primary contention, however, is that when the Oval Office and similar spaces are opened to the press pool, they become nonpublic fora and therefore the White House may not withhold access on the basis of viewpoint. We disagree.

First, the press events to which the AP seeks access do not involve the type of communicative activities that transform a restricted government space into a nonpublic forum. Forum analysis applies only to communicative activities. Where, as here, a small group of journalists is permitted to attend events in restricted White House spaces like the Oval Office, the primary activity is observational newsgathering. [A]t so-called press pool events, journalists are relegated to watching events unfold and very often have no interaction with the President or other officials. At these events, journalists do not expect to have a substantive conversation with officials. Instead, journalists are present just to witness what is said and what the reaction is, and what else is happening in the room. The AP admits as much and identifies the harms from exclusion as the loss of opportunities to gather and quickly disseminate news about the President. Newsgathering may enjoy some First Amendment protections from government interference. But newsgathering is not itself a communicative activity. When journalists are invited to observe events in the Oval Office, they are gathering information for their reporting, which is a noncommunicative step in the production of speech.

Second, the communicative acts identified by the district court cannot transform these restricted White House spaces into nonpublic fora. The AP stressed that the quick dissemination of presidential news is essential to its business model as a global wire service. And the district court concluded that journalists are in fact "speaking" from these limited-access spaces because they transmit stories, observations, and photographs in real time. Without question, such reporting constitutes speech and expressive activity. That speech, however, has little if any nexus to the restricted spaces in which it occurs such that the spaces become nonpublic fora.

In every case in which the Court has concluded a government property constitutes a traditional public forum, designated forum, or even nonpublic forum, there exists a close relationship between the forum and the protected speech. Since Roman times, a forum has been emblematic of a space for citizens to participate in public discussion and dialogue, to exchange ideas, and to engage in political debate. In modern doctrine, the "traditional public forum" is closely tethered to this historical conception: It is a place which, "time out of mind, [has] been used for purposes of assembly, communicating thoughts between citizens, and discussing public questions." *Perry*. In a similar way, a designated public forum is a space the government opens for use by the public as a place for expressive activity.

Even with respect to less conventional nonpublic fora, the Supreme Court has carefully considered the connection between the speech and the forum. In *Cornelius*, the plaintiffs wanted to solicit donations (a form of protected speech) through a charity drive brochure targeted at federal employees. The Court concluded that the charity drive with its government-distributed materials was a nonpublic forum because the nexus between solicitation and the communication of information and advocacy of causes is present in the [charity drive brochure] as in other contexts. The plaintiffs sought access to a particular means of communication, namely, speaking to government workers within the nonpublic forum of the charity drive brochure.

When a small number of press observe presidential events, they are not using the Oval Office as the location or means of communication. And when the White House opens events in the Oval Office to a select group of journalists for observational newsgathering, the journalists generally are not speaking with the President or other officials, nor are they engaged in dialogue with each other. The AP's reporting on presidential events through electronic dissemination of news to editors or the public outside the White House is the only communicative activity at issue. But this activity could occur anywhere and therefore lacks the essential connection to the government space required to create even a nonpublic forum.

We decline to adopt a rule that would turn any government space in which smart phones or computers are allowed into a nonpublic forum simply because individuals can communicate with the outside world by blogging, posting comments and pictures, or other otherwise disseminating messages in real time. Smart phone ownership is ubiquitous. The mere possibility of communicating through the internet while on government property cannot transform every government space into a forum protected by the First Amendment. Indeed, we are not aware of any forum analysis case in which the relevant expressive or communicative activity was directed outside the forum. When the courts determine that government property serves as a forum, the property is the essential situs for the communicative activity.

Third, these spaces should not be classified as nonpublic fora because access to them is tightly controlled and highly selective. Only about one percent of hard pass holders can fit in spaces like the Oval Office. When access to government property is very limited, considerations of viewpoint may be permissible.

At oral argument, the AP agreed that the President or White House could select a group of journalists each day to observe events in these spaces and that such selection would not be subject to forum analysis.

The AP further conceded that the President could abolish the existing press pool or establish a new pool based on different criteria, including viewpoint. And the AP agrees the White House or President can discriminate on the basis of viewpoint in granting exclusive interviews, answering journalists' questions, or selecting journalists to attend an event about a particular subject matter.

The AP's concessions give away the game, because such scenarios cannot be distinguished from so-called press pool events, which are at bottom small press availabilities with the President. Allowing a handful of selected journalists into the President's personal office cannot transform it into the Brady Briefing Room. The AP therefore must place great weight on the historical press pool as the forum to which it seeks access. But as we have already explained, the only potential fora here are the restricted physical spaces, like the Oval Office, to which AP seeks access, not the historical press pool.

Finally, the fact that the President is communicating at these events further distances this context from forum analysis. When the government is speaking, forum analysis is usually inapplicable because while the First Amendment restricts government regulation of private speech, it does not regulate government speech.

Although the White House disclaims primary reliance on the government speech doctrine, the events to which the AP seeks access by their nature involve presidential, *i.e.* government, speech. The messages conveyed in the Oval Office are government speech and opportunities for the President's administration to express its message. Forum analysis is also inappropriate when government speech occurs within a limited space, such as the Oval Office, the essential function of which would be defeated by compelling the President to support private speech on a viewpoint-neutral basis.

The AP's claim to access is inconsistent with longstanding First Amendment principles and would plant the seed of a constitutional case in every decision the White House makes about which reporters to include at presidential events. For the foregoing reasons, the White House is likely to prevail against AP's viewpoint discrimination claim.

[The panel majority also rejected the AP's claim that the White House had impermissibly retaliated against it based on viewpoint]:

Choosing who may observe or possibly speak with the President in these spaces is not the type of action that supports a retaliation claim.

Rather, it is more akin to a decision about how the President wields the bully pulpit.

Our dissenting colleague emphasizes that the denial of a government benefit based on speech is often actionable. While this is generally true, the press pool is in no way a government benefit program. Denying unemployment benefits, tax exemptions, or trademarks on the basis of viewpoint can support a First Amendment retaliation claim. Denying access to observe or speak with the President in his private spaces cannot. The dissent acknowledges that the President may take viewpoint into account when granting interviews to select journalists. Our holding today reflects the fact that granting access to spaces such as the Oval Office is more like granting interviews than like denying unemployment benefits.

Furthermore, in determining whether a First Amendment retaliation claim is actionable, courts may be guided by long settled and established practices. As the AP acknowledges (and the district court recognized), the White House can and does reward journalists with advantages like interviews with the President and the opportunity to ask questions at press events. Such viewpoint-based preferences occur at every level of government in the relationship between elected officials and the press. These pervasive practices simply do not give rise to a retaliation claim, regardless of how valuable the access may be.

PILLARD, Circuit Judge, dissenting

For almost a century, the White House has enabled the White House Press Pool, a limited number of credentialed media organizations, to cover the President at close range from inside the Oval Office, Air Force One, and other government-controlled spaces. White House staff determines which presidential activities and trips the Press Pool covers. But participation in the Press Pool or the broader White House press corps has never been conditioned on the viewpoint expressed outside the Pool by any participating news organization—until now.

The issue here is whether, when the White House authorizes the Press Pool to travel with the President or observe an Oval Office meeting or signing, the White House may exclude journalists or news organizations based on their expression outside the Pool of views the President disfavors. Neither this court nor the Supreme Court has ever upheld the exclusion from a forum or denial of a benefit based on a private recipient's viewpoint outside the forum or benefit program. Because the district court correctly enjoined just such exclusion here, I see no basis for a stay pending appeal.

The panel's stay of the preliminary injunction cannot be squared with longstanding First Amendment precedent, multiple generations of White House practice and tradition, or any sensible understanding of the role of a free press in our constitutional democracy. Both its public-forum and retaliation analyses contravene the fundamental principle that the government may not leverage its allocation of valuable support to punish recipients for the viewpoints they express with their own time and resources.

The right of journalists in the Press Pool to participate free from discrimination based on viewpoint has endured even during the eras of rockiest relations between the White House and the press—during the Watergate investigations, and Independent Counsel Kenneth Starr's investigation of President Bill Clinton. Until this case, Presidents might have openly criticized press coverage they received—including from outlets in the Press Pool—but none had ousted a participant from the Pool based on viewpoint.

No precedent of this court or the Supreme Court countenances denial of a government benefit or exclusion from a government-created program to otherwise eligible participants solely because of disagreement with a participant's point of view expressed outside the benefit or program. Public officials often and inevitably disagree with publicly expressed views of the journalists or news organizations that cover them. Until now, every United States president has had the fortitude to tolerate the presence in the White House and Oval Office of credentialed journalists known to disagree with one or more government-preferred viewpoints. The First Amendment demands no less.

Few constitutional doctrines are as firmly established as the principle that ideologically driven attempts to suppress a particular point of view are presumptively unconstitutional. It is unsurprising, then, that the government could not identify a single case approving viewpoint discrimination—the most egregious form of speech restriction—in circumstances bearing any material similarity to this case. Given government officials' perennial frustration with unflattering press coverage, the absence of supportive precedent for defendants' action is striking.

The prohibition on viewpoint discrimination applies equally to the imposition of penalties and the denial of benefits. The government may not condition receipt of any otherwise-available benefit or opportunity on a recipient's endorsement or avoidance of a particular viewpoint. That rule applies to government benefits generally, including federal funding, tax exemptions, trademarks, government contracts, and public-sector employment. Even where a government program is designed to support a small number of speakers selected on discretionary, aesthetic criteria, it may not impose restrictions intended to punish certain ideas or viewpoints. And even discretionary support to public broadcasters cannot be allocated to curtail expression of a particular point of view.

It is axiomatic that the government may not regulate speech based on its substantive content or the message it conveys. The only exception to the general rule is when the government engages in expression of the government's own viewpoint, that is, when it is engaged in government speech. But defendants expressly disavow that the AP's Stylebook or other references to the Gulf of Mexico constitute government speech. The upshot is that no general program for admitting the press to the White House or the Oval Office can exclude a press outlet based on its viewpoint.

The President's use of the Oval Office as a platform for his official speech does not entail governmental authority to impose viewpoint restrictions on the Press Pool. Even where the government funds private organizations to advance official policy and therefore can control the viewpoint expressed within the funded program, it may not deny support based on disapproval of the recipient's speech outside that program. The government may not require private participants to adopt—as their own—the Government's view on an issue of public concern as a condition of funding. The rule that public funds may be limited to the purpose for which they are granted does not empower the government to impose viewpoint restrictions on grantees' private speech.

Whatever my colleagues mean by emphasizing that Oval Office events "involve" governmental speech because the President typically speaks there, the Press Pool's coverage of those events—let alone the content of the AP's Stylebook—is not governmental speech legitimately subject to official viewpoint control. My colleagues are also wrong that the "essential function" of the Oval Office is "defeated" by the presence of a Press Pool free from viewpoint discrimination. The Press Pool has operated without viewpoint control for almost a century during which presidents have communicated directly from the Oval Office. The purpose of the Press Pool has never been to propagandize for the President, but only to enable reliable news coverage of his leadership. Public officials' prerogative to speak for the government does not include any ability to control private parties' speech on their own behalf, even when that speech relates to the government's message. . . .

Defendants concede that the AP had been barred from the Press Pool solely because of references to the Gulf of Mexico in its own writing. They gave no other, constitutionally defensible basis for the AP's exclusion. And defendants have (correctly) disavowed the argument that their discriminatory treatment of the AP can be understood as regulation of the government's own speech.

The only basis for defendants' action is that the AP had expressed—outside the Oval Office and while speaking in its own capacity with no government support—a point of view that the White House disagreed with and sought to suppress. Even without any forum analysis, that resolves this case.

Forum analysis powerfully reinforces that conclusion. The AP's exclusion from the Press Pool violates the bedrock principle that the government may not exclude private speakers from a government-created forum, even a nonpublic forum, based on their viewpoint. When the government imposes restrictions on the use of public property for private expression, such as by limiting speech only in a specific location, the government must abide by the First Amendment's public forum doctrine. Every type of forum recognized under the First Amendment shares a baseline prohibition on viewpoint discrimination.

The Press Pool readily qualifies as at least a nonpublic forum. Spaces that White House staff open for journalists' newsgathering and nongovernmental communication have consistently been held to be nonpublic forums. The default category in forum analysis is the nonpublic forum, which includes all remaining public property that does not qualify as a traditional, designated, or limited public forum. Nonpublic forums include any government-controlled space that is not by tradition or designation a forum for public communication, but where private expressive activity nonetheless occurs. A space can qualify as a nonpublic forum even if it was not specifically opened for purposes of providing a forum for expressive activity, so long as such private expressive activity occurs.

The White House Press Pool is a forum even when it convenes outside the White House, such as on Air Force One or at Mar-a-Lago. A public "space" may refer to a forum more in a metaphysical than in a spatial or geographic sense, but the same principles are applicable. In a nonpublic forum, the government enjoys the most flexibility to craft rules limiting speech and may reserve such a forum for its intended purposes, communicative or otherwise, but any such limits must be reasonable and not an effort to suppress expression merely because public officials oppose the speaker's view.

The application of nonpublic forum analysis in this case is straightforward. The Press Pool is not materially distinguishable from previously recognized nonpublic forums. There is no principled basis for exempting the press's activities in any White House "press area" from the requirement of viewpoint neutrality. When the White House Press Pool convenes in the Oval Office, just as when the broader press corps convenes in another White House location, it does so to engage in newsgathering. To that end, Pool members communicate text and photos to editors and the broader public, all of which is nongovernmental expressive activity occurring on federal property. Gathering information about government officials in a form that can readily be disseminated to others serves a cardinal First Amendment interest in protecting and promoting the free discussion of governmental affairs.

The fact that the Oval Office is generally closed to the public is simply another way of saying that it is not by tradition or designation a forum for public communication, *i.e.* that it is a nonpublic forum. Government office buildings are paradigmatic nonpublic forums. And the security restrictions applicable to the Oval Office do not alter the calculus. The entire White House is under tight security, but when spaces within are open to White House-credentialed journalists, exclusions are impermissible if based upon the content of the journalist's speech. That same principle applies when the Oval Office is open to the Press Pool.

Defendants' (and the majority's) principal argument is that the President has unlimited discretion to pick which journalists to grant special access unavailable to other members of the press corps. The AP does not assert a right to have the President return its phone calls, or to interact and speak with government officials. What the AP challenges is its reporters' and photographers' exclusion from a government program for which it is otherwise fully eligible and has long participated, based solely on the AP's own expression in its Stylebook and reporting. . . .

The defendants do not engage with those distinctions but sweep them aside to assert a legal prerogative of unprecedented breadth. In their view, when the President deals with the press, he is permitted to consider the nature of a journalist's coverage in deciding how much access to give them. But the "access" to interview government sources . . . should not be conflated with "access" to forums on government property that are established to enable journalists to report on the government's activities. We have held that the White House may not deny those reporters that "special access" solely because they dislike the reporters' viewpoints.

None of this analysis rests on any affirmative right of AP reporters to be present in the Oval Office. Plaintiffs do not argue that the White House is constitutionally obliged to operate a Press Pool[.] But once the government chooses to permit a forum for private expression in a government controlled space, the First Amendment forbids viewpoint-based restrictions on who may participate.

[Judge PILLARD also dissented from the majority's opinion regarding the AP's retaliation claim]:

The government's defense against the retaliation claim is unlikely to succeed for all the same reasons. The majority concludes that the AP suffered no retaliation because its exclusion from the Press Pool was "not a materially adverse action" for First Amendment purposes. The majority reasons that the government did not impose a punishment on the AP or deprive it of property, and so no retaliation occurred. But as discussed above, the exclusion was retributive, and in any event the First Amendment prohibits even the denial of wholly discretionary support or benefits in retaliation for a recipient's exercise of speech rights outside the supported activity or program.

* * *

In granting a stay, my colleagues assert a novel and unsupported exception to the First Amendment's prohibition of viewpoint-based restrictions of private speech—one that not even the government itself advanced. And they accept an equally unprecedented notion of harm to presidential "independence" when professional journalists are "permit[ted] to observe him" from the Press Pool despite the President's disagreement with something their news organization published.

Make no mistake as to why it matters that the panel majority accepts these theories. In the short term, the court allows the White House to rely on viewpoint to exclude the AP from the Press Pool pending a final decision on the merits, a process that typically takes months. And, looking further ahead, if any merits panel were to accept those theories, the result would be a Press Pool—and perhaps an entire press corps—limited during Republican administrations to the likes of Fox News and limited to outlets such as MSNBC when a Democrat is elected. More to the point, if the White House were privileged to exclude journalists based on viewpoint, each and every member of the White House press corps would hesitate to publish anything an incumbent administration might dislike. Factually accurate journalism unflattering to the incumbent administration would not long endure. Purporting to respect the First Amendment while allowing exclusion of journalists from the Press Pool based on viewpoint will quickly erode the independence of any press outlet hoping to retain the chance to cover the White House at close range.

DISCUSSION

1. *Presidents and Press (Dis)Favoritism.* As the majority in *Budowich* observed, Presidents have long granted special access or shown favoritism to media outlets or reporters that provide favorable coverage and denied access to disfavored media. During his first term, President Trump revoked the press credential of a CNN reporter who challenged him during a press conference. A district court ruled that the revocation violated the reporter's due process rights and the White House agreed to restore the credential. President Obama frequently clashed with Fox News. At one point, his White House decided Fox News would not be permitted to interview a high-level agency official—even though the network was part of the press pool assigned to the event. However, when Fox News and other news outlets objected, the White House relented, and Fox was granted access. Recently, the Trump White House barred *The Wall Street Journal* from attending an international trip as part of the press pool based on its reporting on the Jeffrey Epstein matter.

2. *Forum Analysis.* Courts have used the public forum doctrine to resolve a variety of First Amendment claims concerning access to public properties and resources. Forum analysis depends in part on identification of the relevant forum. In *Budowich*, the majority focused on the Oval Office and Air Force One, while the dissent focused on the Press Pool. Which public forum analysis did you find

more persuasive? Note Judge Pillard did not think it was *necessary* to apply the public forum doctrine, but that the doctrine "reinforced" the general principle that government cannot discriminate against speakers based on viewpoint.

3. *"Newsgathering."* The Supreme Court's decisions have recognized a limited First Amendment right of the public and press to gather information. *See, e.g.*, *Branzburg v. Hayes*, 408 U.S. 665, 707 (1972). The majority in *Budowich* recognized a newsgathering right but concluded that merely reporting on events that occur in the Oval Office and on Air Force One were not "expressive" activity for purposes of applying the public forum doctrine. Are reporters recording and disseminating information from the Oval Office engaged in expression?

4. *Retaliation.* As we have seen, a prevalent First Amendment claim in Trump 2.0 litigation is that the administration has retaliated against a speaker for engaging in protected expression. Why does the majority reject that claim in *Budowich*, and why does the dissent think it has merit?

5. *The Pentagon and the Press.* As part of a purported effort to crack down on leaks, the Defense Department adopted a policy that prohibits reporters from obtaining or soliciting any information, including unclassified material, from the Pentagon that the Department does not explicitly authorize for release. The policy also restricts press access to areas within the Pentagon. The Department vowed to revoke the press credentials of any reporter who violated the policy. Several media outlets refused to agree to the restrictions and dozens surrendered their Pentagon press credentials. *The Washington Post*'s Executive Editor stated, "The proposed restrictions undercut First Amendment protections by placing unnecessary constraints on gathering and publishing information."

C. PROBLEM EXERCISE: ACCESS TO AN AGENCY EVENT

Your law firm represents a national newspaper whose reporters were recently barred from attending a "National Immigration Enforcement Summit" sponsored by the Department of Homeland Security (DHS) at its office building in Washington, D.C. The summit was an all-day event devoted to the topic of how the U.S. Immigration and Customs Enforcement (ICE) agency will conduct nationwide sweeps and raids of businesses suspected of employing noncitizens. Your client's newspaper has published stories that have been critical of the current administration's immigration policies, especially the actions of ICE. The president has denounced this reporting on social media as "irresponsible hit pieces by a deranged, leftist, and treasonous newspaper that NO ONE READS." DHS invited Newsmax, Fox News, and other right-leaning news outlets to cover the event but excluded your client's newspaper and other left-leaning outlets. A DHS spokesperson explained that due to security concerns and space limitations inside the venue, DHS could only accommodate ten media representatives. The spokesperson also explained there would be a live stream in a building nearby for those that could not attend the summit. However, one of the outlets reported that a handful of seats were vacant in the press section. Your client believes DHS has violated its First Amendment rights. What advice would you give your client concerning a possible lawsuit challenging the exclusion?

D. BROADCAST MEDIA

As discussed earlier, President Trump has sued media outlets for defamation, consumer fraud, and election interference based on their reporting and editorial actions. One of the lawsuits, against CBS, centered on an interview of Vice President and then-presidential candidate Kamala Harris on the program *60 Minutes*. While the lawsuit *and* a merger application filed by CBS's parent, Paramount, were both pending, the Federal Communications Commission investigated whether

CBS violated federal law when it edited Harris's answers to interview questions. The FCC investigation was precipitated by a Complaint filed by the Center for American Rights (CAR). The following are excerpts from the Complaint.

Before the
FEDERAL COMMUNICATIONS COMMISSION

In re Complaint Against WCBS-TV

COMPLAINT

INTRODUCTION

"Rigging or slanting the news is a most heinous act against the public interest—indeed, there is no act more harmful to the public's ability to handle its affairs. In all cases where we may appropriately do so, we shall act to protect the public interest in this important respect." *In Re Complaints Covering CBS PROGRAM "HUNGER IN AMERICA,"* 20 F.C.C.2d 143, 151 (Oct. 15, 1969). Broadcasters are public trustees licensed to operate in the public interest and, as such, may not engage in intentional falsification or suppression of news.

This complaint concerns an act of significant and substantial news alteration, made in the middle of a heated presidential campaign. Moreover, in this instance we have the clear external evidence of outtakes necessary for this Commission to act. WCBS TV aired the Sunday CBS morning news show "Face the Nation" on Sunday, October 5. It also aired the CBS program "Sixty Minutes" on Monday, October 6. The two programs featured the same question asked to Vice President Kamala Harris, with two completely different answers.

In the first clip, CBS journalist Bill Whitaker asks the Vice President about Israeli Prime Minister Benjamin Netanyahu: "But it seems that Prime Minister Netanyahu is not listening." In that clip, Harris replies: "Well, Bill, the work that we have done has resulted in a number of movements in that region by Israel that were very much prompted by or a result of many things, including our advocacy for what needs to happen in the region." In the second clip, Whitaker asks the exact same question. But in this clip, Harris replies: "We are not gonna stop pursuing what is necessary for the United States to be clear about where we stand on the need for this war to end."

Same interview, same question, two completely different answers.

Under this Commission's long-standing precedent, CBS retains the right to exercise news judgment when editing its material. And that kind of editing is normal in the context of a news magazine style show like "Sixty Minutes." However, CBS crosses a line when its production reaches the point of so transforming an interviewee's answer that it is a fundamentally different answer. This CBS may not do. Here, CBS has taken a single question and transformed Harris' answer such that the general public no longer has any confidence as to what the Vice President actually said in response to the query.

Strong and prompt action by the Commission is necessary to restore public confidence in the broadcast and to clarify this matter of national interest and importance.

WCBS's VIOLATION OF 47 U.S.C. § 309(a)

News distortion is incorporated in the public-interest standard for broadcasters, 47 U.S.C. § 309(a). "[T]o violate the news distortion policy, the distortion must be about a significant matter and not merely something trivial or incidental." Lili Levi, *Reporting the Official Truth: The Revival of the FCC's News Distortion Policy*, 78 Wash. U. L. Q. 1005, 1023 (2000). Here, the question is incredibly consequential—U.S. foreign policy toward the Middle East in the middle of a war—and the timing is also significant: weeks before a presidential election, and with a candidate who has sat for very few news interviews.

The Complainant is not asking the Commission to censor CBS News or to invade CBS News' free speech. *See* 42 U.S.C. § 326. The U.S. Supreme Court has squarely held that Commission does not transgress Section 326 by reviewing licensees' past conduct under the public-interest standard. *FCC v. Pacifica Found.*, 438 U.S. 726, 735 (1978). Rather, the Court has held that the Commission acts appropriately in executing Congress's desire "to assure that the public receives through this medium a balanced presentation of information on issues of public importance." *FCC v. League of Women Voters*, 468 U.S. 364, 377 (1984).

CONCLUSION

The FCC has had a policy against "news distortion" in over-the-air broadcast (local TV and radio stations) news for over 50 years. Here, CBS engaged in news distortion by editing its news program to such a great extent that the general public cannot know what answer the Vice

President actually gave to a question of great importance on a matter of national security policy.

* * *

[The FCC initially dismissed CAR's complaint, concluding that CBS had not engaged in news distortion. However, the agency subsequently decided to *reopen* the inquiry. The following are excerpts from comments submitted by the Foundation for Individual Rights and Expression (FIRE), in response to an FCC notice seeking public comments on CAR's news distortion allegations.]

Before the
FEDERAL COMMUNICATIONS COMMISSION
Washington, D.C. 20554

In the Matter of)
News Distortion Complaint)
MB Docket No. 25-73)
Involving CBS Broadcasting Inc.,)
Licensee of WCBS, New York, NY)

Comments of the Foundation for Individual Rights and Expression

This proceeding is a political stunt. Neither the Center for American Rights' (CAR) complaint nor this Commission's decision to reopen its inquiry accords with how the agency has understood and applied its broadcast regulations ever. To the contrary, the Commission has made clear it "is not the national arbiter of the truth," *Complaints Covering CBS Program "Hunger in America,"* 20 F.C.C.2d 143, 151 (1969), and it has strictly avoided the type of review sought here because "[i]t would involve the Commission deeply and improperly in the journalistic functions of broadcasters." *Complaint Concerning the CBS Program "The Selling of the Pentagon,"* 30 F.C.C.2d 150, 152 (1971). The staff's initial dismissal of CAR's complaint was obviously correct.

For the Commission to reopen the matter and to seek public comment turns this proceeding into an illegitimate show trial. This is an adjudicatory question, not a rulemaking, and asking members of the public to "vote" on how they feel about a news organization's editorial policies is both pointless and constitutionally infirm. Prolonging this matter is especially unseemly when paired with FCC review of a pending merger application involving CBS's parent corporation and the fact that President Trump is currently involved in frivolous litigation over the same *60 Minutes* broadcast. In this context, this proceeding is precisely the kind of unconstitutional abuse of regulatory authority the Supreme Court unanimously condemned in *NRA v. Vullo*, 602 U.S. 175 (2024).

The CAR complaint rests on a fundamental misunderstanding of the Commission's limited role in regulating broadcast journalism and fails to grasp the basic elements of the news distortion policy as the FCC historically has defined and applied it. This agency has never asserted the authority to police news editing and has rightly observed that it would result in a "quagmire" even to try. *Hunger in America*, 20 F.C.C.2d at 150. The news distortion policy simply does not involve itself with "a judgment as to what was presented, as against what should have been presented," *Network Coverage of the Democratic Nat'l Convention*, 16 F.C.C.2d 650, 657–58 (1969), yet that is CAR's sole complaint. And even if CBS's editorial decisions in *60 Minutes* fell within the range of activities governed by the news distortion policy, the CAR complaint is utterly deficient. It does not present any "extrinsic evidence" of news distortion as the policy requires, and the full unedited transcript of the interview in question shows the network's editing did not alter the substance of the answers given. CAR's complaint merely reflects its own editorial preferences, which cannot justify this inquiry.

Even if the FCC's news distortion policy somehow authorized the Commission to act as editor-in-chief, as CAR imagines, the Communications Act and the First Amendment prohibit such intrusion into journalistic decisions. The Act expressly denies to the FCC "the power of censorship" as well as the ability to promulgate any "regulation or condition" that interferes with freedom of speech. 47 U.S.C. § 326. The FCC accordingly has interpreted its powers narrowly so as not to conflict with the First Amendment. And whatever limited authority the Commission might have possessed in the era the news distortion policy was created has diminished over time with changes in technology. Any attempt in this proceeding to apply a more robust view of the Commission's public interest authority to include an ability to review and dictate individual news judgments would stretch the FCC's public interest mandate to the breaking point.

Ultimately, no FCC policy can override the First Amendment's fundamental bar against the government compelling editors and publishers "to publish that which 'reason tells them should not be published.'" *Miami Herald Publ'g Co. v. Tornillo*, 418 U.S. 241, 256 (1974). "For better or worse, editing is what editors are for; and editing is selection and choice of material." *CBS, Inc. v. Democratic Nat'l Comm.*, 412 U.S. 94, 120 (1973). The news distortion policy still exists only because of the exceedingly limited role the Commission has given it over the years, and this proceeding is not a vehicle for expanding its reach.

Finally, this proceeding itself is an exercise in unconstitutional jawboning. The Commission must heed the Supreme Court's recent reminder that the "'threat of invoking legal sanctions and other means of coercion . . . to achieve the suppression' of disfavored speech violates the First Amendment." *Vullo*, 602 U.S. at 180. The purpose and timing of this inquiry are both obvious and unjustifiable. Launching a politically fraught investigation based on such a paper-thin complaint in these circumstances is alone a compelling example of regulatory abuse. But to resurrect the flimsy complaint after it was fully and properly interred by staff dismissal, and to do so in support of the President's private litigation position, is all but a signed confession of unconstitutional jawboning. The Commission can begin to recover some dignity only by dropping the matter immediately.

Even if CBS's editorial decisions in *60 Minutes* fell within the range of activities governed by the news distortion policy, the CAR Complaint is woefully deficient. The Commission recognized long ago it cannot be "the national arbiter of the truth," and its news distortion policy has an "extremely limited scope." *Galloway v. FCC*, 778 F.2d 16, 21 (1985). Investigation is warranted only "where extrinsic evidence has been presented to the Commission suggesting that a licensee has staged or culpably distorted the presentation of a news event." *Democratic Nat'l Convention*, 16 F.C.C.2d at 657.

The Public Notice is premised on the conceit that compiling this record and investigating CBS for its news judgment is necessary to serve the "public interest." But this ignores that the Communications Act expressly withholds from government the power to "interfere with the right of free speech by means of radio communication." 47 U.S.C. § 326. This denies to the FCC "the power of censorship" as well as the ability to promulgate any "regulation or condition" that interferes with freedom of speech. *Id.* These policies "were drawn from the First Amendment itself [and] the 'public interest' standard necessarily invites reference to First Amendment principles." *CBS, Inc.* 412 U.S. at 121. Consequently, the

Supreme Court has stressed that "the First Amendment must inform and give shape to the manner in which Congress exercises its regulatory power in this area." *FCC v League of Women Voters of Cal.*, 468 U.S. 364, 378 (1984). Although the Court historically interpreted the law to give some greater leeway to regulate broadcasting compared to traditional media, the public interest standard has never permitted the level of intrusion into the editorial process that this proceeding represents.

DISCUSSION

1. *Broadcast Licensees and the "Public Interest."* President Trump has suggested that regulators should consider revoking the licenses of broadcasters that air negative coverage of or commentary about him. "I have read someplace that the networks were 97 percent against me," he said. "I get 97 percent negative, and yet I won and easily." President Trump continued, "I would think maybe their license should be taken away." Congress charged the FCC with ensuring that broadcast licensees act in the "public interest." As FIRE observed in its comments, that does not grant the agency a general authority to review the *content* of broadcasts or the viewpoints they express. However, it does empower the agency to investigate "news distortion." Based on the CAR complaint and the FIRE submission, what is your understanding of "news distortion"?

2. *Editorial Discretion.* After initially resisting the FCC's demand for full transcripts of its interview with Vice President Harris, CBS acquiesced and provided the transcript to the agency. Further, as part of its settlement of the civil lawsuit brought by President Trump, CBS agreed to make public complete written transcripts of *all* future interviews with presidential candidates. As FIRE's comments note, the Supreme Court has recognized that media outlets have a First Amendment right to editorial discretion. Access to the transcripts may further the public's interest in obtaining full and accurate information. However, CBS's concession may set a negative precedent in terms of the media's editorial independence. Should CBS have agreed to release the transcripts?

3. *Leveraging Multiple Proceedings.* As discussed in Part A., Donald Trump sued CBS News for its editorial actions relating to the broadcast of the Harris *60 Minutes* interview. Trump alleged unlawful acts

of "election and voter interference through malicious, deceptive, and substantial news distortion." After Trump was elected, CBS's parent company Paramount Global sought the Trump Administration's approval of a proposed merger with Skydance Media. In addition to (now President) Trump's civil lawsuit, the FCC proceeding discussed above was also pending as the FCC reviewed the merger application. Paramount later settled the president's lawsuit. FIRE's comments included the following allegation:

> Bottom line, the Commission's request for public comment lacks any legitimate regulatory rationale, but its *realpolitik* purpose is sadly transparent. This proceeding is designed to exert maximum political leverage on the CBS network at a time when President Trump is engaged in frivolous litigation against it over the same *60 Minutes* broadcast, with the FCC using other regulatory approvals the network needs to exert added pressure.

4. *Late Night Television*. Shortly after he criticized CBS's settlement with President Trump on air, late night television host Stephen Colbert was informed that his show would not be renewed. Another late night host, Jimmy Kimmel, was suspended for comments he made about the murder of Charlie Kirk, a right wing political activist and media personality. In the leadup to Kimmel's suspension, the Federal Communications Commission Chair, Brendan Carr, said in a podcast interview that ABC would face consequences for Kimmel's comments: "We can do this the easy way or the hard way," Carr said. Kimmel's show returned after a brief suspension. Both CBS and ABC maintained that their actions were based on business considerations.

5. *Network Shakeups and Editorial Changes*. During Trump 2.0, some networks have made leadership and other personnel changes in response to the administration's criticisms of their coverage and practices. CBS installed Bari Weiss, an anti-woke crusader, opinion writer, and longtime critic of mainstream media, as its new editor-in-chief. The executive producer of "60 Minutes" resigned, claiming that the network had interfered with his journalistic independence. CBS also hired a conservative policy analyst with no experience overseeing news coverage to act as an "ombudsman" reviewing com-

plaints about its coverage. The installation of an ombudsman was one of Skydance's commitments to the Trump administration as the company sought to merge with Paramount. In addition, again in response to criticism from the Trump Administration, networks have altered their editorial policies. For example, CBS's "Face the Nation" agreed not to edit recorded interviews after the administration accused the network of deceptively altering an interview with Homeland Security Secretary Kristi Noem.

E. INVESTIGATING THE PRESS

The Federal Communications Commission (FCC) is not the only federal agency that can investigate and sanction the media. The following materials relate to an investigation of Media Matters for America by the Federal Trade Commission (FTC). The FTC opened its investigation of Media Matters, a watchdog group that has published critical reports about the social media platform X, based on alleged collusion with advertisers. Media Matters claimed the FTC's investigation was in retaliation for its critical reporting about X and its fact-checking of conservative media. The excerpts following the doctrinal synopsis are from Media Matters' memorandum in support of its motion for a preliminary injunction.

DOCTRINAL SYNOPSIS: FIRST AMENDMENT RETALIATION

- The First Amendment prohibits government officials from subjecting an individual to retaliatory actions for speaking out or engaging in protected expression.
- To prevail on a First Amendment retaliation claim, Plaintiff must show (1) they engaged in conduct protected under the First Amendment; (2) Defendants took some retaliatory action sufficient to deter a person of ordinary firmness in Plaintiff's position from speaking again; and (3) there is a causal link between the exercise of a constitutional right and the adverse action.

IN THE UNITED STATES DISTRICT COURT
FOR THE DISTRICT OF COLUMBIA

MEDIA MATTERS FOR AMERICA)
)
v.)
)
FEDERAL TRADE COMMISSION)

Plaintiff's Memorandum in Support of Motion for Preliminary Injunction

INTRODUCTION

Plaintiff Media Matters for America has been the target of an ongoing retaliatory campaign because powerful government actors disapprove of its journalism. This Court has already halted two unlawful state-level investigations into Media Matters [in Texas and Missouri]. The Federal Trade Commission ("FTC") has now stepped in, launching a similar—and indeed, broader—investigation in response to the same protected speech that the state-level investigations sought to squelch. This Court should prevent the FTC from leveraging the power of the federal government to punish Media Matters for its speech.

Covering a time frame triple the length of the Texas Civil Investigative Demand (CID), the FTC CID attempts to probe all aspects of Media Matters' operations, including its editorial process, finances, internal research, and external communications. Media Matters filed this case, claiming that the FTC's CID, like the State AGs' CIDs, is unconstitutional because it retaliates against Media Matters for its protected speech in violation of the First Amendment and because it impermissibly probes into Plaintiff's journalistic activities in violation of the First and Fourth Amendments. Media Matters now moves for a preliminary injunction against the FTC's CID and investigation.

Media Matters is likely to succeed on its First Amendment retaliation claim because multiple factors make clear that the FTC issued its CID in response to Media Matters' protected speech. Additionally, there is no sound justification for the CID, further confirming that it was not issued for any legitimate investigative purpose. The FTC has no statutory authority to enforce the antitrust laws against a nonprofit like Media Matters. And the FTC has never offered a sound basis for suspecting that Media Matters has violated any antitrust law. Though several FTC officials have publicly accused Media Matters of participating in an "advertiser boycott" of X, the only evidence they point to is public advocacy and reporting by Media Matters concerning X—which is protected speech, not a call for an unlawful boycott. And, critically, multiple administration allies have also publicly called on people to cease doing business with certain companies, including MSNBC, and yet it does not appear that the FTC has investigated them. That strongly suggests that the decision to issue a CID to Media Matters was not driven by a genuine concern about unlawful "boycotts."

Put simply, too many factors justify the inference that the FTC issued its CID because Media Matters did what the Constitution permits: express its views on matters of significant public concern. Media Matters is thus likely to prevail on its First Amendment retaliation claim.

BACKGROUND

Since it was established in 2004, Media Matters has published articles on extremism and bias in the news. As part of its mission to address misinformation, Media Matters has reported on the spread of misinformation and extremist rhetoric (including neo-Nazi images, antisemitic conspiracy theories, and racial slurs) on websites that host user-generated content, including, but not limited to, Facebook, Instagram, YouTube and X.

In its articles, Media Matters has stated that those sites have a responsibility to the public to monitor and remove false or extremist user content. Its reporting became even more important in 2022, when Elon Musk submitted a bid to purchase Twitter, retracted that bid, and was sued by Twitter to hold him to his offer. Media Matters' President Angelo Carusone publicly stated that Musk's stated goal of sharply reducing content moderation on Twitter would turn it into a "cauldron[] of misinformation and abuse." Mr. Carusone also warned that advertisers would not be interested in a no-holds-barred version of Twitter; "[a]dvertisers want to know that their ads are not going to appear alongside extremists, that they're not going to be subsidizing or associating with the types of things that would turn off potential customers[.]"

Those warnings set the stage for what eventually became a nearly two-year campaign to silence Media Matters and stifle its coverage of political extremism and misinformation online.

Musk completed his purchase of Twitter in October 2022. Almost immediately, he dismantled the site's content moderation systems, drastically reduced staff responsible for removing hate speech, eliminated infrastructure policies targeted at flagging misinformation and violent content, and reinstated accounts known for white supremacist rhetoric. These guardrails gone, the number of posts containing once-banned content predictably ballooned. For example, slurs against gay men and Black Americans on the site increased by 58 and 200 percent, respectively. And the use of the n-word increased nearly 500% in the twelve hours after Musk officially bought the site.

The private sector response came quickly, too. Advertisers saw the rapid increase in conspiracy theories and hate speech on X and, hesitant to have their products displayed next to posts that would offend the vast majority of their customers, pulled their advertisements from the site. X's revenue plummeted. Prominent conservatives like Mike Davis—well-known friend of FTC Chairman Andrew Ferguson and vocal advocate for using the legal system to punish political opponents—blamed Media Matters. He viewed Media Matters' warnings to advertisers as a "cancer to free speech," and encouraged Musk to "nuke [Media Matters'] and all staff accounts."

By July 2023, X's advertising revenue was reportedly down 50% compared to the prior year. Advertising revenue for X in the United States in particular apparently dropped even further in the following months, falling to a level as much as 60% lower than the prior year by September 2023. And the blowback against Media Matters grew in turn. Jon Schweppe, a longtime critic of Media Matters and proponent of using antitrust litigation as a "political solution" to create "a free and honest public square" online, posted in June 2023 a restatement of his view that "Media Matters wants to weaponize powerful institutions to censor conservatives." Within months of that post, Schweppe became Senior Policy Advisor to FTC Chairman Andrew Ferguson. Jake Denton, now the FTC's Chief Technology Officer, agreed with Schweppe, calling Media Matters "an organization devoted to pressuring companies into silencing conservative voices."

Media Matters did not back down. In 2023, Plaintiff published at least fourteen articles about Musk and X, many of which showed that X displayed advertisements next to extremist content. Numerous media outlets reported on the same topic.

Musk claimed that "activist groups like Media Matters try to use their influence to attack our revenue streams by deceiving advertisers on X." He insisted that Media Matters "manipulate[d]" advertisers and the public by "curat[ing]" and "contriv[ing]" in order to "find a rare instance of ads serving next to the content they chose to follow," i.e. extremist content.

The FTC's focus on Media Matters began with President Trump's elevation of Andrew Ferguson to FTC Chairman in January 2025. Prior to being selected for the role of Chairman, Ferguson had already made plain his views on content moderation in his role as an FTC Commissioner. In a September 2024 dissenting statement from an FTC report, Ferguson described decisions to remove user-generated content as an "Orwellian" "censorship regime." In November of that year, immediately following the election, he began publicly chiding advertisers who were hesitant to work with X for fear that their ads might run alongside offensive user content. Ferguson rebranded their lawful, independent economic decisions as impermissible "advertiser boycotts," stating that "antitrust enforcers should take this seriously." He stated in an interview that "one of the most important things the FTC can do to promote free speech is to keep a very close eye on" such advertiser behavior. In a leaked document setting out his qualifications to be FTC Chairman, Ferguson promised to "investigate and prosecute" so-called "advertiser boycotts."

Once he became Chairman, Ferguson made good on that promise. He started with an FTC Request for Information in which the agency sought public comment on "technology platform censorship." Ferguson made clear that this request was targeted at advocates for online content moderation such as Media Matters. Ferguson's own words showed that his objection to content moderation was driven by his disagreement with the viewpoint of the content moderators. Speaking at the University of Chicago, he attributed the FTC's public comment request to the concern that "platforms [can] engage in censorship—whether on their own initiative, in collusion with each other, or at the behest of left-wing public officials, regulators, advertisers, or other DNC interest groups."

Ferguson is not alone. He has surrounded himself with like-minded senior officials, who have unabashedly accused Media Matters of "censorship." As noted above, Ferguson brought on Jon Schweppe as Senior Policy Advisor and Jake Denton as FTC Chief Technology Officer. Both had long targeted Media Matters, claiming that it "want[ed] to weaponize powerful institutions to censor conservatives," (Schweppe), was "the scum of the [E]arth," (Schweppe), and supposedly "pressur[ed] companies into silencing conservative voices," (Denton). To round out the group, Ferguson hired Joe Simonson as FTC Director of Public Affairs. Simonson believed that Media Matters was out to "cancel" conservative voices and praised X's litigation against Media Matters. He called Media Matters reporters "stupid and resentful Democrats who went to like American University and didn't have the emotional stability to work as an assistant press aide for a House member."

Ferguson and his allies thus believed that Media Matters' journalism and advocacy were suppressing the views that they favored. The FTC CID demands documents, data, and information dating back to January 1, 2019 (i.e., more than six years ago). And the FTC CID demands essentially every document relating to content moderation created by Media Matters during that expansive timeframe, including the following:

- "all documents that Media Matters either produced or received in discovery in any litigation between Media Matters and X Corp. related to advertiser boycotts since 2023."
- "all documents relating to other entities that purport to track, categorize, monitor, analyze, evaluate, or rate news, media, sources, platforms, outlets, websites, or other content publisher entities for 'brand suitability,' 'reliability,' 'misinformation,' 'hate speech,' 'false' or 'deceptive' content, or similar categories."
- "all communications between Media Matters and more than a dozen online advocates against online misinformation and hate speech."
- "all communications between Media Matters and any other person regarding any request for Media Matters to label any news, media, sources, outlets, platforms, websites, or other content publishers entities for 'brand suitability,' 'reliability,' 'misinformation,' 'hate speech,' 'false' or 'deceptive' content, or similar categories, regardless of whether the request was fulfilled."

These requests strike deep into the core of Media Matters' journalistic and nonprofit mission. For example, Media Matters was founded in part to combat misinformation and employs reporters for exactly that purpose; the CID seeks all documents relating to other entities that track and monitor misinformation. It further demands all communications about online monitoring—a clear attempt to determine Media Matters' sources at social media companies and likeminded outside entities, including other civil society organizations, that communicated about sites like X.

The weight of the FTC CID has already had a real and material impact on Media Matters, its journalists, and their collective First Amendment rights. For instance, recently, X's artificial-intelligence chatbot, Grok, began to spew antisemitic tropes following Musk's statement that he improved the chatbot, and that users "should notice a difference when [they] ask [it] questions." Although this type of story is normally Media Matters' bread-and-butter reporting, it has refrained from reporting it due to the ongoing campaign of retribution against it from entities hoping to curry favor with Musk. Similarly, Media Matters journalists have refrained from publishing the types of stories about media ties at the FTC that they would have published even during the first Trump administration. With the federal investigation ongoing, all articles about the FTC and its connections to Musk are flagged for additional approval and review so that management can decide whether the publication is worth the risk of additional retaliation. On an individual level, journalists at Media Matters are self-censoring to avoid punishment for their affiliation with the organization. Staff members are less willing to investigate newsworthy ties between federal agencies and partisan media organizations.

Media Matters' content moderation advocacy has also been stifled. Other organizations committed to combating misinformation and hate speech online have limited their communication with Media Matters, including by no longer engaging with Media Matters for public-facing advocacy like sign-on letters. Also due to the investigations and litigations, Media Matters has also refrained from sharing its research into X and X's advertisers, which it used to share freely with other research organizations. To give a concrete example, Elon Musk made headlines yet again in early July of this year when he reprogrammed X's AI Chatbot, Grok, in part because of its reliance on Media Matters as a source. A week later, Grok had deemed itself "MechaHitler," and was posting antisemitic conspiracy theories in response to posts across the platform. In years past, Media Matters would have conducted research and reporting on those posts and shared its findings with the public, reporters, and other organizations. Because of the FTC's ongoing "boycott" investigation, Media Matters was forced to sit on the sidelines for yet another national story. This goes to the core of Media Matters' messaging capabilities and has made it more difficult for the organization to retain staff.

The onslaught of government investigations has predictably restricted Media Matters financially. MMFA has amended or curtailed communications with partner organizations in a myriad of ways to avoid exposing them to or ensnaring them in ongoing litigation or investigations.

ARGUMENT

The law is settled that the First Amendment prohibits government officials from subjecting an individual to retaliatory actions for speaking out. The journalistic activities that precipitated the FTC's CID are undoubtedly protected by the First Amendment. They involved research and reporting on topics of public concern—including the rise of extremist content on X—which goes to the core of the First Amendment.

The Supreme Court has held that government actors "cannot attempt to coerce private parties in order to punish or suppress views that the government disfavors." *Nat'l Rifle Ass'n of Am. v. Vullo*, 602 U.S. 175, 180 (2024). Defendants, through their investigation and CID, have taken action sufficient to deter a person of ordinary firmness in Plaintiff's position from speaking again. Here, the FTC has issued a burdensome CID—enforceable through a petition in federal court—that calls for several categories of sensitive materials, conduct that would plainly deter a person of ordinary firmness in Plaintiff's position from speaking again. That is particularly true here given the larger retribution campaign that serves as the backdrop for the FTC's CID.

Courts have found that a government investigation is sufficient to chill protected speech. The predictable—and intended—chilling effect of the FTC's investigation and CID is reinforced by the power federal law vests in the agency to punish Plaintiff for noncompliance, including seeking judicial enforcement of the CID, *see* 15 U.S.C. § 49, even though, as a nonprofit, Media Matters should be exempt from FTC enforcement actions. Moreover, in contrast to ordinary litigation, where Media Matters can resist burdensome discovery through the rules of civil procedure, the FTC's broad investigative prerogatives are sweeping and the protections for CID recipients are minimal. An FTC CID need only be reasonably relevant to its stated investigative purpose.

Finally, Plaintiff's speech has already been chilled by Defendants' conduct, confirming that Defendants' conduct would deter a person of ordinary firmness from engaging in protected speech. The participation of a federal agency in this campaign has magnified its capacity to stifle Media Matters' speech.

The FTC issued its CID because of Media Matters' constitutionally protected speech. Evidence sufficient to show causation can take many forms. A plaintiff can, for example, point to suspicious timing linking protected speech and government action, demonstrate that the government's justification for its action is pretextual, or show that the government's reasoning for its action has changed over time.

Here, multiple factors justify the inference that the FTC issued the CID because of government disapproval of Plaintiff's reporting on Musk and its public advocacy in favor of content moderation: (1) comments from key officials concerning Media Matters and the suspicious timing of the CID; (2) the connections between the substance of the FTC's CID and prior state AG CIDs and the conduct they sought to deter; (3) the lack of a legal basis for an FTC investigation into Media Matters; and (4) the FTC's decision to investigate Media Matters while apparently declining to investigate many others—including allies of the administration—that have also publicly called on persons and entities to cease doing business with certain companies.

DISCUSSION

1. *Preliminary Injunction.* The district court granted Media Matters' motion for preliminary injunction. *See Media Matter for America v. Federal Trade Commission*, Civil Action No. 25-1959 (SLS), ___ F. Supp. 3d ___, 2025 WL 2378009 (D.D.C., Aug. 15, 2025). The court explained:

> Speech on matters of public concern is the heartland of the First Amendment. The principle that public issues should be debated freely has long been woven into the very fabric of who we are as a Nation. Without it, our democracy stands on shaky ground. It should alarm all Americans when the Government retaliates against individuals or organizations for engaging in constitutionally protected public debate. And that alarm should ring even louder when the Government retaliates against those engaged in newsgathering and reporting.
>
> . . . On the merits, the Court finds that Media Matters is likely to succeed on its First Amendment retaliation claim. Media Matters engaged in quintessential First Amendment activity when it published an online article criticizing Mr. Musk and X. And the Court finds that the FTC's expansive CID is a retaliatory act. There can be no doubt that such a

CID would deter a reporter of ordinary firmness from speaking again. Indeed, the FTC's CID has had its intended effect. Because of the CID, Media Matters has decided against pursuing certain stories about the FTC, Chairman Ferguson, and Mr. Musk. Finally, given the comments by Chairman Ferguson and his colleagues about Media Matters, the timing of the CID, and evidence of pretext, Media Matters is likely to show that retaliatory animus was the but-for cause of the FTC's CID.

2. *Leveraging Agency Power.* A variety of administrative agencies can be used to investigate, coerce, and sanction media outlets. During Trump 2.0, the Labor Department, the Federal Communications Commission and the Federal Trade Commission have all been involved in investigations and other actions against media. As noted in the Introduction, harnessing agency power has helped the Trump 2.0 Administration broaden the effects of the President's Executive Orders.

3. *Retaliation Redux.* As readers are no doubt aware by now, allegations of retaliation for protected expression have been among the most common themes in litigation against the Trump Administration. One possible reason is that administration officials, including President Trump, have communicated a desire to retaliate against political enemies on social media and in other contexts. As Media Matters' brief shows, this makes it easier for plaintiffs to establish the necessary "causal link" between the alleged retaliatory action and their expression.

4. *Media Subpoenas.* In its preliminary injunction papers, Media Matters argued that the FTC's investigation violated both its Fourth and First Amendment rights. The Supreme Court has recognized that subpoenas to newspapers and other media raise significant constitutional concerns. Thus, where "the materials sought to be seized" by an administrative subpoena even "may be protected by the First Amendment," the requirements of the Fourth Amendment are applied with "scrupulous exactitude." *Zurcher v. Stanford Daily*, 436 U.S. 547, 564 (1978). Media Matters argued that "compliance with the FTC's CID would require it to disclose its finances, editorial process, newsgathering activities, affiliations with likeminded entities

that monitor extremist content, and other material that is protected from disclosure by the First Amendment."

5. *Partisanship and Media Regulation*. The Trump Administration has targeted or sanctioned many individuals and organizations aligned with the political left, including elite law firms, universities, and Democratic officials. It has also targeted organizations that raise campaign funds for Democratic candidates, including Media Matters and ActBlue. *See* Presidential Memorandum, *Investigation Into Unlawful "Straw Donor" and Foreign Contributions in American Elections* (Apr. 24, 2025) (singling out ActBlue).

7

THE FREE FLOW OF INFORMATION

A popular Government, without popular information, or the means of acquiring it, is but a Prologue to a Farce or a Tragedy; or, perhaps, both.

—**JAMES MADISON**

This final chapter examines restrictions on the distribution of information. The free flow of information facilitates important First Amendment values including self-government, the search for truth in a variety of marketplaces of ideas, and individual self-fulfillment.[1] As First Amendment doctrines recognize, individuals and organizations must be free to gather, disseminate, and receive information. President Trump's Executive Orders, and agency actions implementing them, have significantly affected the public's access to data, the scientific process, academic freedom, the functions of libraries, parks, and museums, and public broadcasting. In contrast to prior chapters, most of the governmental actions discussed in this chapter have not given rise to First Amendment claims. Nevertheless, the administration's actions affect critical First Amendment interests in production, dissemination, and receipt of information.

DOCTRINAL SYNOPSIS: INFORMATION FLOW

- As a general matter, the First Amendment protects the right to gather, produce, distribute, and receive information.
- Supreme Court decisions recognize that government is prohibited from "limiting the stock of information from which members of the public may draw" and that "the State may not, consistently with the spirit of the First Amendment, contract the spectrum of available knowledge."
- However, the Court has not recognized a First Amendment right to access *all* information in the possession of government.

A. ACCESS TO INFORMATION AND DATA

Prior chapters have examined the broad effects of President Trump's Executive Orders regarding "DEI," gender, American history, and patriotism. These Orders have announced Executive Branch policies regarding their respective subjects and directed agencies to enforce them by, for example, opening investigations and terminating federal funding.

Trump 2.0 directives and agency actions have also limited the public's access to a wide range of information and data. The federal government is an important source of public information on issues relating to public health, the environment, scientific research, American history, and a host of other matters. In general, executive agencies can determine what information and messages they will communicate, including on their websites and at other properties the federal government owns or operates. The information and viewpoints naturally will change, depending in part on who is in the White House. However, President Trump's Executive Orders have resulted in unique restrictions on access to information by the public, the press, scientists, farmers, and others.

As soon as he assumed office, President Trump directed federal agencies to remove public-facing references to "DEI," "gender ideology," "environmental justice," and other disfavored topics or concepts.[2] Agencies across the federal government scrubbed websites of offending terms, language, studies, and other information. Some of these efforts were comical. For example, the Department of Defense removed material about the

"Enola Gay," the aircraft that dropped the atomic bomb on Hiroshima, apparently because the aircraft's *name* was no longer acceptable.[3]

Many other deletions suggested a more serious effort to delete or remove valuable information. The Defense Department deleted information about Jackie Robinson, the Tuskegee Airmen, Navajo Code Talkers, and female fighter pilots.[4] Arlington Cemetery's website "lost" pages on Black veterans, women in service, and the Civil War.[5] In some instances, agency officials later indicated some of these deletions were in error, perhaps the effort of overzealous officials or overinclusive search terms. However, the intentionality and breadth of the purge soon became apparent.

In compliance with President Trump's Executive Orders, agencies removed materials that even hinted American history was anything other than uplifting and positive. For example, the National Park Service removed information about the internment of Japanese Americans, the Tuskegee Airmen, and the Stonewall Uprising for gay rights.[6] The National Park Service's web page on the Underground Railroad was revised to characterize the Railroad as an example of "cross-racial cooperation in the fight for racial equality."[7] A review of federal government websites showed agencies across government had "softened descriptions of some of the most shameful moments of the nation's past."[8] For those who rely on government websites and resources to obtain information about American history, agency enforcement of President Trump's directives created an incomplete and inaccurate record.

The federal government is also an important source of scientific, demographic, and other kinds of data. Academic researchers, scientists, health care providers, urban planners, and others rely on datasets produced and managed by federal agencies. In response to President Trump's Executive Orders, web pages, studies, and datasets that included terms like "health equity, "environmental justice," "artificial intelligence bias," "diversity," and other forbidden terms and phrases simply disappeared.[9] The U.S. Census Bureau deleted links to reports on gender identity and sexual orientation.[10] The Bureau of Prisons deleted a breakdown of transgender inmates in federal prisons.[11] The Centers for Disease Control removed from its website public health data and information concerning contraception, abortion, HIV, and suicide risk for transgender persons.[12] Several agencies also removed references to studies and information pertaining to LGBT people. Finally, the Department of Justice removed information relating to transgender victims of sexual assault.

The White House and federal agencies also removed data concerning climate change from agency websites and databases. The Environmental Protection Agency, the White House Council on Environmental Quality, and the Office of Science and Technology Policy deleted several climate resources and datasets.[13] Among other topics, the affected data addressed climate change challenges for "*marginalized*" communities, a buzz word that apparently suggested the data was related to "DEI." The White House also ordered the Department of Agriculture to take down *all* websites referencing the climate crisis, including data farmers rely upon in planting and harvesting crops.

Federal agencies appear to have implemented President Trump's Orders by conducting a whole-of-government artificial intelligence-facilitated search for offending terms such as "gender," "equity," and "disparate impact." Agencies have since restored some portion of the materials they initially deleted. However, it is difficult and perhaps in some cases impossible to know whether and to what extent other deletions have occurred or may occur in the future. Again, this information is invaluable to health care providers, scholars, and scientists in a variety of fields.

As indicated, the federal government can choose to communicate what it wishes, including on agency websites. The First Amendment does not entitle the public or others to access specific information—although some federal statutes may limit the government's authority to remove or delete certain information. As a general matter, implementation of Trump 2.0 Executive Orders has restricted the free flow of historical, scientific, and other information. The administration's actions have broadly and purposefully "limit[ed] the stock of information from which members of the public may draw."[14]

DISCUSSION

1. *Politics and Information Flow.* Consider the following comments by a data scientist and a head of libraries:

   > While database updates and website changes are routine, this is probably the first time Americans are witnessing deletion weaponized on a large scale as a political tool. These deletions undermine basic good government—and the historical record. Democratic governments need far more robust legal frameworks and safeguards for data that is essential to citi-

> zens' well-being. Scientific practices may change, policies may shift, and history may be debated, but the record of government should endure, regardless of who holds power.

Nanna Bonde Thylstrup and Richard Ovenden, *Politicians Shouldn't Get to Delate Inconvenient Facts*, N.Y. Times (Apr. 11, 2025).

2. *Preserving Information.* Consider the various audiences or potential recipients of agency information, and how alterations to government websites might affect them. Should there be a First Amendment *right* to access at least certain kinds of governmental information, something akin to a "right to remember"? Can and should Congress enact a law requiring the Executive Branch to maintain and preserve some government databases? If so, which databases, for how long, and under what standards?

3. *Presidential Records.* Congress has recognized certain information is critically important in terms of maintaining governmental transparency. For example, the Presidential Records Act of 1978 (PRA), 44 U.S.C. §§ 2201–2209, requires that Presidents and Vice Presidents retain certain records and provide them to the National Archives. Congress passed the PRA in the aftermath of the Watergate scandal that ended Richard Nixon's presidency. After bitterly complaining about the role of the National Archives in a criminal investigation relating to his retention of classified documents, President Trump fired the National Archivist and put Secretary of State Marco Rubio in charge of the National Archives. The President did not provide a reason for the Archivist's termination. What effect might presidential control of the National Archives have on governmental recordkeeping, transparency, and accountability?

4. *Statutory Data Protections.* Some courts have invalidated Trump 2.0 agency data removals on *statutory* grounds. A district court granted a temporary restraining order to Doctors for America, a nonprofit organization of physicians and medical trainees, which challenged the removal of certain health-related datasets from agency websites. *Doctors For America v. Office of Personnel Management*, 766 F. Supp.3d 39 (D.D.C. 2025). In *Doctors for America*, the court concluded that the agency had violated the Administrative Procedure Act by failing to engage in "reasoned decision-making" before deleting the healthcare data. *Id.* at 53. It also determined that the data

removal had caused irreparable harm to teachers and physicians who relied on these materials. *Id.* at 54. In another case, a group of farmers successfully sued to have climate-related data restored to the Department of Agriculture's website, again on the ground that the agency failed to comply with statutory requirements. The agency then agreed to restore the data. *See* Karen Zraick, *Farmers Sued Over Deleted Climate Change Data. So the Government Will Put It Back*, N.Y. TIMES (May 12, 2025).

B. MUSEUMS, PARKS, AND LIBRARIES

Museums, public parks, and public libraries are all critically important to the distribution of information about American history, culture, and other subjects. President Trump has issued an Executive Order addressing the content of displays at museums and parks. He also issued an Executive Order that directed the elimination of the Institute of Museum and Library Services (IMLS), which is the only federal agency dedicated to funding library services in the U.S. The IMLS supports libraries through funding grants, research, and policy development. Finally, the Defense Department has implemented the president's Executive Orders on "DEI" and gender in ways affecting classroom instruction and students' access to library books. The following materials consider the effects of these executive actions on the free flow of information.

1. Historical Narratives

President Trump has issued several Executive Orders that affect the distribution of information about American history. In *Restoring Truth and Sanity to American History*, the President declared:

> Over the past decade, Americans have witnessed a concerted and widespread effort to rewrite our Nation's history, replacing objective facts with a distorted narrative driven by ideology rather than truth. This revisionist movement seeks to undermine the remarkable achievements of the United States by casting its founding principles and historical milestones in a negative light.[15]

The President's *Restoring Truth and Sanity* Order applies to "the Smithsonian Institution and its museums, education and research centers, and the National Zoo."[16] More broadly, it directs federal agencies to "restore Federal sites dedicated to history, including parks and museums, to solemn and uplifting public monuments that remind Americans of our extraordinary heritage, consistent progress toward becoming a more perfect Union, and unmatched record of advancing liberty, prosperity, and human flourishing."[17]

"Museums in our Nation's capital," the President has asserted, "should be places where individuals go to learn—not to be subjected to ideological indoctrination or divisive narratives that distort our shared history."[18] Accordingly, President Trump directed the Vice President and other Administration officials to "remove improper ideology from such properties."[19] He also directed no future funding be provided for displays that "degrade shared American values, divide Americans based on race, or promote programs or ideologies inconsistent with Federal law."[20]

Section 4 of the Order responds to the backlash against and removal of Confederate statutes in the wake of George Floyd's murder in 2020. It directs the Secretary of the Interior to:

> (a) determine whether, since January 1, 2020, public monuments, memorials, statues, markers, or similar properties within the Department of the Interior's jurisdiction have been removed or changed to perpetuate a false reconstruction of American history, inappropriately minimize the value of certain historical events or figures, or include any other improper partisan ideology;
>
> (b) take action to reinstate the pre-existing monuments, memorials, statues, markers, or similar properties, as appropriate and consistent with [federal laws]; and
>
> (c) take action, as appropriate and consistent with applicable law, to ensure that all public monuments, memorials, statues, markers, or similar properties within the Department of the Interior's jurisdiction do not contain descriptions, depictions, or other content that inappropriately disparage Americans past or living (including persons living in colonial times), and instead focus on the greatness of the achievements and progress of the American people or, with

respect to natural features, the beauty, abundance, and grandeur of the American landscape.

President Trump has also issued three other Executive Orders that have affected the presentation of historical information and narratives. As discussed in Chapter 4, these Orders broadly directed that federal funds not be used to support or promote "DEI," "gender ideology," or "unpatriotic education" at federally funded K-12 schools.[21] As discussed above, executive agencies have relied on these Orders to remove disfavored information and data about race, gender, and other subjects from agency websites and databases. There is some overlap between and among the Executive Orders. For example, the *Restoring Truth and Sanity* Order directs that museums "celebrate the achievements of women in the American Women's History Museum and do not recognize men as women in any respect in the Museum."[22]

President Trump's Executive Orders will have a significant effect on what historical information visitors to the Nation's museums and national parks will receive. Employees at the National Park Service (NPS) have been ordered to report any items or displays that may be inconsistent with the President's *Restoring Truth and Sanity* or other Executive Orders.[23] The NPS has also invited visitors to parks and museums to suggest revisions or removals.

According to a review of items identified as part of this process, flagged materials have included books about slavery, the Civil War, civil rights, the first Native American cabinet secretary, George Washington's ownership of slaves, and other items that mention or discuss the history of racism or sexism in the United States.[24] Agency websites, signs, educational films, displays, panels, and other materials have been scoured for potentially offending material, which may be subject to removal or revision in line with the president's Executive Orders. Reporting indicates that some National Park Service employees, concerned that their failure to flag offending items will cost them their jobs, have painted with a broad brush. As in other contexts, the breadth and ambiguity of the Executive Orders has produced a degree of over-compliance.

The Interior Department has insisted that its review process "reinforces our commitment to telling the full and accurate story of our nation's past."[25] Not everyone agrees. For example, a group of historians, librarians and data experts at the University of Minnesota launched a "Save our Signs" project, encouraging people to post images of signs to preserve information that could be removed.[26] Their website proclaims, "Real history is not just happy stories."[27]

DISCUSSION

1. *Government Speech and Information Flow.* Under the government speech doctrine, the Executive Branch can express and advance its preferred historical narratives and exclude those it does not wish to communicate or support. Historians or others whose displays or depictions are removed by federal officials from national museums or parks generally cannot object on First Amendment grounds. Although the President's directives restrict the free flow of information to the significant part of the American public visiting national parks, no visitor has a First Amendment right to insist that specific historical information or materials be displayed on governmental properties.

2. *History and Historians.* As noted, professional historians and other information professionals have expressed concerns about President Trump's *Restoring Truth and Sanity* order. The American Historical Association issued a statement that included the following comments:

   > Historians explore the past to understand how our nation has evolved. We draw on a wide range of sources, which helps us to understand history from different angles of vision. Our goal is neither criticism nor celebration; it is to understand—to increase our knowledge of—the past in ways that can help Americans to shape the future.
   >
   > The stories that have shaped our past include not only elements that make us proud but also aspects that make us acutely aware of tragedies in our nation's history. No person, no nation, is perfect, and we should all—as individuals and as nations—learn from our imperfections.

   "Historians Defend the Smithsonian," *Approved by AHA Council*, March 31, 2025.

3. *Historical Truths.* According to a Fact Sheet accompanying the *Restoring Truth and Sanity* Executive Order, President Trump declared that he "is fighting back by reestablishing truth in the historical

narrative." Critics have responded that the administration is seeking to declare historical half-truths and present a sanitized version of American history. Is the problem not the attempt to achieve some balance in the American narrative, but rather that a government official is dictating that balance by defunding and controlling information centers? Is there any difference between a governmental command to *remove* Confederate statues and a government command to *re-install* them?

4. *Civic Institutions.* President Trump's efforts to override museum and information experts and impose historical "truths" is part of a broader campaign to control civic institutions including the Bar, universities, the press, and libraries. What, if anything, do these institutions have in common?

---

2. Libraries and Information Access

Like its museums and parks, America's public libraries facilitate the free flow of information and the distribution of knowledge. Libraries provide books and many other educational resources to the public. In 1996, Congress established the Institute of Museum and Library Services to "create strong libraries and museums that connect people with information and ideas" that envision "a democratic society where communities and individuals thrive with broad public access to knowledge, cultural heritage, and lifelong learning."[28] One of President Trump's Executive Orders effectively eliminated the IMLS.[29]

Meanwhile, other Trump Executive Orders have affected school libraries operated by federal departments. In a recent lawsuit, students challenged the exclusion of library books at Department of Defense schools.

The Department of Defense Education Activity (DoDEA) provides pre-kindergarten, elementary, and secondary education to approximately 67,000 dependents of military personnel around the world. In response to President Trump's Executive Orders banning "gender ideology" and "discriminatory equity ideology" from federally funded education, DoDEA placed hundreds of school library books in "quarantine" and reviewed them for permanent removal. (Additionally, DoDEA educators were instructed to revise their curricula to remove discussions of gender, race, immigration, and various facets of developmental health.)

In *E.K. and S.K. v. Dept. of Defense Education Activity*, No. 1:25-cv-00637-PTG-IDD (E.D. Va.), parents of children attending DoDEA schools challenged the book removals and limits on classroom discussions. The excerpts below, which focus on the library book "quarantines," are from the parties' preliminary injunction pleadings.

Memorandum in Support of Plaintiffs' Motion for a Preliminary Injunction

INTRODUCTION

In public schools serving military families around the globe, the Government is quarantining books from school libraries and scrubbing references to race and gender from the curriculum. In January 2025, President Trump issued Executive Orders targeting "gender ideology" and "discriminatory equity ideology" across federal agencies, the military, and K-12 schools. The Department of Defense Education Activity ("DoDEA"), the civilian subagency tasked with running schools on military bases, moved swiftly to comply. DoDEA has removed hundreds of books from circulation, including canonical and award-winning titles like *To Kill a Mockingbird* and *Julian Is a Mermaid*. Plaintiffs, twelve DoDEA students ranging from pre-kindergarten to eleventh grade, are suffering ongoing and irreparable harm because of this egregious Government censorship.

The Supreme Court has long recognized that public school students have a First Amendment right to access information in public libraries and in school curricula. In *Board of Education v. Pico*, ("*Pico*"), the Supreme Court, in a plurality opinion, set forth the principle that the First Amendment provides guardrails against Government attempts to turn public school libraries into "partisan or political" battlegrounds. *Bd. of Educ. v. Pico*, 457 U.S. 853 (1982).

Plaintiffs seek a preliminary injunction to protect students' First Amendment right to receive information and ideas free from political and ideological censorship. The Court should declare DoDEA's actions to enforce the Executive Orders unconstitutional and order DoDEA to revoke its memoranda implementing EO guidance; restore quarantined books to school shelves; and prohibit further book and curricular removals based on those materials' perceived connection to "gender ideology" and "discriminatory equity ideology."

ARGUMENT

"Our Constitution does not permit the official suppression of ideas." *Pico*, 457 U.S. at 871 (plurality op.). When the government singles out specific ideas for suppression, just for the sake of suppressing disfavored views, courts are required to intervene.

As a corollary to the First Amendment's protection against government censorship of speech, it also protects listening and learning. It is long-established that the Government may not infringe on "the right to receive information and ideas." *Stanley v. Georgia*, 394 U.S. 557, 564 (1969); *Lamont v. Postmaster Gen.*, 381 U.S. 301, 306–07 (1965) (holding that the First Amendment protects Americans' right to receive "communist political propaganda" through the mail). Since students do not shed their constitutional rights to freedom of speech or expression at the schoolhouse gate, *Tinker v. Des Moines Indep. Cmty. Sch. Dist.*, 393 U.S. 503, 506 (1969), it follows that students also maintain their First Amendment right to access information at school. Indeed, while "all First Amendment rights accorded to students must be construed in light of the special characteristics of the school environment," *Pico*, 457 U.S. at 868, the "vigilant protection of constitutional freedoms is nowhere more vital than in the community of American schools." *Tinker*, 393 U.S. at 512.

For more than forty years, the First Amendment has constrained public schools' libraries from removing books based on political disagreements. In its only case addressing public school library holdings, the Supreme Court made clear that "school officials may not remove books for the purpose of restricting access to the political ideas or social perspectives discussed in them, when that action is motivated simply by the officials' disapproval of the ideas involved." *Pico*, 457 U.S. at 879–80 (J. BLACKMUN, concurring); *id.* at 872 (plurality op.).

In *Pico*, parents in a New York school district had obtained a list of "objectionable" books at a conservative education conference. Upon learning that some of the listed books were present in the district's libraries, members of the school board aligned with the concerned parents directed the removal of nine books. Students who had been denied access to the library books sued to vindicate their First Amendment rights.

A plurality of the Supreme Court held that "local school boards may not remove books from school library shelves simply because they dislike the ideas contained in those books and seek by their removal to 'prescribe what shall be orthodox in politics, nationalism, religion, or other matters of opinion.'" *Id.* at 872 (plurality opinion) (quoting *W. Va. Bd. of Educ. v. Barnette*, 319 U.S. 624, 642 (1943)). In so doing, the plurality made clear that "the First Amendment rights of students may be directly and sharply implicated by the removal of books from the shelves of a school library." *Pico*, 457 U.S. at 866. The plurality opinion recognized that "just as access to ideas makes it possible for citizens generally to exercise their rights of free speech and press in a meaningful manner, such access prepares students for active and effective participation in the pluralistic, often contentious society in which they will soon be adult members." *Id.* at 868.

It is hard to overstate the reverence for school libraries held by the members of the *Pico* court. The plurality highlighted that "the special characteristics of the school library make that environment especially appropriate for the recognition of the First Amendment rights of students." *Id.* It recognized that "[a] school library, no less than any other public library, is a place dedicated to quiet, to knowledge, and to beauty.' *Id.* The plurality further emphasized that "students must always remain free to inquire, to study and to evaluate, to gain new maturity and understanding" and that "[t]he school library is the principal locus of such freedom." *Pico*, 457 U.S. at 868–69. In a school library "a student can literally explore the unknown, and discover areas of interest and thought not covered by the prescribed curriculum. The student learns that a library is a place to test or expand upon ideas presented to him, in or out of the classroom." *Id.* at 869.

At the same time, the plurality recognized that school officials "rightly possess significant discretion to determine the content of their school libraries." *Pico*, 457 U.S. at 870. Government defendants had "argue[d] that they must be allowed unfettered discretion to 'transmit community values' through the Island Trees schools." *Id.* at 869. The plurality recognized that it could "not deny that local school boards have a substantial legitimate role to play in the determination of school library content," but explicitly rejected their "claim of absolute discretion to remove books from their school libraries." *Id.* at 869.

The plurality opinion stands for the proposition that the discretion necessarily afforded to school officials to decide on school library contents "may not be exercised in a narrowly partisan or political manner." *Id.* at 870. As such, whether school officials' "removal of books from their school libraries denied [student plaintiffs] their First Amendment rights depends upon the motivation behind petitioners' actions." *Id.* at 871.

The plurality then outlined constitutional versus impermissible motivations for removing books. "If [government defendants] intended by their removal decision to deny [student plaintiffs] access to ideas with which [the government] disagreed, and if this intent was the decisive factor in [the government's] decision, then [government defendants] have exercised their discretion in violation of the Constitution." *Id.* Perhaps anticipating an ideological purge akin to what is happening in DoDEA schools, the plurality provided the hypothetical example of "an all-white school board, motivated by racial animus, decid[ing] to remove all books authored by blacks or advocating racial equality and integration." *Id.* 870–71. In such a situation, the plurality said, "few would doubt that the order violated the constitutional rights of the students denied access to those books." *Id.*

By contrast, the plurality recognized that "an unconstitutional motivation would not be demonstrated if it were shown that [government defendants] had decided to remove the books at issue because those books were pervasively vulgar [. . . or] the removal decision was based solely upon the 'educational suitability' of the books in question." *Id.* at 871. The plurality opinion pointed out that it "would be a very different case if the record demonstrated the [government] had employed established, regular, and facially unbiased procedures for the review of controversial materials." *Id.* at 874. Instead, the school board's "removal procedures were highly irregular and ad hoc–the antithesis of those procedures that might tend to allay suspicions regarding [government officials'] motivations." *Id.* at 875. Ultimately, the plurality concluded that the Island Trees School Board's "decision to remove the books rested decisively upon disagreement with the constitutionally protected ideas in those books, or upon a desire on [the School Board's] part to impose upon the students of the Island Trees High School and Junior High School a political orthodoxy to which petitioners and their constituents adhered." *Id.*

Even though *Pico* yielded four separate opinions, none of which is joined by five justices, a majority of Justices on the *Pico* Court agreed that removing books from school libraries implicates students' First Amendment rights. Post-*Pico*, circuit courts have noted the fractured opinions, but the plurality's holding continues to be applied by circuit courts. Even courts that emphasize that *Pico* is technically nonbinding stop short of rejecting its guidance.

Because the First Amendment prohibits ideological book removals in public school libraries, DoDEA's censorship pursuant to the Executive Orders and implementing instructions must be enjoined. Plaintiffs seek an injunction against the Government's removal of books based on political disagreements with what the government refers to as "gender ideology" and "discriminatory equity ideology"—*i.e.*, exactly the sorts of "partisan or political" reasons that *Pico* forbids. The Court should enjoin Defendants from removing more books from DoDEA libraries pursuant to Executive Orders and restore the prior status quo by ordering that all quarantined books be restored to circulation.

Defendants' Memorandum of Law in Opposition to Plaintiffs' Motion for a Preliminary Injunction

INTRODUCTION

In America's federalist system, it is the public authorities, like school boards, that are charged with administering the nation's public schools. Moreover, the Supreme Court has repeatedly cautioned that federal courts do not have a role in refereeing the conflicts that might arise regarding educational matters in the school system as those can and should be worked out at the local level. Yet, despite these well-entrenched principles in American jurisprudence, Plaintiffs invite this Court to serve as the Superintendent of five schools within the Department of Defense Education Activity ("DoDEA") school system for choices concerning books in their libraries.

Plaintiffs cannot establish a clear likelihood of success on the merits of their Free Speech claims. As ample case law shows, curating a library collection is an act of government speech. It is therefore not subject to rigorous scrutiny under the First Amendment's Free Speech Clause. Even if that were not the case, Plaintiffs cannot establish that DoDEA schools' reviews were motivated by any impermissible reason other than a pedagogical concern for its schoolchildren. Pursuant to the President's Executive Orders and the educational objectives of the Department, the book reviews were undertaken to implement DoDEA's current pedagogical approach to teaching schoolchildren regarding gender and sexuality and to better promote an inclusive environment. There is nothing constitutionally improper in that decision.

ARGUMENT

At the outset, "public education in our Nation is committed to the control of state and local authorities," and as such, federal courts should not "intervene in the resolution of conflicts which arise in the daily operation of school systems." *Tinker v. Des Moines Ind. Cmty. Sch. Dist.*, 393 U.S. 503, 507 (1969). To that end, the Supreme Court "has repeatedly emphasized the need for affirming the comprehensive authority" of the schools and their officials "to prescribe and control conduct in the schools." *Id.* "This standard is consistent with our oft-expressed view that the education of the Nation's youth is primarily the responsibility of parents, teachers, and state and local school officials, and not of federal judges." *Hazelwood Sch. Dist. v. Kuhlmeier*, 484 U.S. 260, 273 (1988). Yet despite these clear principles, Plaintiffs nevertheless ask this Court to weigh the specific educational merits of DoDEA's ongoing review of its library book collections in the five DoDEA schools that Plaintiffs attend.

Despite Plaintiffs' demand, they have no recourse under the First Amendment's Free Speech Clause to challenge DoDEA schools' reviews of their library collections. [This activity is] government speech and therefore "do[es] not . . . trigger the First Amendment rules designed to protect the marketplace of ideas." *Walker v. Tex. Div. Sons of Confederate Veterans, Inc.*, 576 U.S. 200, 207 (2015).

There is no doubt that curating a library is an expressive act performed by the government. Curating a library collection for schoolchildren accounts for, among other things, selecting age-appropriate materials that are suitable for schoolchildren's educational needs. At DoDEA specifically, the library in each school is individual to the school and all libraries endeavor to provide a well-balanced collection that supports the school's curriculum, reflects the interests of the local school community, and supports special needs and programs. As the Supreme Court's decision in *Moody v. NetChoice, LLC*, 603 U.S. 707, 728 (2024) illustrates, curation qualifies as an expressive act. Indeed, "[d]eciding on the third-party speech that will be included in or excluded from a compilation—and then organizing and presenting the included items—is expressive activity of its own." *Id.* at 731. This is what DoDEA librarians and educators do when curating their library collections, evaluating a host of criteria to determine whether a book is educationally appropriate.

The inclusion, or exclusion, of certain materials reflects DoDEA's expressive act of speech that it wishes to convey to its audience—here, schoolchildren. DoDEA's libraries are thus like the social media platforms in *Moody*, for DoDEA's libraries "combin[e] 'multifarious voices' to create a distinctive expressive offering." 603 U.S. at 738. *Cf. United States v. Am. Libr. Ass'n, Inc.*, 539 U.S. 194, 204 (2003) (Rehnquist, C.J., plurality op.) ("[L]ibraries collect only those materials deemed to have the requisite and appropriate quality.").

Accordingly, DoDEA's expressive act of curating its libraries is a form of government speech exempted from significant scrutiny under the Free Speech Clause of the First Amendment. As such, DoDEA "has the right to speak for itself" and may thus curate its library collection in the manner it sees best for educating its schoolchildren. *Pleasant Grove City v. Summum*, 555 U.S. 460, 467 (2009) (quotation omitted).

Under Plaintiffs' theory, every individual book acquisition and removal are potentially subject to judicial scrutiny if a library patron believes there has been an act of viewpoint discrimination. If this were so, understandably, such challenges would grind DoDEA's educational mission to halt—slowing the process by which DoDEA schools curate their collections at best, or at worst, incentivizing DoDEA to cease providing libraries to its schoolchildren altogether.

Though Plaintiffs may disagree with the Government's current speech in this context, it is the democratic electoral process that nevertheless first and foremost provides a check on government speech.

Plaintiffs are incorrect that the Supreme Court's decision in *Pico* governs this case. At best, *Pico*'s precedential holding is as follows: given the factual disputes in the record, summary judgment was not properly granted to the school district. *See Pico*, 457 U.S. at 883–84 (White, J., concurring in the judgment).

Many courts agree that *Pico* supplies no precedential value. [description of lower court decisions omitted] Thus, the plurality opinion does not control this case.

Even if Plaintiffs were correct that *Pico*'s plurality opinion applies, DoDEA's reviews of the five libraries' resources withstand scrutiny under that standard. Per the *Pico* plurality, school boards cannot constitutionally exercise their discretion to determine the content of school libraries "in a narrowly partisan or political manner." *Pico*, 457 U.S. at

870 (Brennan, J., plurality op.). Not only must the school board's motive be "narrowly partisan or political," but this "unconstitutional" intent must be "the decisive factor in the board's decision." *Id.* at 871. Stated differently, the constitutionally impermissible motive was the but for cause of the decision. Examples of impermissible motives the plurality identified were: "[i]f a Democratic school board, motivated by party affiliation, ordered the removal of all books written by or in favor of Republicans;" or "if an all-white school board, motivated by racial animus, decided to remove all books authored by blacks or advocating racial equality and integration." *Id.* at 870–71. By contrast, the *Pico* plurality indicated that it would be "perfectly permissible" for a school board to remove books based on the "educational suitability" of the book. *Id.* at 871.

Plaintiffs have not identified that any decision was "narrowly partisan" or politically motivated. In Plaintiffs' view, without much by way of supporting evidence, the Executive Orders "are based on what the current presidential administration deems to be politically incorrect." But such a conclusory assertion does not definitively establish that "narrowly partisan" motivations were the "decisive factor" as to any one book. Only the pedagogical concern of ensuring that students receive instruction on the biological binary of sex and promoting inclusivity values through merit (and thereby eliminating any remaining vestiges of discrimination) motivated the change in course and drive the continued reviews until final decisions are made.

It is a significant logical leap to conclude that teaching students about the binary sexes is a "narrowly partisan" act—as the *Pico* plurality defined the term—given the state of debate and discourse of the last several years. The same is true with respect to teaching and building an inclusive environment based on values and merit rather than immutable traits. The former is grounded in established scientific understanding and the latter comports with the Supreme Court's understanding of equal treatment in federally-funded school systems. *See Students for Fair Admissions, Inc. v. President & Fellows of Harvard Coll.*, 600 U.S. 181, 231 (2023) ("In other words, the student must be treated based on his or her experiences as an individual—not on the basis of race.").

Plaintiffs' claims of partisanship are further dispelled given the systematic reviews that DoDEA is employing for the collections in the five schools. With the identification for review complete, subject matter experts at DoDEA in each content area made a recommendation for each identified material that was further vetted. As that process has concluded, each of the identified materials is then subjected to an even more focused review that assesses the educational and pedagogical value of each resource prior to making a recommendation for final disposition of these materials. Once the entirety of these reviews is completed, final recommendations will be presented to the Director of DoDEA, who will in turn provide her final assessments and recommendations to the deciding official. In sum, DoDEA supplied at least three layers of secondary review for each of the materials to assess their educational and pedagogical value before a determination is made. This three-layer review makes this case quite different from *Pico* and thereby underscores the lack of narrowly partisan motivations in this case.

DISCUSSION

1. *Preliminary Injunction* The district court granted plaintiffs' motion for preliminary injunction. *E.K. and S.K. v. Department of Defense Education Activity*, ___F. Supp. 3d ___, 2025 WL 2969560 (E.D. Va., Oct. 20, 2025). The court rejected the argument that the government's book removals were a form of government speech. It also concluded the removals were motivated by partisan interests rather than pedagogical concerns.

2. *Public School Library Book Removals.* As the briefs in *E.K.* show, the state of the law in terms of removal of public school library books is not clear. Although several lower courts have issued decisions in book removal cases, the decision in *Pico* is the Supreme Court's *only* precedent on the subject. What precedential weight or value should lower courts assign to *Pico*?

3. *Public Library Book Removals.* Conflicts have also arisen over the removal of books from public libraries *not* affiliated with public schools. Here, too, lower courts have reached different conclusions regarding the application of *Pico* and First Amendment doctrines. In a recent decision, the full U.S. Court of Appeals for the Fifth Circuit concluded that public library patrons do not have a First Amendment right to challenge the removal of books from public libraries. *See Little v. Llano County*, 138 F.4th 834 (5th Cir. 2025) (*en banc*). In *Little*, the Fifth Circuit observed that there is no "brave new right to receive information from the government in the form of taxpayer-funded

library books." The court also held that *Pico* did not establish a binding precedent. Further, a plurality of the appeals court's judges concluded that the selection and removal of public library books constituted government speech. Among the titles at issue in *Little* were Isabel Wilkerson, *Caste: The Origins of Our Discontent*; Susan Campbell Bartoletti, *Called Themselves the KKK: The Birth of an American Terrorist Group*; Tillie Walden, *Spinning*; Maurice Sendak, *In the Night Kitchen*; and Robie Harris, *It's Perfectly Normal: Changing Bodies, Growing Up, Sex and Sexual Health*.

4. *Censorship and the free flow of information*. The Fifth Circuit majority in *Little* wrote, "Take a deep breath, everyone. No one is banning (or burning) books. If a disappointed patron can't find a book in the library, he can order it online, buy it from a bookstore, or borrow it from a friend." Does the (assumed) ability to locate a source *somewhere* make the decision to remove it from the public library any less censorious?

C. SCIENTIFIC RESEARCH

The production and distribution of scientific information are vitally important to the free flow of information. President Trump has issued an Executive Order, *Restoring Gold Standard Science*.[30] The Order accused prior administrations of politicizing science, including with regard to the Covid-19 pandemic and climate change studies.[31] The president stated that his administration is "committed to restoring a gold standard for science" and "restor[ing] the American people's faith in the scientific enterprise and institutions that create and apply scientific knowledge in service of the public good."[32]

The *Gold Standard* Order directed federal agencies to "practice data transparency, acknowledge relevant scientific uncertainties, [be] transparent about the assumptions and likelihood of scenarios used, approach scientific findings objectively, and communicate scientific data accurately."[33] To further these ends, however, President Trump's directive put political appointees in charge of vetting scientific research and gave them the authority to "correct scientific information," control the manner in which it is communicated to the public, and "discipline" those who run afoul of the Trump Administration's scientific standards.[34] Before he became Secretary of the U.S. Department of Health and Human Services, Robert F. Kennedy, Jr. said of medical journals: "I'm going to litigate against you under the racketeering laws, under the general tort laws" and "I'm going to find a way to sue you unless you come up with a plan right now to show how you're going to start publishing real science and stop retracting the real science and publishing the fake pharmaceutical science by these phony industry mercenaries."[35]

Scientists have expressed concerns that the *Gold Standard* and other presidential directives, including those relating to "DEI" and gender, insert politics into research and provide a pretext for discounting or ignoring scientific evidence that does not comport with the Trump Administration's politics.[36] The administration has taken various actions that highlight and, in some cases, corroborate these concerns. Consider the following examples:

- Scientists at the National Institutes of Health (NIH) and others working outside government have complained that administration officials have censored their work based on prohibited terms or concepts and barred them from giving interviews about studies contradicting the administration's positions.[37]
- A federal prosecutor sent a "letter of inquiry" to medical journals, asking about their selection process for scientific articles and suggesting they may be falsifying their results or engaging in corrupt practices.[38]
- The Trump Administration terminated or threatened to terminate billions of dollars in federal funding for universities, including support for scientific and medical research—without regard to whether the research meets "Gold" or any other scientific standards.
- The NIH has terminated funding for more than 100 research grants involving transgender people.[39]
- The Trump Administration has laid off thousands of researchers, frozen grants from the National Science Foundation, and announced plans to eliminate entire agency science and research departments.[40]

As this partial list shows, the *Gold Standard* Executive Order and agency implementing actions have threatened the free flow of information. As in other areas, scientists and researchers have self-censored to avoid sanction. Universities have canceled lectures based on concerns that the "anti-government" tone of presentations might upset the Trump Administration.[41] And legal counsel at hospitals have warned staff not to use "triggering" words like "vulnerable" or "diverse" to describe their patients during treatment or in presentations.[42]

President Trump's Executive Orders are part of a *system* of speech regulation rather than a series of isolated directives. For example, the *Gold Standard* Order is not the only presidential order that affects scientific inquiry. Consider the following decision, which addressed federal agencies' decisions to remove scientific papers from a governmental online portal because they contained disfavored terms and concepts regarding *gender*, which was the subject of another Executve Order.

DOCTRINAL SYNOPSIS: VIEWPOINT NEUTRALITY

- "If there is any fixed star in our constitutional constellation, it is that no official, high or petty, can prescribe what shall be orthodox in politics, nationalism, religion, or other matters of opinion or force citizens to confess by word or act their faith therein." *West Virginia Bd. of Education v. Barnette* (1943)
- Speech regulations that suppress disfavored viewpoints are *presumptively* invalid: they are valid only if narrowly tailored to further compelling governmental interests.

Schiff v. Office of Personnel Management

784 F. Supp. 3d 380 (D. Mass. 2025)

SOROKIN, J.

The plaintiffs in this action are physicians and professors who challenge the removal of articles they authored from an online patient-safety resource launched and hosted by the federal government. They allege violations of their First Amendment rights arising from the implementation by three government agencies of an Executive Order concerning "gender ideology." The plaintiffs are likely to succeed in proving that the removal of their articles was a textbook example of viewpoint discrimination by the defendants in violation of the First Amendment.

Background

In 1999, Congress created the Agency for Healthcare Research and Quality ("AHRQ") within the Department of Health and Human Services ("HHS"). 42 U.S.C. § 299(a). AHRQ's purpose is to enhance the quality and effectiveness of health services through the establishment of a broad base of scientific research and promotion of improvements in clinical and health system practices. Congress required the Secretary of HHS to "facilitate the creation of, and maintain, a network of patient safety databases that provides an interactive evidence-based management resource for providers, patient safety organizations, and other entities." § 299b-23(a). AHRQ was tasked with using information gathered via the network to "analyze national and regional statistics, including trends and patterns of health care errors." § 299b-23(c). Congress further directed that "information resulting from such analyses shall be made available to the public." *Id.*

Early on, AHRQ sought to leverage the power of the internet to build upon a tradition within the medical profession of learning from mistakes by discussing them with colleagues at in-person "morbidity and mortality" ("M&M") conferences. AHRQ initiated an online series of case studies serving as a nationwide, ongoing M&M conference aimed at discussing and preventing diagnostic errors. Two years later, in 2005, AHRQ launched the Patient Safety Network ("PSNet"), a continuously updated Web-based portal designed to fill the need for a comprehensive information resource for those working in patient safety. By 2007, thousands of subscribers received PSNet's weekly newsletter. In 2015, AHRQ merged its series of case studies into PSNet to create a unified patient-safety resource. PSNet's editors estimated in 2024 that the site received more than three million page views annually.

A form on PSNet allowed practitioners to submit information about medical errors they encountered, including a general description of the patient, relevant events and factors contributing to the error, the effects of the error on the patient, and suggestions for avoiding similar errors in the future. The editorial team would review submissions, selecting cases to feature on PSNet based on their clinical and educational value, among other criteria. Subject-matter experts were then identified and invited to write a case study, or commentary, about the error and lessons to be learned from it. Expert commentary published on PSNet contained a standard disclaimer informing readers that the content did not represent the views of AHRQ or HHS.

Dr. Gordon Schiff is a practicing physician and an Associate Professor of Medicine at Harvard Medical School. Dr. Celeste Royce is a practicing physician and an Assistant Professor of Obstetrics, Gynecology, and Reproductive Biology at Harvard Medical School. During their decades-long careers, Drs. Schiff and Royce have each researched and written about patient safety. Each has authored commentaries related to their areas of practice that were selected for publication on PSNet. One PSNet commentary by Dr. Royce and one by Dr. Schiff are particularly relevant here, as recent events involving those commentaries gave rise to this lawsuit.

Following a conference she co-led in January 2020, Dr. Royce co-authored a commentary on a case study concerning a delayed diagnosis of endometriosis. The draft commentary was submitted to PSNet in early May 2020. An editorial process ensued, during which feedback centered on ensuring the commentary focused on the diagnostic process (as opposed to "the details of endometriosis" or "other medical issues"). Dr. Royce and her co-author revised the draft to align more closely with the patient safety focus of PSNet, and the commentary was published on PSNet in June 2020. The commentary concluded with a series of "Take-Home Points," the last of which was:

> Although not germane to this particular case, it is important to note that endometriosis can occur in trans and non-gender-conforming people and lack of understanding this fact could make diagnosis in these populations even more challenging. Therefore, endometriosis should be considered in the differential diagnosis for any person presenting with chronic abdominal or pelvic pain.

This language appeared in the draft commentary when it was first submitted to PSNet; it was not the subject of any discussion or feedback during the editing process. The published version of the commentary includes a standard disclaimer specifying that the authors were responsible for its contents, which "do not necessarily represent the views of AHRQ" and should not be understood "as an official position of AHRQ or" HHS.

In September 2021, Dr. Schiff and two co-authors submitted to PSNet a draft commentary on assessing suicide risk. The draft was accepted for publication, and an editorial process followed during which a series of revisions occurred through November 2021 in response to peer review and feedback. The commentary was published on PSNet in January 2022. In a section entitled "Approaches to Improving Safety," the commentary noted the importance of "having knowledge of which populations are at higher risk of suicide." It went on: "High risk groups include male sex, being young, veterans, Indigenous tribes, lesbian, gay, bisexual, transgender, queer/questioning (LGBTQ)." A footnote supporting this list of high-risk groups directed readers to an article in the *Journal of the American Medical Association*. This language was not challenged, nor its scientific accuracy or relevance questioned, during the editorial process. Dr. Schiff's commentary was also published with the standard disclaimer.

The day his second term in office began, President Donald Trump issued an executive order entitled "Defending Women From Gender Ideology Extremism and Restoring Biological Truth to the Federal Government" ("the EO"). Federal agencies were obligated to "remove all statements, policies, regulations, forms, communications, or other internal and external messages that promote or otherwise inculcate gender ideology." *Id.* § 3(e).

On January 29, 2025, OPM's Acting Director issued a memorandum entitled "Initial Guidance Regarding [the EO]" ("OPM Memo"). The OPM Memo directed agencies to "[t]ake down all outward facing media (websites, social media accounts, etc.) that inculcate or promote gender ideology" ("Takedown Directive").

Two days later, on the first deadline set by the OPM Memo, the Acting Secretary of HHS issued a memorandum with the subject line "Action: Initial Guidance Regarding [the EO]" ("HHS Memo"), requiring all "HHS Operating and Staff Divisions" to "tak[e] prompt actions" complying with and implementing the EO and the OPM Memo. The HHS Memo was accompanied by a form each division was required to complete and submit by February 6, 2025. A flurry of activity followed. Among the recipients of the HHS Memo was Margie Shofer, AHRQ's Division Director of General Patient Safety. Shofer received the HHS Memo the day it issued and promptly learned that AHRQ's Office of Communications was removing all web content that mentions gender and transgender topics in response to the Takedown Directive.

In short order, Shofer received a list of publications from PSNet that had been identified for removal using word searches targeting terminology that potentially conflicted with the EO and [the] OPM Memo's directives. Shofer narrowed the list to include only that content that was associated with the issues outlined in the [EO]. Nothing in the record sheds light on what criteria Shofer used to narrow the list. Her team sent the narrowed list to the contractor providing technical support for PS-Net and instructed the contractor to remove the identified articles from the website. Dr. Schiff received an email from PSNet's co-Editor in Chief, Dr. Patrick Romano, notifying him that his commentary on assessing suicide risk had been removed from PSNet "due to a perception that it violates the White House policy on websites 'that inculcate or promote gender ideology.'" Dr. Romano attached a copy of the OPM Memo to his email. In an ensuing exchange, Dr. Romano explained that AHRQ had been instructed to interpret the OPM Memo as requiring the removal of "anything with the words 'transgender,' 'nonbinary,' or 'gender identity,'" and that this also rendered the acronym LGBTQ "problematic because it includes that letter T for 'transgender.'"

Dr. Romano emailed Dr. Royce to notify her that her endometriosis commentary had been removed from PSNet, citing the same "perception" that had led to the removal of Dr. Schiff's article days earlier. In this email, Dr. Romano added that Dr. Royce's "publication ha[d] not been deleted," but was "simply archived so it can be restored to public access at a future time." Meanwhile, in response to a request from PSNet's technical-support contractor, Shofer agreed to try and explore whether the articles could be republished if their content were adjusted. The result of that exploration was communicated to the impacted authors, including Drs. Royce and Schiff, in an email from Dr. Romano sent on February 6, 2025. Per that email:

> AHRQ has received approval to re-post your original commentaries, which we have been discussing over the last several days. However, the condition is the removal of the problematic words—i.e., the words "transgender" and "LGBTQ." In the case of [Dr. Schiff's] commentary, this entails simply editing out just three words from a list of risk factors for suicide. In the case of [Dr. Royce's] commentary, this entails editing out just the very last sentence. These conditions are nonnegotiable.

Dr. Romano went on to say that "a prominent editor's note" would appear on the restored articles disclosing that they had been "updated to comply with" the EO.

Dr. Schiff responded later that day, declining to change his article. In his view, the required revision would have eliminated "evidence-based peer reviewed information" and "censor[ed] truth out to be replaced by nontruth." He offered to correct any factual inaccuracies that the government could identify and support with data or other evidence. Dr. Royce responded the next morning, saying she would not agree to delete the identified sentence from her commentary but would "be okay with" revising it to say "endometriosis can occur in any woman and is a rare but possible diagnosis in men." Her proposal elicited a series of responses from Dr. Romano. He wrote to reiterate that deletion of the sentence was "non-negotiable." He also conveyed "the Administration's view" that "endometriosis is not a possible diagnosis in men."

Because Drs. Schiff and Royce did not agree to the alterations required as conditions of reposting, their commentaries on suicide risk and endometriosis, respectively, remain unavailable on PSNet.

Analysis

There is no dispute that, for First Amendment purposes, PSNet is a limited public forum. *See Pleasant Grove City v. Summum*, 555 U.S. 460, 470 (2009) (describing settings in which private speech occurs on government property, including when "a government entity" creates "a forum that is limited to use by certain groups or dedicated solely to the discussion of certain subjects"). In such a forum, a government entity may impose restrictions on speech that are reasonable and viewpoint neutral. Though the government may reserve a limited public forum for its intended purposes, any regulation on speech it imposes must be "reasonable" and cannot amount to "an effort to suppress expression merely because public officials oppose the speaker's view." *Perry Educ. Ass'n v. Perry Loc. Educators' Ass'n*, 460 U.S. 37, 46 (1983). Thus, restrictions on private speech in a limited public forum must satisfy two conditions: reasonableness and viewpoint neutrality. If a restriction is reasonable but is not viewpoint-neutral—or vice versa—it will not withstand First Amendment scrutiny.

In their papers, the defendants mostly focused on arguing that the defendants had imposed reasonable restrictions on speech that were required by the EO. Their reasonableness argument is a nonstarter. Even if it were right—and it is not, for reasons the Court will mention in a moment—that would not diminish the plaintiffs' likelihood of success. The record establishes that the defendants' implementation of the EO produced restrictions on speech that are not viewpoint neutral. The defendants made no meaningful argument to the contrary in their papers, and they admitted at the motion hearing that AHRQ's actions in response to the Takedown Directive amounted to viewpoint discrimination.

The bedrock principle of viewpoint neutrality demands that the government not suppress speech where the real rationale for the restriction is disagreement with the underlying ideology or perspective that the speech expresses. The essence of viewpoint discrimination is a governmental intent to intervene in a way that prefers one particular viewpoint in speech over other perspectives on the same topic. That is precisely what Drs. Schiff and Royce have alleged—and persuasively supported with declarations and other exhibits.

The commentaries were removed from PSNet because of their expressive content. By the defendants' admission, they implemented the Takedown Directive by performing word searches to identify all publications that used certain words the defendants deemed inconsistent with the policy expressed in the EO. Items containing those words were removed without advance notice to the authors or PSNet's editors. Deletion of the offending words or sentences was a nonnegotiable prerequisite for reposting. Even passing references to people who identify themselves as transgender were deemed contrary to the perspective regarding gender identity set forth in the EO. Because the plaintiffs refused to change the content of their commentaries by removing words that acknowledged the existence of people who identify themselves as transgender, the defendants did not repost them.

This is a flagrant violation of the plaintiffs' First Amendment rights as private speakers on a limited public forum. The defendants' only response on this point is an assertion that the requirement of viewpoint neutrality is not absolute. Essentially, the defendants urge the Court to find that their admitted viewpoint discrimination did not rise to the level of a constitutional violation here. They offer no authority supporting this position, because there is none.

Because of the plaintiffs' powerful showing of viewpoint discrimination, the Court need not delve deeply into whether the restriction at issue here was reasonable. It suffices for present purposes to observe that the defendants' assertions of reasonableness are expressed generally, without regard to the patient-safety purpose of PSNet. The defendants do not engage with, let alone meaningfully respond to, the authorities cited by the plaintiffs explaining that reasonableness must be evaluated in light of the purpose served by the forum. The defendants have offered no evidence or argument showing the decisions to remove the commentaries had anything to do with patient safety. To the contrary, the record suggests their removal, and the revisions required as a condition of re-posting, undermine patient safety.

DISCUSSION

1. *Government and Expertise.* Defending the need to preserve the independence of experts and expertise from governmental control, Robert Post has observed, "A state that controls our knowledge controls our minds." Robert C. Post, *Democracy, Expertise, Academic Freedom: A First Amendment Jurisprudence For The Modern State* 33 (Yale Univ. Press, 2012). Post warned that "a state that can manipulate the production of disciplinary knowledge can set the terms of its own legitimacy." *Id.* He connected these concerns to the principle of "democratic competence," or "the cognitive empowerment of persons within public discourse, which in part depends on their access to disciplinary knowledge." *Id.* at 34. Consider how these concerns are implicated by the Trump Administration's actions relating to science and scientific inquiry.
2. *Politicizing Science.* Some critics have asserted that the Trump Administration has politicized science and scientific inquiry. *See, e.g.*, Katherine J. Wu, '*This Is Not How We Do Science, Ever*,' N.Y. Times (Apr. 25, 2025). The federal government can choose to fund scientific research consistent with its general policies and priorities, even if that means excluding other projects. For example, a Democratic President may want to fund public research on firearms-related injuries, while a Republican President may want to focus on other priorities. What, then, are the appropriate or necessary limits on governmental regulation of scientific expertise?
3. *Unconstitutional Scientific Conditions.* As it has in other areas, the Trump Administration has relied on access to federal funding to control scientific inquiry. For example, it has terminated research funding for projects that relate to or rely on race and gender. The Ninth Circuit has denied a stay of a district court order enjoining the federal government from terminating research grants based on "DEI" and "gender ideology" provisions in Executive Orders. *Thakur v. Donald J. Trump*, 148 F. 4th 1096 (9th Cir. 2025). The court concluded the viewpoint-based grant terminations likely violated the First Amendment. One

commentator has argued that even if the government can choose which areas of scientific inquiry to fund, *ideological* restrictions on ongoing scientific research impose unconstitutional conditions. *See* Kendra Albert, *Facts and Feelings: First Amendment Challenges to Mandated Ideological Compliance for Scientific Grants*, Knight First Amendment Institute (June 17, 2025). According to Albert, these restrictions "are not only programmatically unrelated to the funding of scientific research, they are fundamentally incompatible with the scientific process. The purpose of scientific research is to find out facts about the world, and scientific progress depends upon the ability to publish one's results and to trust the accuracy of prior work."

4. *Preserving Scientific Independence.* Assuming partisan intervention in the scientific process is a problem, how can researchers and scientists respond? Regarding access to funding, it might be possible to obtain *private* resources rather than rely on public funding. As *Schiff* and *Thakur* show, some executive actions may also be redressable through litigation. As in other contexts, the potential scope of the remedy is an issue. *Schiff* applies to specific datasets or papers. However, in *Thakur* courts authorized a class action by all grantees whose funding was terminated based on "DEI" and gender considerations. As noted in other contexts, litigation is expensive and time-consuming. Moreover, given the President's broad authority to affect personnel, spending, and other conditions at federal agencies involved in scientific research, the First Amendment may not be a very effective means of preserving scientific independence. What other checks might be available?

D. PROBLEM EXERCISE: REPRESENTING A SCIENTIST

Dr. Barbara Baker, who works at a large public research university, has just received an email from the National Institutes of Health (NIH). The email informed Dr. Baker that a grant for a research project she leads at her LGBTQ+ Policy Lab has been terminated because it "involves transgender issues." According to the NIH email: "Research programs based on gender identity are often unscientific, have little identifiable return on investment, and do nothing to enhance the health of many Americans." The letter cited President Trump's Executive Order, *Defending Women From Gender Ideology Extremism and Restoring Biological Truth to the Federal Government* (Jan. 30, 2025). Dr. Baker strongly disagrees with NIH's assessment of the value of her research. In fact, she believes her study is critical to understanding and treating transgender suicide, which is a pressing public health concern. Dr. Baker has come to you for legal advice concerning how to respond to the NIH letter and grant termination. What advice would you give her?

E. PUBLIC BROADCASTING

Public broadcasting has long played an important role in terms of facilitating information flow, both inside the United States and across the globe. Among other things, publicly funded broadcasts provide educational and other valuable programming, including shows like "Sesame Street" that teach children how to read and count. This content is part of a once robust, but rapidly shrinking, media environment. Local affiliate stations, which are especially important to rural communities, often lack access to community news and other vital information.[43] For decades, public broadcasting has filled that gap.

Publicly funded broadcasts also reach global audiences. Outlets like Voice of America and Radio Free Europe/Radio Liberty, which rely on federal funding to broadcast in foreign nations, have facilitated the distribution of information. Critically, these stations reach audiences in nations that lack robust free speech and press freedoms. Among other vital functions, Voice of America and Radio Free Europe/Radio Liberty serve as a check on authoritarian regimes by publishing non-state-approved news and information.[44]

In the U.S., those on the political right have long contended that publicly funded broadcasting censors conservative viewpoints. They have urged Congress to terminate funding for public television and radio. Responding to these concerns, President Trump signed an Executive Order, *Ending Taxpayer Subsidization of Biased Media*, in which he declared that government funding of private sources of non-commercial media is "corrosive."[45] The Order, which terminated all federal funding for PBS and NPR, alleged the outlets had failed to provide "fair, accurate, unbiased, and nonpartisan news."[46] President Trump also issued Executive Orders that effectively dismantled Voice of America and Radio Free Europe/Radio Liberty and ordered the firing of most of these broadcasters' employees.[47] Again, he justified these directives by accusing the outlets of broadcasting "anti-Trump" content. Voice of America and Radio Free Europe challenged President Trump's Executive Orders on statutory and separation of powers grounds. At the time of publication, these lawsuits were pending.[48]

PBS and NPR also filed federal lawsuits to prevent termination of their federal funding. They argued that President Trump violated the First Amendment by retaliating against them based on their viewpoints. They also alleged the President had imposed an unconstitutional condition on federal funding, by requiring all member stations to sever ties with PBS and NPR. As usual, President Trump had communicated his views on social media: "NPR and PBS, two horrible and completely biased platforms (Networks!), should be DEFUNDED by Congress, IMMEDIATELY. Republicans, don't miss this opportunity to rid our Country of this giant SCAM, both being arms of the Radical Left Democrat Party. JUST SAY NO AND, MAKE AMERICA GREAT AGAIN!!!" While their lawsuits were pending, Congress voted to terminate federal funding for both NPR and PBS.[49]

Congress enacted the Public Broadcasting Act of 1967, which created NPR and PBS, because it determined that broad access to free, high-quality, *independent* public radio and television programming produced and aired by private entities for the benefit of all Americans was a public good. Whatever their faults or supposed biases, these media outlets play a crucial role in providing educational, news, and other programming to communities across the U.S. While NPR and PBS do not rely heavily on federal funding, the loss of over $1 billion will substantially affect their operations. The loss will be most acutely felt by the broadcasters' local member stations, which are highly dependent on federal funding to serve their communities.

Defunding and dismantling public broadcasting stations further erodes a media ecosystem that has been plagued by layoffs and other financial setbacks. In characteristic fashion, President Trump justified his actions as a means of cancelling long-disfavored press institutions.

Like law firms, universities, Bar organizations, newspapers, and other targets, President Trump attacked public broadcasting stations because of his antipathy toward the content of their coverage. Congress went along, notwithstanding that when it created PBS and NPR, it sought to protect them from precisely this sort of political interference.

The President's and Congress's actions will substantially suppress the free flow of information on the nation's airwaves, especially in rural communities with few other reliable sources of information. What is more, these governmental actions will undermine civic institutions that provide independent reporting and programming to American audiences. If upheld, President Trump's actions against Voice of America and Radio Free Europe will shrink America's global influence and cede the global airwaves to authoritarian regimes, who will use that space to expand their influence.

CONCLUSION

The Trump Era, which at this point has lasted nearly a full decade, has been one of the most consequential for freedom of speech and freedom of the press in American history. All Americans should be concerned about how not just the current occupant of the Oval Office has used the powers of the presidency to retaliate against speakers and chill expression, but the potential roadmap these actions have created for future presidents.

The First Amendment has long been a powerful check against repressive laws and authoritarian impulses. What do the materials in the book tell us about the robustness of speech and press freedoms once put to the stress test of Trump 2.0? Since there are undoubtedly more trials to come, this assessment is necessarily preliminary. However, based on events so far, *three* general conclusions seem warranted.

First, executive power can pose unique threats to freedom of expression. Trump 2.0 has demonstrated that whole-of-society expressive harms can emanate directly from campaigns orchestrated by the White House. As President Trump has shown, with the simple stroke of a pen (and a zealously compliant federal bureaucracy) presidents can broadly threaten freedom of expression. President Trump's Executive Orders have affected not only speech within the Executive Branch but the expressive and associative rights of law firms, corporations, universities, artists, libraries, reporters, broadcasters, nonprofit associations, scientists, and others. Because of Trump 2.0, we now have a better understanding of how executive power can affect things like access to data, academic freedom, legal advocacy, immigration, and scientific inquiry. There are, as well, important separation of powers lessons. Although the principal function of the presidency is to *execute* the laws passed by Congress, President Trump has not generally relied on Congress. Indeed, in certain contexts, his administration has ignored or even violated federal laws. First Amendment freedoms are even more precarious when the Legislative Branch fails to stand up to the Chief Executive.

Second, Trump 2.0 has revealed that litigation and First Amendment doctrines are only a partial antidote for aggressive uses of executive power. As we have seen, speakers have successfully relied on First Amendment doctrines and standards to obtain at least preliminary relief from some Trump 2.0 directives and agency actions. However, First Amendment doctrines and rights have not been sufficient to prevent the widespread erosion of First Amendment rights and the free flow of information. One reason is that targets of executive action—law firms, universities, corporations, scientists, and the press—have often chosen *not* to resist executive edicts. Although there have been exceptions, anticipatory compliance and obeisance have been widespread. Another reason First Amendment litigation may be ineffectual is that courts do not always recognize that jawboning, financial coercion, vague edicts, and threats of reprisal violate free speech rights. Finally, even when they conclude violations have occurred, courts have found it difficult to fashion effective remedies. The Supreme Court has limited the judiciary's power to grant nationwide relief. And owing to the government speech principle, courts generally cannot order the federal government and its officials not to make threatening or retributive statements that can broadly chill expression. In sum, although plaintiffs have prevailed in some early cases, this has not prevented many law firms from turning away clients, broadcasters from self-censoring, international students from self-deporting, or scientific papers from being deleted, withdrawn or, worse still, never written.

Third, the First Amendment is necessary, but will not be sufficient, to preserve American democracy. First Amendment doctrines and rights are important for protecting collective interests in self-government and the search for truth, as well as the free flow of information. However, these values also rest on respect for the rule of law and democratic governance. As this book goes to print, President Trump has taken actions to militarize the federal government's response to civil unrest by deploying federalized National Guard and active military troops to cities including Los Angeles and Chicago. He has compared himself to a king, bragged about taking protesters' First

Amendment rights away, asserted he has "the right to do anything I want to do," and mused from the Oval Office that some Americans may want a dictator to rule.[1] In his second term, President Trump has acted pursuant to a theory of executive power that vests in him the authority to order criminal investigations of political opponents, terminate billions of dollars in appropriated funds, delete scientific and other data, and impose military rule in response to protests. Arrayed against this exercise of mostly unchecked power, by a *president* who is "drawing all power into [his] impetuous vortex," the First Amendment sometimes appears to be a mere "parchment barrier[]."[2]

On a more hopeful note, studying the use of executive power and its relation to First Amendment rights suggests potential reforms. In terms of the First Amendment, Trump 2.0 has highlighted new ways governments can chill or suppress expression. Specifically, the administration has relied on "jawboning" and other less formal means of pressuring or coercing speakers and has sought to revive a right/privilege distinction that treats First Amendment rights as a matter of grace. Courts will need to be more aware of how executive retaliation, funding denials, and threatened investigations chill expression and violate First Amendment rights. Further, Trump 2.0 also supports the argument that courts must reign in the concept of "government speech," which Trump Administration officials have repeatedly invoked to mask the regulatory effects of their actions. Trump 2.0 should also produce renewed interest in the free expression harms associated with vague governmental policies and pronouncements. Although vagueness doctrine has traditionally been concerned mostly with *statutory* enactments, courts must now apply it to executive edicts and policies.

The Supreme Court also has critically important unfinished business. It should clarify the limits on the Executive Branch's authority to detain and deport noncitizens based on their political viewpoints. Trump 2.0 actions in this area have relied on the outdated and untenable position that the government can censor and suppress the political expression of noncitizens. The Court should formally repudiate the Cold War era precedents the Trump Administration has relied on to detain and deport noncitizens, which failed to protect even the First Amendment rights of American citizens.

Finally, to turn one final time to the separation of powers, Trump 2.0 has demonstrated the acute need for *legislation* reigning in executive authority across a wide range of areas including federal funding, data preservation, scientific research, and removal of lawfully resident aliens. For the reasons already stated, courts alone cannot bear the burden of preserving First Amendment freedoms.

ACKNOWLEDGMENTS

First and foremost, I want to thank Ron Collins. Without his support and encouragement, this book would not exist. To say that I was reluctant to work on a *second* book about Donald Trump and the First Amendment is an understatement. Ron convinced me that a project like this, which focuses on recording and, more importantly, learning from the First Amendment conflicts of Trump 2.0, was not just worthwhile but necessary.

I also want to thank Keith Sipe, Carolina Academic Press's publisher, for believing in and publishing the book.

Thanks to Stephen Solomon and Susanna Granieri at First Amendment Watch, for hosting my updated repository of Trump 2.0 First Amendment-related Executive Orders, litigation documents, and commentary. I relied on this source, which Ron Collins encouraged and contributed to, when researching and writing the book.

Last but not least, great thanks to William & Mary Law School and my Dean, Benjamin Spencer, for financially and otherwise supporting the project.

NOTES

INTRODUCTION

1. For discussion of the various First Amendment controversies during President Trump's first term, *see* TIMOTHY ZICK, THE FIRST AMENDMENT IN THE TRUMP ERA (Oxford Univ. Press, 2019).

2. *See* Executive Order 14149, 90 Fed. Reg. 8243, *Restoring Freedom of Speech and Ending Federal Censorship* (Jan. 20, 2025).

3. Charlie Savage, *Trump Baselessly Claims He "Took the Freedom of Speech Away" from Flag Burners*, N.Y. TIMES (Oct. 9, 2025), https://www.nytimes.com/2025/10/09/us/politics/trump-freedom-of-speech-flag-burning.html.

4. *See, e.g.*, Sonja R. West, *Suing the President for First Amendment Violations*, 71 OKLA. L. REV. 321 (2018).

5. *See* GEOFFREY R. STONE, PERILOUS TIMES. FREE SPEECH IN WARTIME: FROM THE SEDITION ACT OF 1798 TO THE WAR ON TERRORISM (2005).

6. *Id.*

7. *See* JOHN W. DEAN, BLIND AMBITION: THE WHITE HOUSE YEARS (Open Road Media, 2016).

8. *See Murthy v. Missouri*, 603 U.S. 43 (2024) (dismissing First Amendment claims against the federal government on standing grounds).

9. *See* Carlos Lozada, *Trump Just Reached a Historic Milestone*, N.Y. TIMES (Apr. 1, 2025), https://www.nytimes.com/2025/04/01/opinion/trump-executive-orders-presidential-power.html.

10. *See* Executive Order No. 14339, 90 Fed. Reg. 42421, *Additional Measures to Address the Crime Emergency in the District of Columbia* (Aug. 25, 2025).

11. *See* Isabelle Murray, Soo Rin Kim, and Adam Carlson, *Trump, who told supporters "I am your retribution," now says, "I'm being indicted for you,"* ABC NEWS (Jun. 26, 2023), https://abcnews.go.com/Politics/trump-told-supporters-retribution-now-im-indicted/story?id=100386551.

12. John W. Dean, *Memorandum from John Dean Titled "Dealing with our Political Enemies,"* August 16, 1971, UNC LIBRARIES (accessed June 30, 2025), https://exhibits.lib.unc.edu/items/show/7896 (emphasis added).

13. *See* Executive Order No. 14263, 90 Fed. Reg. 15615, *Addressing Risks from Susman Godfrey* (Apr. 9, 2025); Executive Order No. 14250, 90 Fed. Reg. 14549, *Addressing Risks from WilmerHale* (Mar. 27, 2025); Executive Order No. 14246, 90 Fed. Reg. 13997, *Addressing Risks from Jenner & Block* (Mar. 25, 2025); Executive Order No. 14237, 90 Fed. Reg. 13039, *Addressing Risks from Paul Weiss* (Mar. 14, 2025); Executive Order No. 14230, 90 Fed. Reg. 11781, *Addressing Risks from Perkins Coie* LLP (Mar. 6, 2025).

14. *See* Presidential Memorandum, *Addressing Risks Associated with an Egregious Leaker and Disseminator of Falsehoods* (Apr. 9, 2025); Presidential Memorandum, *Addressing Risks from Chris Krebs and Government Censorship* (Apr. 9, 2025).

15. *See* Teddy Rosenbluth, *"Vaguely Threatening": Federal Prosecutor Queries Leading Medical Journal*, N.Y. TIMES (Apr. 25, 2025), https://www.nytimes.com/2025/04/25/health/nejm-prosecutor-letter.html?smid=nytcore-ios-share&referringSource=articleShare.

16. *See, e.g.*, Natalie Sherman and Nadine Yousif, *Disney faces US investigation over DEI practices*, BBC (Mar. 29, 2025), https://www.bbc.com/news/articles/c62k20l5x24o.; Devlin Barrett, *Trump's Old Grudge Fuels Swipe at a New Law Firm*, N.Y. TIMES (Mar. 25, 2025), https://www.nytimes.com/2025/03/25/us/politics/trump-executive-order-law-firm-jenner-block.html?smid=nytcore-ios-share&referringSource=articleShare; Eliza Shapiro, *Immigration Authorities Arrest Pro-Palestinian Activist at Columbia*, N.Y. TIMES (Mar. 9, 2025), https://www.nytimes.com/2025/03/09/nyregion/ice-arrests-palestinian-activist-columbia-protests.html?smid=nytcore-ios-share&referringSource=articleShare; Nate Raymond, *Harvard doctors sue over Trump removal of articles mentioning LGBTQ health issues*, REUTERS (Mar. 12, 2025), https://www.reuters.com/legal/government/harvard-doctors-sue-over-trump-removal-articles-mentioning-lgbtq-health-issues-2025-03-12/.

17. *See* Stephaine Saul, *Harvard Sues Trump Administration Over Threats to Cut Funding*, N.Y. TIMES (Apr 21, 2025), https://www.nytimes.com/2025/04/21/us/harvard-lawsuit-trump-administration.html?smid=nytcore-ios-share&referringSource=articleShare.

18. *See A Statement from Constitutional Law Scholars on Columbia*, NEW YORK REVIEW (Mar. 20, 2025), https://www.nybooks.com/online/2025/03/20/a-statement-from-constitutional-law-scholars-on-columbia/.

19. *See, e.g.*, Sara Weissman, *What Does the Education Department's DEI Guidance Really Mean?*, INSIDE HIGHER ED. (Mar. 4, 2025), https://www

.insidehighered.com/news/government/politics-elections/2025/03/04/what-does-eds-new-dei-guidance-really-mean?utm_source=Inside+Higher+Ed&utm_campaign=09b8c3a1fe-DNU_2021_COPY_02&utm_medium=email&utm_term=0_1fcbc04421-09b8c3a1fe-237226025&mc_cid=09b8c3a1fe&mc_eid=402d71d225.

20. *See* Ryan Quinn, *AAUP Opposes "Anticipatory Obedience" to Trump, GOP*, Inside Higher Ed (Jan. 24, 2025), https://www.insidehighered.com/news/quick-takes/2025/01/24/aaup-opposes-anticipatory-obedience-trump-gop?utm_source=Inside+Higher+Ed&utm_campaign=1358bfd60a-DNU_2021_COPY_02&utm_medium=email&utm_term=0_1fcbc04421-1358bfd60a-237226025&mc_cid=1358bfd60a&mc_eid=402d71d225.

21. Ronald K.L. Collins, *Free speech in an age of fear: The new system of loyalty oaths*, First Amendment News (Apr. 3, 2025), https://www.thefire.org/news/blogs/ronald-kl-collins-first-amendment-news/free-speech-age-fear-new-system-loyalty-oaths.

22. Repression-through-intimidation is not limited to Executive Orders. President Trump has also filed several lawsuits against newspapers, pollsters, and others to extract settlements and weaken the press. The administration has also relied on agency investigations and other regulatory leverage against media entities. *See, e.g.*, David Enrich, *Trump's New Line of Attack Against the Media Gains Momentum*, N.Y. Times (Feb. 7, 2025), https://www.nytimes.com/2025/02/07/business/media/trump-media-lawsuits.html?smid=nytcore-ios-share&referringSource=articleShare.

23. *See* Jenny Gross, *N.Y.U. Langone Cancels Doctor's Speech, Citing Anti-Government Tone*, N.Y. Times (Apr. 2, 2025), https://www.nytimes.com/2025/04/02/nyregion/nyu-doctor-speech-canceled.html?smid=nytcore-ios-share&referringSource=articleShare.

24. Joseph Goldstein, *Fearing Trump, Hospital Shuns "Trigger" Words Like "Diverse,"* N.Y. Times (Mar. 19, 2025), https://www.nytimes.com/2025/03/19/nyregion/nyu-langone-trigger-words-trump-dei.html?smid=nytcore-ios-share&referringSource=articleShare.

25. *See* Edward Rubin, *What's Wrong with Langdell's Method, and What to Do About It*, 60 Vand. L. Rev. 609, 661–664 (2007).

26. *See* Alan Blinder, *University of Minnesota, Under Federal Scrutiny, Limits Its Political Speech*, N.Y. Times (Mar. 14, 2025), https://www.nytimes.com/2025/03/14/us/university-of-minnesota-political-speech.html?smid=nytcore-ios-share&referringSource=articleShare; Matthew Goldstein, *Five More Big Law Firms Reach Deals With Trump*, N.Y. Times (Apr. 12, 2025), https://www.nytimes.com/2025/04/11/business/trump-law-firms-kirk

land-ellis-latham-watkins.html?smid=nytcore-ios-share&referringSource=articleShare.

27. *See Trump v. CASA*, 145 S. Ct. 2540, 2550 (2025) (concluding district courts are not authorized to issue universal injunctions).

CHAPTER 1

1. *See* Genevieve Lakier, *Chilling Effects, Trump's Anti-DEI Executive Orders, and the Role of the Courts (or why the Fourth Circuit Decision in National Association of Diversity Officers v. Trump is wrong)*, BALKINIZATION (Mar. 19, 2025), https://balkin.blogspot.com/2025/03/chilling-effects-trumps-anti-dei.html.

2. *See, e.g.*, Rosenberger v. Rector and Visitors of Univ. of Va., 515 U. S. 819, 829 (1995) (explaining that regulation of speech based on "the specific motivating ideology or the opinion or perspective of the speaker" violates the First Amendment).

3. *See Pleasant Grove City, Utah v. Summum*, 555 U.S. 460, 467 (2009) ("The Free Speech Clause restricts government regulation of private speech; it does not regulate government speech.").

4 *Id.*

5. *Id.*

6. *See Reed v. Town of Gilbert*, 576 U.S. 155, 168–69 (2015).

7. *Id.* at 171.

8. *Rosenberger*, 515 U.S. at 829.

9. *Id.*

10. *W. Va. State Bd. of Educ. v. Barnette*, 319 U.S. 624, 642 (1943).

11. *See* Peter Wehner, *Trump's Appetite for Revenge Is Insatiable*, THE ATLANTIC (Mar. 20, 2025), https://www.theatlantic.com/ideas/archive/2025/03/political-enemy-retribution-efforts/682095/.

12. *Hartman v. Moore*, 547 U.S. 250, 256 (2006).

13. *Id.* at 259.

14. *Id.* at 260.

15. *Connally v. General Construction Co.*, 269 U.S. 385, 391 (1926).

16. *Grayned v. City of Rockford*, 408 U.S. 104, 108 (1972). Regarding the problem of expressive chill, *see generally* Frederick Schauer, *Fear, Risk and the First Amendment: Unraveling the Chilling Effect*, 58 B.U. L. REV. 685 (1978).

17. *Grayned*, 408 U.S. at 108.

18. *Id.*

19. *Speiser v. Randall*, 357 U. S. 513, 526 (1958).

20. *See, e.g., Gibson v. Florida Legis. Investigation Comm.*, 372 U.S. 539, 556–57 (1963); *Shelton v. Tucker*, 364 U.S. 479, 486 (1960); *Barenblatt v. United States*, 360 U.S. 109, 137–38 (1959) (Black, J., dissenting); *Speiser v. Randall*, 357 U.S. 513, 525–26 (1958); *Sweezy v. New Hampshire*, 354 U.S. 234, 246–50 (1957); *Wieman v. Updegraff*, 344 U.S. 183, 195 (1952) (Frankfurter,]., concurring). *See also NAACP v. Button*, 371 U.S. 415,433–34 (1963); *Bates v. City of Little Rock*, 361 U.S. 516, 524 (1960); *NAACP v. Alabama*, 357 U.S. 449, 462–63 (1958).

21. *Button*, 371 U.S. at 432.

22. *See, e.g.*, Genevieve Lakier, *Enforcing the First Amendment in an Era of Jawboning*, Univ. of Chi. L. Rev. (forthcoming, 2026).

23. *Id.*

24. *National Rifle Association of America vs. Vullo*, 602 U.S. 175, 189 (2024).

25. *Id.* at 193.

26. *Id.*

27. *Id.* at 189 (citation omitted).

28. *See Murthy v. Missouri*, 603 U.S. 43 (2024).

29. *See generally* Kathleen M. Sullivan, *Unconstitutional Conditions*, 102 Harv. L. Rev. 1421 (1989).

30. *See, e.g., Legal Svs. Corp. v. Velazquez*, 531 U.S. 533, 542 (2001) (concluding that when the government provides funds to facilitate private speech, it cannot deny funds based on the speaker's viewpoint).

31. *Agency for Int'l Dev. v. Alliance for Open Society Int'l, Inc.*, 570 U.S. 205 (2013).

32. The example is from Cass R. Sunstein, *Our Money or Your Life! Higher Education and the First Amendment*, Harv. L. Rev. Forum (forthcoming 2025).

33. Michael C. Dorf, *Conditional Funding Can Raise Difficult Legal Questions. Trump's Freezes Don't.*, Knight First Amendment Institute at Columbia University (May 13, 2025), https://knightcolumbia.org/blog/conditional-funding-can-raise-difficult-legal-questions-trumps-freezes-dont.

34. *Id.*

35. *See* Rachel Riedl and Stephen Yale-Loehr, *Our Foreign Students Are Terrified, and They're Right to Be*, N.Y. Times (Apr. 19, 2025), https://www.nytimes.com/2025/04/19/opinion/international-students-ice-deportations-universities.html?smid=nytcore-ios-share&referringSource=articleShare.

36. *See Bridges v. Wixon*, 326 U.S. 135, 148 (1945).

37. *Harisiades v. Shaughnessy*, 342 U.S. 580 (1952).

38. *See* Erwin Chemerinsky, The First Amendment 137–39 (Aspen Publishing, 3rd ed. 2024) (observing that, following the era in which *Harisiades* was decided, "by the mid-1960s, the Court appeared to be much more protective of speech," and describing the since-developed "incitement test" requiring "a likelihood of imminent harm").

39. *See American-Arab Anti-Discrim. Comm. v. Reno*, 70 F.3d 1045 (9th Cir. 1995), *rev'd on other grounds*, 525 U.S. 471 (1999) ("read properly, *Harisiades* establishes that deportation grounds are to be judged by the same standard applied to other burdens on First Amendment rights"). *See also Parcham v. INS*, 769 F.2d 1001 (4th Cir. 1985).

40. *See Price v. INS*, 962 F.2d 836 (9th Cir. 1991) ("[T]he Court has historically afforded Congress great deference in the area of immigration and naturalization. . . . [I]n the exercise of its broad power over immigration and naturalization, 'Congress regularly makes rules that would be unacceptable if applied to citizens'"); *Bluman v. FEC* (D.C.C. 2011) (Kavanaugh, J.), *aff'd without opinion* (U.S. 2012) ("The Court has further indicated that aliens' First Amendment rights might be less robust than those of citizens in certain discrete areas. *See Harisiades.*").

41. *See, e.g., Reno v. American-Arab Anti-Discrimination Committee*, 525 U.S. 471 (1999) (holding that unlawfully present aliens could not bring selective enforcement claims based on the First and Fifth Amendments).

42. *See Garrison v. Louisiana*, 379 U.S. 64, 77 (1964) (urging government to promote, through its laws and regulations, "the paramount interest in a free flow of information to the people").

43. *See* William E. Lee, *The Supreme Court and the Right to Receive Expression*, 1987 Sup. CT. REV. 303.

44. Alexander Meiklejohn, Political Freedom: The Constitutional Powers of the People (Harper, 1960).

45. Thomas Emerson, The System of Freedom of Expression (Random House, 1970).

46. *New York Times Co. v. Sullivan*, 376 U.S. 254, 270 (1964).

47. *See, e.g., Va. Pharmacy Bd. v. Va. Consumer Council*, 425 U.S. 748, 756 (1976) ("Freedom of speech presupposes a willing speaker. But where a speaker exists, as is the case here, the protection afforded is to the communication, to its source and to its recipients both.") (footnote omitted)

48. *See, e.g., Island Trees Sch. Dist. v. Pico*, 457 U.S. 853, 870 (1982) (plurality) (concluding school boards possess broad discretion to remove library books but that discretion "may not be exercised in a narrowly partisan or political manner"); *Keyishian v. Board of Regents*, 385 U.S. 589, 603 (1967) (recognizing academic freedom is "a special concern of the First Amendment"). For a discussion of the importance of the free flow of information

produced by experts, *see* ROBERT C. POST, DEMOCRACY, EXPERTISE, ACADEMIC FREEDOM: A FIRST AMENDMENT JURISPRUDENCE FOR THE MODERN STATE (Yale Univ. Pess, 2012).

49. *See* William E. Lee, *The Supreme Court and the Right to Receive Expression*, 1987 SUP. CT. REV. 303.

50. *First Nat'l Bank of Boston v. Bellotti*, 435 U.S. 675, 783 (1978).

51. *Stanley v. Georgia*, 394 U.S. 557, 564 (1969).

52. *Lamont v. Postmaster Gen.*, 381 U.S. 301, 306 (1965); *Griswold v. Connecticut*, 381 U. S. 479, 482 (1965).

53. *Garrison v. Louisiana*, 379 U.S. 64, 77 (1964).

54. *See Pleasant Grove City v. Summum*, 555 U.S. 460 (2009) (recognizing the government's freedom to express its own views without regard to content neutrality requirements).

55. *Citizens United v. FEC*, 558 U.S. 310, 339 (2010).

56. *See, e.g.*, *Houchins v. HQED, Inc.*, 438 U.S. 1, 9 (1978) ("This Court has never intimated a First Amendment guarantee of a right of access to all sources of information within government control.").

57. *See, e.g.*, *Rust v. Sullivan*, 500 U.S. 173, 193 (1991) (upholding federal law restricting abortion advocacy and counseling in the context of a federally funded program).

CHAPTER 3

1. *See* Executive Order 14151, 90 Fed. Reg. 8339, *Ending Radical and Wasteful Government DEI Programs and Preferencing* (January 20, 2025); Executive Order 14173, 90 Fed. Reg. 8633, *Ending Illegal Discrimination and Restoring Merit-Based Opportunity* (Jan. 21, 2025).

2. Exec. Order 14151, § 1.

3. *Id.* § 2.

4. *Id.* § 2(b)(i).

5. Exec. Order 14173, § 3(b)(ii).

6. *Id.* § 3(c)(ii).

7. *Id.* § 4(a).

8. *Id.* § 3(b)(iv).

9. *Id.* § 4(b)(ii).

10. *Id.* § 4(b)(ii); § 5.

11. *See* Executive Order 14168, 90 Fed. Reg. 8615, *Defending Women From Gender Ideology Extremism and Restoring Biological Truth to the Federal Government*, § 1 (Jan. 20, 2025).

12. *Id.* § 2.

13. *Id.* § 1.

14. *Id.*
15. *Id.* § 2(f).
16. *Id.* § 3(g).
17. Id. § 3(b).
18. *Id.* § 3(d).
19. *Id.* § 3(e).
20. Executive Order 14183, 90 Fed. Reg. 8757, *Prioritizing Military Excellence and Readiness* § 1 (Jan. 27, 2025).
21. *Id.*
22. *Id.*
23. *Id.* § 2.
24. *See* Executive Order 14190, 90 Fed. Reg. 8853, *Ending Radical Indoctrination in K-12 Schooling*, § 3(b)(ii) (Jan. 29, 2025).
25. Executive Order 14253, 90 Fed. Reg. 14563, *Restoring Truth and Sanity to American History* (Mar. 27, 2025), § 1.
26. *Id.*
27. *Id.* § 2.
28. *Id.* § 4.
29. *See Fact Sheet: President Donald J. Trump Restores Truth and Sanity to American History* (March 27, 2025).
30. Executive Order 14190, § 3(b)(ii) (Jan. 29, 2025).
31. *Id.* § 2 (d)(i).
32. *Id.* § 2 (b)(viii).
33. Executive Order 14161, 90 Fed. Reg. 8451, *Protecting the United States from Foreign Terrorists and Other National Security and Public Safety Threats*, §§ 1(a)-(b) (Jan. 30, 2025).
34. *Id.* § 3(f).
35. Exec. Order 14151, § 3(b)(iv) (emphasis added).
36. *Id.*, § 2.

CHAPTER 4

1. *See* Executive Order No. 14151, 90 Fed. Reg. 8339, *Ending Radical And Wasteful Government DEI Programs And Preferencing* (January 20, 2025); Executive Order No. 14173, 90 Fed. Reg. 8633, *Ending Illegal Discrimination and Restoring Merit-Based Opportunity* (Jan. 21, 2025).

CHAPTER 5

1. Executive Order 14161, 90 Fed. Reg. 8451, *Protecting the United States from Foreign Terrorists and Other National Security and Public Safety Threats*, § 1(b) (Jan. 30, 2025).

2. Executive Order 14188, *Additional Measures to Combat Anti-Semitism*, 90 Fed. Reg. 8847, § 1 (Feb. 3, 2025).

3. *Id.* § 2.

4. *Id.* § 3 (e).

5. *See Fact Sheet: President Donald J. Trump Takes Forceful and Unprecedented Steps to Combat Anti-Semitism*, The White House (Jan. 30, 2025), https://perma.cc/GY4H-7ASR.

6. Issuance of visas, 8 U.S.C. § 1201(i) (1952).

7. After several months, a court concluded that Mahmoud Khalil had been detained in retaliation for pro-Palestine expression and ordered his release. Jonah E. Bromwich, *Mahmoud Khalil Must Be Released on Bail, Federal Judge Orders*, N.Y. TIMES (June 20, 2025), https://www.nytimes.com/2025/06/20/nyregion/mahmoud-khalil-release-order.html.

CHAPTER 6

1. *See* MARVIN KALB, ENEMY OF THE PEOPLE: TRUMP'S WAR ON THE PRESS, THE NEW MCCARTHYISM, AND THE THREAT TO AMERICAN DEMOCRACY (Brookings Institution Press, 2018).

2. *See* Hadas Gold, *Donald Trump: We're going to "open up" libel laws*, POLITICO (Feb. 26, 2016), https://www.politico.com/blogs/on-media/2016/02/donald-trump-libel-laws-219866.

3. Associated Press, *A federal judge has dismissed Trump's defamation case against CNN over "the Big Lie,"* CNN (July 30, 2023), https://www.npr.org/2023/07/30/1190983801/a-federal-judge-has-dismissed-trumps-defamation-case-against-cnn-over-the-big-li.

4. Michael R. Sisak, *Donald Trump ordered to pay The New York Times and its reporters nearly $400,000 in legal fees*, ASSOCIATED PRESS (Jan. 12, 2024), https://apnews.com/article/trump-new-york-times-taxes-lawsuit-slapp-f39342501d9a2a5cfd36181f9f336215.

5. Graham Kates, *Trump sues Des Moines Register over poll, promises more lawsuits against news outlets after ABC News settlement*, CBS NEWS (Dec. 17, 2024), https://www.cbsnews.com/news/trump-threatens-lawsuit-des-moines-register-poll-media/.

6. *See* Michael M. Grynbaum, *Trump Threatens to Sue The Times and CNN Over Iran Reporting*, N.Y. TIMES (June 26, 2025), https://www.nytimes.com/2025/06/26/business/media/trump-iran-new-york-times-cnn.html.

7. *See* Nandita Bose and Jonathan Stempel, *Trump Sues Wall Street Journal over Epstein report, seeks $10 billion*, REUTERS (July 19, 2025), https://www.reuters.com/world/us/trump-sues-wall-street-journal-over-epstein-report-seeks-10-billion-2025-07-19/.

8. Daisuke Wakabayashi and Michael C. Grynbaum, *Trump Sues The New York Times for Articles Questioning His Success*, N.Y. Times (Sept. 16, 2025), https://www.nytimes.com/2025/09/16/business/media/trump-lawsuit-new-york-times.html?smid=nytcore-ios-share&referringSource=articleShare.

9. Michael R. Sisak, *Donald Trump ordered to pay The New York Times and its reporters nearly $400,000 in legal fees*, Associated Press (Jan. 12, 2024), https://apnews.com/article/trump-new-york-times-taxes-lawsuit-slapp-f39342501d9a2a5cfd36181f9f336215.

10. *Id.*

11. Donald J. Trump v. New York Times Co., __ F. Supp. 3d __, 2025 WL 2680597 (M.D. Fla., Sept. 19, 2025).

12. *See generally* Anthny Lewis, Make No Law: The Sullivan Case and the First Amendment (Knopf, 1992).

13. *New York Times Co. v. Sullivan*, 376 U.S. 254 (1964).

14. *Id.* at 280.

15. *See, e.g., Curtis Publishing Co. v. Butts*, 388 U.S. 130 (1967).

16. *Sullivan*, 376 U.S. at 278.

17. *See* Adam Liptak and Eileen Sullivan, *Trump, Angry Over Woodward Book, Renews Criticism of Libel Laws*, N.Y. Times (Mar. 30, 2017), https://www.nytimes.com/2017/03/30/us/politics/can-trump-change-libel-laws.html.

18. *See* David Folkenflick and Mary Yang, *Fox News settles blockbuster defamation lawsuit with Dominion Voting Systems*, NPR (Apr. 18, 2023), https://www.npr.org/2023/04/18/1170339114/fox-news-settles-blockbuster-defamation-lawsuit-with-dominion-voting-systems.

19. *See* Michael R. Sisak, *ABC agrees to give $15 million to Donald Trump's presidential library to settle defamation lawsuit*, Associated Press (Dec. 14, 2024), https://apnews.com/article/abc-trump-lawsuit-defamation-stephanopoulos-04aea8663310af39ae2a85f4c1a56d68.

20. *See* Benjamin Mullin, Michael M. Grynbaum, Lauren Hirsch and David Enrich, *Paramount to Pay Trump $16 Million to Settle "60 Minutes" Lawsuit*, N.Y. Times (July 2, 2025), https://www.nytimes.com/2025/07/02/business/media/paramount-trump-60-minutes-lawsuit.html.

21. *See, e.g., Miami Herald Publishing Co. v. Tornillo*, 418 U.S. 241, 258 (1974) ("The choice of material to go into a newspaper, and the decisions made as to limitations on the size and content of the paper, and treatment of public issues and public official—whether fair or unfair—constitute the exercise of editorial control and judgment.").

22. Joe Flynt, *Trump Expects $20 Million More in Ad Dollars From "60 Minutes" Settlement*, The Wall Street Journal (July 22, 2025), https://www.wsj.com/business/media/trump-60-minutes-cbs-settlement-5e3f1ce0

?gaa_at=eafs&gaa_n=ASWzDAh67Hh0CINbvW5fPK8H63AIEIKDOHI5LMVcFl9AaPoUnMYcVh5SXxUn1M6PfbI%3D&gaa_ts=688660d2&gaa_sig=zysytoCabvHrFcHQT5aJE8Ik0kN2QMhAazCDj7EEnSy-QfJX-iNRm_9pGXwSCAtGBjj_apZwnNXnGSORM2Nj5w%3D%3D.

23. *See* Ashley Ahn, *Lawmakers Question Whether CBS Canceled Colbert's Show for Political Reasons*, N.Y. Times (July 18, 2025), https://www.nytimes.com/2025/07/18/us/politics/stephen-colbert-canceled-trump-lawmakers.html?smid=nytcore-ios-share&referringSource=articleShare.

CHAPTER 7

1. Collective or societal interests in self-government and the search for truth, which were first discussed in early Supreme Court opinions by Justices Brandeis and Holmes, have become part of a First Amendment value system that looks beyond the individual speaker's interest in communicating. *See Whitney v. California*, 274 U.S. 357, 371 (1927) (Brandeis, J., concurring); *Abrams v. United States*, 250 U.S. 616, 624 (1919) (Holmes, J., dissenting).

2. *See* Executive Order 14151, 90 Fed. Reg. 8339, *Ending Radical and Wasteful Government DEI Programs and Preferencing* (January 20, 2025); Executive Order 14173, 90 Fed. Reg. 8633, *Ending Illegal Discrimination and Restoring Merit-Based Opportunity* (Jan. 21, 2025); Executive Order 14168, 90 Fed. Reg. 8615, *Defending Women From Gender Ideology Extremism and Restoring Biological Truth to the Federal Government* (Jan. 20, 2025).

3. *See* Conor Murray, *Enola Gay Aircraft—And Other Historic Items—Inaccurately Targeted Under Pentagon's Anti-DEI Purge*, Forbes (Mar. 7, 2025), https://www.forbes.com/sites/conormurray/2025/03/07/enola-gay-aircraft-and-other-historic-items-inaccurately-targeted-under-pentagons-anti-dei-purge/.

4. *See* Chris Boccia and Luis Martinez, *DOD says it 'mistakenly removed' Jackie Robinson, other content from website amid DEI purge*, ABC News (Mar. 19, 2025), https://abcnews.go.com/Politics/dod-mistakenly-removed-jackie-robinson-content-website-amid/story?id=119955477.

5. *See* Tim Balk, *Arlington Cemetery Website Loses Pages on Black Veterans, Women and Civil War*, N.Y. Times (Mar. 14, 2025), https://www.nytimes.com/2025/03/14/us/politics/arlington-cemetery-website-dei.html?smid=nytcore-ios-share&referringSource=articleShare.

6. *See* Brian Bennett, *Federal Webpages Go Dark as Trump Administration Removes Public Data*, Time (Jan. 31, 2025), https://time.com/7211965/trump-federal-websites-data/.

7. *See* John Swaine and Jeremy B. Merrill, *Amid anti-DEI push, National Park Service rewrites history of Underground Railroad*, Washington Post (Apr. 6, 2025), https://www.washingtonpost.com/investigations/2025/04/06

/national-park-service-underground-railroad-history-slavery/?utm_campaign=wp_post_most&utm_medium=email&utm_source=newsletter&carta-url=https%3A%2F%2Fs2.washingtonpost.com%2Fcar-ln-tr%2F41f8040%2F67f2a2f28670807363c8476b%2F5df3c2709bbc0f414f218d72%2F11%2F51%2F67f2a2f28670807363c8476b.

8. *Id.*

9. *See* Catherine Rampell & Amanda Shendruk, *A sample of the government webpages Trump doesn't want you to see*, WASHINGTON POST (Feb. 9, 2025), https://www.washingtonpost.com/opinions/interactive/2025/sample-government-webpages-trump-doesnt-want-you-see/.

10. *See* Jonathan J. Cooper, *A list of government web pages that have gone dark to comply with Trump orders*, ASSOCIATED PRESS (Jan. 31, 2025), https://apnews.com/article/government-websites-changes-trump-transgender-dei-orders-383fc983c6ca48804f1404cbc61ee9e9.

11. *Id.*

12. *Id.*

13. *See* National Security Archive, *Disappearing Data: Trump Administration Removing Climate Information From Government Websites* (Feb. 6, 2025), https://nsarchive.gwu.edu/briefing-book/climate-change-transparency-project-foia/2025-02-06/disappearing-data-trump.

14. *First Nat'l Bank of Boston v. Bellotti*, 435 U.S. 675, 783 (1978).

15. Executive Order 14253, 90 Fed. Reg. 14563, *Restoring Truth and Sanity to American History* (Apr. 3, 2025), § 1.

16. *Id.* § 2.

17. *Id.* § 1.

18. *Id.*

19. *Id.* § 2.

20. *Id.* § 1.

21. *See* Executive Order 14151, 90 Fed. Reg. 8339, *Ending Radical and Wasteful Government DEI Programs and Preferencing* (January 20, 2025); Executive Order 14168, 90 Fed. Reg. 8615, *Defending Women From Gender Ideology Extremism and Restoring Biological Truth to the Federal Government*, § 1 (Jan. 20, 2025); Executive Order 14190, 90 Fed. Reg. 8853, *Ending Radical Indoctrination in K-12 Schooling*, § 3(b)(ii) (Jan. 29, 2025).

22. Exec. Order 14253, § 2(b)(ii).

23. *See* Jake Spring, *Park gift shops could remove books on slavery and the Civil War*, WASH. POST (July 25, 2025), https://www.washingtonpost.com/climate-environment/2025/07/25/parks-gift-shops-banned-books/?utm_campaign=wp_the7&utm_medium=email&utm_source=newsletter&carta-url=https%3A%2F%2Fs2.washingtonpost.com%2Fcar-ln-tr%2F43cda06%2F688

3615d300b04282953cd07%2F598a8940ade4e26514fd512c%2F30%2F109%2F6883615d300b04282953cd07.

24. *Id.*

25. *Id.*

26. *Save Our Signs, Celebrate All-American History*, https://sites.google.com/umn.edu/save-our-signs/home?authuser=0.

27. *Id.*

28. Museum and Library Services Act of 1996, P.L. 104-208, title VII, § 702, 110 Stat. 3009-295.

29. *See* Executive Order 14238, 90 Fed. Reg. 13043, *Continuing the Reduction of the Federal Bureaucracy*, § 2(a)(iv) (Mar. 14, 2025).

30. Executive Order 14303, 90 Fed. Reg. 22601, *Restoring Gold Standard Science* (May 23, 2025).

31. *Id.* § 1.

32. *Id.*

33. *Id.*

34. *Id.* § 7(a).

35. *Id.*

36. *See* Leila Fadel, *How the Trump administration is impacting the First Amendment rights of scientists*, NPR "Morning Edition" (Apr. 14, 2025), https://www.npr.org/2025/04/14/nx-s1-5349473/trump-free-speech-science-research.

37. *See* Alice Callahan, *Leading Nutrition Scientist Departs N.I.H., Citing Censorship*, N.Y. Times (Apr. 16, 2025), https://www.nytimes.com/2025/04/16/well/kevin-hall-nutrition-retirement-nih-censorship-rfk-maha.html?smid=nytcore-ios-share&referringSource=articleShare.

38. *See* Teddy Rosenbluth and Rebecca Robbins, *Trump-Allied Prosecutor Sends Letters to Medical Journals Alleging Bias*, N.Y. Times (Apr. 18, 2025), https://www.nytimes.com/2025/04/18/health/trump-martin-us-attorney-medical-journals.html?smid=nytcore-ios-share&referringSource=articleShare.

39. *See* Katherine J. Wu, *"This Is Not How We Do Science, Ever,"* N.Y. Times (Apr. 25, 2025), https://www.theatlantic.com/health/archive/2025/04/-trump-kennedy-science-government-propaganda/682569/?utm_campaign=atlantic-daily-newsletter&utm_content=20250424&utm_source=newsletter&utm_medium=email&utm_term=The+Atlantic+Daily.

40. *See* Heather Souvaine Horn, *Life in a Warming World, The New Republic* (Apr. 21, 2025), https://newsletter.tnr.com/index.php?action=social&chash=c6335734dbc0b1ded766421cfc611750.1658&s=b7fe3607754d2fc83dcc045235a66ee7.

41. *See* Jenny Gross, *NYU Langone Cancels Doctor's Speech, Citing Anti-Government Tone*, N.Y. Times (Apr. 2, 2025), https://www.nytimes.com/2025/04/02/nyregion/nyu-doctor-speech-canceled.html?smid=nytcore-ios-share&referringSource=articleShare.

42. *See* Joseph Goldstein, *Fearing Trump, Hospital Shuns "Trigger" Words Like "Diverse,"* N.Y. Times (Mar. 19, 2025), https://www.nytimes.com/2025/03/19/nyregion/nyu-langone-trigger-words-trump-dei.html?smid=nytcore-ios-share&referringSource=articleShare.

43. *See* Megan Mineiro, *Public Broadcast Cuts Hit Rural Areas, Revealing a Political Shift*, N.Y. Times (Aug. 26, 2025), https://www.nytimes.com/2025/08/26/us/politics/public-broadcast-cuts.html?smid=nytcore-ios-share&referringSource=articleShare.

44. *See* Paul Sonne, Alina Lobzina and Milana Mazaeva, *Its Journalism Challenged Autocrats. Trump Wants to Silence It*, N.Y. Times (Apr. 16, 2025),

45. Exec. Order No. 14290, 90 Fed. Reg. 19415, *Ending Taxpayer Subsidization of Biased Media* (May 1, 2025).

46. *Id.*

47. *See* Executive Order 14238, 90 Fed. Reg. 13043, *Continuing the Reduction of the Federal Bureaucracy* (March 14, 2025); *Presidential Statement, The Voice of Radical America* (March 15, 2025).

48. *See* Katherine Long, *Voice of America director sues over the outlet's closure*, Politico (Mar. 26, 2025), https://www.politico.com/news/2025/03/26/voice-of-america-shutdown-lawsuit-027972.

49. *See* Jim Rutenberg, *Conservatives Get the PBS and NPR Cuts They've Wanted for Decades*, N.Y. Times (Jul. 18, 2025), https://www.nytimes.com/2025/07/18/business/media/npr-pbs-funding-cuts-republicans.html?smid=nytcore-ios-share&referringSource=articleShare.

CONCLUSION

1. *See* Chris Cameron, *Deploying National Guard to Chicago? Trump Says He Has "The Right to Do Anything I Want to Do,"* N.Y. Times (Aug. 26, 2025), https://www.nytimes.com/2025/08/26/us/politics/trump-national=-guard-chicago-dictator.html.

2. James Madison, *Federalist No. 48,* The Federalist Papers (Cooke ed. 1961).

INDEX